Macroeconomics

Wynne Godley worked on the British economy
in the Treasury for fourteen years, becoming
deputy director of its Economic Section in 1967,
responsible for the economic analysis and
forecasting on which the Treasury's fiscal and
monetary policy was based. He also made a
detailed study of public expenditure planning.
Since 1970 he has been director of the Department
of Applied Economics at Cambridge where he
has concentrated on economic policy questions.

Francis Cripps studied economics at Cambridge
then, after two years working in Thailand, became
a junior lecturer in the Cambridge faculty in 1967.
He stopped teaching in 1971 in order to do full-
time research.

During the 1970s Godley, Cripps and their
colleagues in the Cambridge Economic Policy
Group became known for their critiques of
government policy, their warnings of disasters
into which the UK economy was plunging, and
their eclectic model and research methods which
distanced them from prevailing fashions of the
decade – monetarism and econometrics. They are
now regarded internationally as unorthodox but
creative champions of the Keynesian tradition.

Masterguides

Macroeconomics, Wynne Godley and Francis Cripps
Ethology, Robert A. Hinde
Religion, Leszek Kolakowski
Social Anthropology, Edmund Leach

FORTHCOMING
Sociology, Daniel Bell
Developmental Psychology, Jerome Bruner
Law, Ronald Dworkin
Sociolinguistics, Dell Hymes
Music, Joseph Kerman
Cognitive Psychology, George Miller
The Philosophy of Language, John Searle
Moral Philosophy, Bernard Williams

Wynne Godley and Francis Cripps

Macroeconomics

Fontana Paperbacks

First published by Fontana Paperbacks 1983

Set in 10 on 11¾ Linotron Times

Charts by Illustra

A hardback edition is published by
Oxford University Press

Made and printed in Great Britain
at The University Press, Oxford

Contents

Part VI   Developments of the model

Acknowledgements

Our first acknowledgement is to our colleagues in the Cambridge Economic Policy Group who have worked with us on economic policy problems for the last ten years; and to the Social Science Research Council who have supported us so generously throughout. The ideas in this book, although theoretical, were learned in the course of modelling work undertaken during this period and in the course of conversations with Professor Kaldor.

We owe special debts to Michael Anyadike-Danes, Kenneth Coutts and David Vines who each made important creative contributions. We owe another special debt to Neville Norman who advised us to build our narrative exposition around charts and indicated how this might be achieved.

Bryan Hopkin, Robert Neild and Hashem Pesaran all read through successive drafts and made many effective comments on substance and presentation.

Joyce Leverett typed and edited six completely different drafts of the book over a period of eighteeen months, often through several weekends at a stretch, and never showed any sign of impatience.

The whole thing was Frank Kermode's idea and he has been a kind and supportive disciplinarian.

Notation

Capital letters denote values in current money terms.

Small letters denote inflation-accounted real values in base-period purchasing power.

Symbols with a circumflex denote disaggregated values (e.g., for a single business or group of institutions within the private sector).

The prefix Δ denotes the absolute change in a variable between the beginning and end of a period.

The prefix % denotes the percentage change in a variable between the previous period and the current period.

The suffix ′ denotes measures related to costs of production.

The subscript -1 denotes opening stocks or, more generally, values lagged 1 period.

End-period stocks

Inventories
    I   value of inventories in current money terms
  IVA inventory valuation adjustment

Financial assets and liabilities
    A   financial assets (broad definition)
  BB bonds held by banks
  BD bank deposits
  BP bonds held by the private sector
    D   total debt

FA   financial assets (narrow definition)
GD   government debt
LI   loans outstanding on inventories
MON   money
PD   private debt
PL   personal loans
RA   reserve assets

Flows

Income
II   profits
T   tax revenue net of grants and subsidies
WB   total wage bill
Y   aggregate national income
YG   government income less grants, subsidies and
         interest payments
YP   private disposable income

Expenditure on goods and services
B   external balance
E   aggregate national expenditure
FE   aggregate final purchases
G   government expenditure
LFE   loan-financed expenditure
M   imports and external transfer payments
PC   personal consumption
PE   private final purchases
X   exports and external transfer receipts
YFE   income-generated expenditure

Financial
RVA   private asset revaluations
TA   private asset transactions
TGD   new government debts less repayments
TPD   new private debts less repayments

Volumes

q	output at base-period market prices
riv	real inventory revaluation
tr	net real external transfer receipts
tt	real terms of trade effects

Costs and prices

C	total current costs
HC	total historic costs
p	price deflator for final purchases
px	price deflator for exports at cost
pm	price deflator for imports at cost
R	nominal interest rate
S	sales revenue
UC	costs per unit of output
W	wage cost per unit of output at market prices
%p	rate of price inflation
%W	rate of cost inflation

Ratios

α	steady-state private assets/income
β	steady-state private liabilities/income
γ	inventories/final sales
ϵ	real payments/real stock of loans
θ	net government income/aggregate income
κ	inventories/historic costs
λ	profits/cost of final sales
μ	imports/aggregate income
ϕ	speed of adjustment of private stocks of assets
σ	base-period market price expenditure/base-period cost
τ	net tax revenue/income or net sales tax/expenditure

Introduction

Macroeconomics is the study of how whole economic systems function. What is ultimately at issue are such things as the determination of national income, output, inflation and unemployment – those things which, in peacetime, are of predominant concern to the public and by which they judge the success or failure of governments.

The content of this book is almost entirely theoretical. A natural question for the reader to ask is whether abstract theory can conceivably make any significant contribution to the real and frightening predicament – chronic recession, unemployment and inflation – now afflicting the world economy.

Our objective is most emphatically a practical one. To put it crudely, economics has got into an infernal muddle. This would be deplorable enough if the disorder was simply an academic matter. Unfortunately the confusion extends into the formation of economic policy itself. It has become pretty obvious that the governments of many countries, whatever their moral or political priorities, have no valid scientific rationale for their policies. Despite emphatic rhetoric they do not know what the consequences of their actions are going to be. Moreover, in a highly interdependent world system this confusion extends to the dealings of governments with one another who now have no rational basis for negotiation.

Perspective

The twenty-five years which followed the Second World War was a period of remarkable success with regard to all the main objectives of macroeconomic policy. There was, at least in developed countries, a nearly continuous expansion of real income and output. Even countries which grew relatively slowly, like the USA and UK, still grew fast enough to more than double their standard of living in the quarter century. In many countries there was virtual full employment. Inflation was generally below 5% per annum.

During this period it came to be thought by most people including ourselves, that postwar prosperity was the consequence of the adoption by governments of 'Keynesian' policies, the essence of which was that total real demand was controlled by decisions about taxation and public expenditure; total demand would, up to the limits set by the capacity of the factories and machines in the economy, determine the flow of output and with it employment and unemployment. According to this view, governments could safely adopt full employment as a target while disregarding any imbalance in the budget – that is, any excess of public spending over revenue receipts. Monetary policy didn't matter much. The quantity of money itself was a residual number thrown up by everything else that happened which could (it was thought) be safely ignored: indeed through much of the successful period statistics relating to what are now called 'monetary aggregates' (stocks of money and various other financial assets) were not regularly available.

There always existed a 'monetarist' school of thought who dissented passionately from the ideas just outlined. They believed that the rate of inflation in the 1950s and 1960s, though it now seems so moderate, was unacceptably high; that there was something almost morally wrong with deficit financing by governments; that so far from the quantity of money being unimportant, it occupied a crucial role in determining the rate of inflation and that the government's first priority should be to control its rate of growth. The monetarist challenge was not very effective when economic performance was generally accepted to be satisfactory.

However at the beginning of the 1970s economic performance in almost all developed countries deteriorated in a spectacular way. Growth of output and real income fell sharply and in our country even went into reverse for prolonged periods. Unemployment rose to levels which, it had been believed, would never again occur. And, into the bargain, inflation accelerated very sharply, with annual rates often in double figures.

As this deterioration proceeded, the monetarist school, having been 'dissidents' during the Keynesian era, effected an extremely successful counterrevolution. At the policy level the governments of most developed countries, generally supported by public opinion, became converted to the idea that it was *impossible* for them to control output and unemployment. All they could do, the new story went, was create conditions (including the elimination of inflation) in which enterprise could flourish.

But the monetarist counterrevolution was also extremely successful at the level of ideas. The Keynesian orthodoxy, which had ruled the roost for so long with a confidence amounting to hubris, was suddenly thrown on the defensive. Our view now (though not at the time) is that, apart from the new political mood, the main reason for the success which monetarism had as a system of ideas was that the Keynesian orthodoxy as then taught and practised was indeed incomplete and inadequate. In particular it did not properly incorporate money and other financial variables.*

It must quickly be noted that a distinguished tradition of scholarly investigation into the treatment of money and financial institutions within a broadly Keynesian framework has existed throughout; the names Modigliani, Blinder and Solow, Tobin and Buiter, Turnovsky spring to mind as among the most creative contributors to it. Yet much of the work in this tradition was too complex to be easily incorporated into textbooks or into the econometric models which advisers of governments used for forecasting and policy analysis. One thing which perhaps made the monetarists' attack so effective was that other people could only give vague or complicated answers to simple questions like how money is created and what functions it fulfils. That such questions tended to produce tormented replies testifies to the

* A very informative and also entertaining account of the debate at that time is Harry G. Johnson's 'The Keynesian revolution and the monetarist counter-revolution', *AER*, May 1971.

power of some monetarist insights as well as to gaps or flaws in the previous orthodoxy.

Yet the fact that monetarists exposed these weaknesses and developed a new expertise for analysis of domestic and international finance does not mean that their own characterization of the functioning of whole economic systems was, itself, complete or correct. Their contention that the real economy is essentially governed by 'supply side' or real factors while monetary policy determines money stocks and flows led them naturally to conclude that inflation was the residual of the system. They expressed this view succinctly by saying that monetary policy and monetary policy alone was the cause of inflation and occasionally to deny that trade unions have any effect on inflation at all. But their failure to pin down the mechanism left them exposed in turn. 'Inflationary expectations' only thinly papered over the gaps in their description.

Our own concern with the monetarist/Keynesian controversy has arisen not so much from participating in the learned debate as from ten years' work trying to build and operate models of the British economy and its international context which would contribute to analysis of the serious practical problems which our country faces. We found quite early on that there was indeed something deficient in most macroeconomic models of the time, including our own, in that they tended to ignore constraints which adjustments of money and other financial assets impose on the economic system as a whole. Our first attempt to formalize the nature of these constraints consisted of the 'New Cambridge' hypothesis* originally published in 1974. This attracted some attention at the time but never gained acceptance, being too crudely conceived and expressed to carry conviction as a realistic representation of the central driving mechanism of a complex modern economy. Yet the New Cambridge hypothesis is the grandfather of the theory presented in the first half of this book.

* A clear account of the New Cambridge hypothesis and its relationship to the views of at least one other school of thought is McCallum and Vines, 'Cambridge and Chicago on the Balance of Payments', *Economic Journal*, June 1981.

Our present synthesis may be broadly characterized by saying that we make a 'monetarist' financial system (based on the behaviour of stocks of money, financial assets and debts) drive a 'Keynesian' flow system based on the response of expenditure to income.

We adumbrate a theory of inflation as a process which may be affected by fiscal and monetary policy but which has a strong dynamic of its own. Yet under well-defined conditions the 'Keynesian' flow part of the system can determine real income and output, irrespective of inflation.

It remains to emphasize that the material presented here is introductory in its nature. What we are hoping to do is establish a logical framework for the analysis of macroeconomic phenomena which is coherent and simple* enough to rinse away some of the sheer confusion which surrounds the subject at present, thereby facilitating orderly and creative work on the problems of stagnation, unemployment and inflation which threaten to get progressively worse through the next decade.

Plan of the book and how to use it

The exposition will proceed at four different levels. The main text contains a *narrative* exposition of the key interdependent macroeconomic processes in which symbols will in general only be used to summarize simple logical relationships, and no reader should be put off by the mere spectacle of such algebra. The narrative exposition is illustrated throughout by *charts* as an aid to intuitive understanding. Then the appendices to most chapters contain formal *analytic* representations of the sequential processes for those people who wish to satisfy themselves that our model must indeed work exactly as we assert, given our assumptions. The algebra here represents causally interdependent processes which are sometimes quite complicated but considered as

---

* But while the material presented here is, we believe, reasonably self-contained there are a number of extremely important subjects which we have not discussed. Of these the most egregious are, perhaps, employment, unemployment and productivity.

algebra is hardly ever taken beyond elementary level. Finally the analytic solutions are used to generate *numerical simulations* of the development of whole economic systems by making specific assumptions about policies and behavioural relationships. We attach great importance to these simulations as they can always be reproduced using only a pocket calculator. Some readers may develop an understanding of all our major contentions more readily by reproducing these numbers or generating alternative solutions with different policies or behavioural assumptions because purely narrative exposition of interdependent processes is always complex and liable to ambiguity. By carrying out their own simulations readers may also gain a sense of what is involved in macroeconomic forecasting for policy purposes.

Chapters 1 and 2 explain how concepts like national income, aggregate output, debt and financial assets can be defined in such a way that they all 'add up' in money terms in a mutually consistent way. The fact that money stocks and flows must satisfy accounting identities in individual budgets and in an economy as a whole provides a fundamental law of macroeconomics, analogous to the principle of conservation of energy in physics. But adding-up constraints are obviously not sufficient to determine what will actually happen. For this we must add behavioural assumptions about how people and institutions operate within such budgetary constraints. Since human behaviour is so varied, our objective will be to establish principles of analysis which capitalize on adding-up constraints so as to confine behavioural processes to a relatively small number of variables each of which can then be the object of empirical study. The smaller the number of behavioural variables which govern how the system *must* function in view of the logical constraints, the more powerful will be our theory as a model for organizing and interpreting data. We shall demonstrate how a whole economy, thought of as a very complicated interdependent system evolving through time, would have to function if quite a small number of behavioural variables followed simple plausible rules. Any reader who masters this approach will at least have some idea of what to look at in a real-life economy.

Having mastered accounting concepts and the general

methodology, the reader must work carefully through Part II of the book (Chapters 3 to 5) which sets out a simplified model of a complete economic system. These chapters introduce principles which are essential for later parts of the book. First, in Chapter 3, there is the question of how individual households or businesses adjust their spending and financial assets subject to the budget constraint set by their income and access to borrowing. In Chapter 4 there is an example of how financial assets can be created by the borrowing which finances the working-capital requirements of businesses. Putting the two processes together in Chapter 5, we see how income and expenditure in the economy as a whole will be 'driven' by debt creation. Once having grasped these chapters the reader will have a basic understanding of how money is created and what its role is in a complete economic system.

The third part of the book tackles fiscal and monetary policy. Since money (and kindred financial assets) play such an important role in the economy, governments and central banks try to ensure by various devices that the right amount is generated on suitable terms. Chapter 6 shows how the government's own budget comes into the story and Chapter 7 examines the compatibility of monetary policies with budget decisions. Chapter 8 looks at mechanisms by which monetary policies may be implemented.

Having given a framework for analysing money and financial assets, we proceed in Part IV to the study of inflation. Here, too, adding-up constraints obtain. Chapter 9 shows how costs (including profits) must add up to form the prices at which goods and services are sold or, what is the same thing, how different types of income add up to form aggregate income. Without yielding any strong theory of the ultimate causes of inflation, this at least enables us to see how inflation relates to problems of income distribution (Chapter 10).

Whatever the mechanisms causing inflation, it is always possible to interpret money accounts for income, expenditure, assets and debts in 'real' purchasing power terms, allowing for changes in the general level of costs and prices. Part V uses the method of inflation accounting (described in Chapter 11) to express propositions from earlier chapters of the book in real terms. This leads directly to the most important concept of monetary macroeconomics – the concept of *aggregate real demand* which governs how much output can be produced and sold. In Chapter 12 we reach the firm conclusion that aggregate real demand is the crucial determinant of total production and real income. This proposition follows logically from the role of money and other financial assets in any modern economy. Although readers new to the subject may have found the preceding chapters hard work, we hope that they will agree that the concept of aggregate real demand is a worthwhile reward.

The last part of the book takes steps towards realism by introducing quite a wide range of debts and assets and the implications of capital gains or losses (Chapter 13) and external or 'balance of payments' transactions (Chapter 14). The latter chapter offers a second crucial insight which once again follows more-or-less inexorably from the role of money in modern economies. This is the paramount importance of 'foreign trade performance', suitably defined, in determining real demand – and hence output and real income – in an open economy. The reader who has persisted this far will then have grasped virtually all of what the authors have learned about macroeconomics at the level of general theory. The results about which we are confident may seem sparse. But in economics, which involves the study of human behaviour, general results are hard won. If people could be confident about the limited general conclusions we have reached, there would at least be *some* basis for rationality in the formulation of macroeconomic policies.

PART I

Concepts and methods

1 National accounts

This chapter introduces concepts which will be used in this book. It emphasizes that definitions of national income, expenditure and output, although generally chosen to make it as easy as possible to reach conclusions about major objectives of macro-economic policy, are in the last resort arbitrary. What is essential, if the interrelationships between macroeconomic variables are to be systematically explored, is that the definitions should be chosen such that logical consistency is preserved. It is noted that any divergence between income and expenditure on goods or services by individual agents or sectors implies the existence of a stock of money (or other financial asset) which implies, in turn, the existence of debt on an exactly equal scale. The chapter finishes with an introduction to the relationships between stocks, flows and time lags.

The choice of subject matter

Out of the infinitely complex configuration of human activities unfolding through time, the subject matter of macroeconomics concerns one narrow group which may broadly be characterized as the purchase, sale and production of goods and services, together with associated income and transfers (including taxes), and transactions in financial and tangible wealth. We say 'broadly' because the boundary of the terrain is in the last resort arbitrary.

Let us start with income and expenditure and then proceed to consider financial assets and debts, coming finally to physical volumes of production and sales.

Total money income and expenditure

It is extremely useful to choose definitions such that total income and expenditure in any year, month, day or second are identically equal to one another; they will be – because we choose to define them so that they are – two different ways of looking at the same process. We are only going to admit into the category of flows called income things which have an exact counterpart in the category of flows called expenditure.*

What items should be included in the two categories?

The answer depends on the purpose for which the accounts are to be used and on the ease with which logical consistency can be maintained.

A reasonably general category of expenditure consists of sales and purchases of goods and services which have a counterpart in terms of money payments. This could include *all* expenditure on goods and services by households and businesses and by the government. But, in order to preserve a meaningful identity with income it is best to exclude 'intermediate' transactions within industry and commerce – such as the sale of steel and components to car manufacturers or wholesale goods to retailers. This leaves what are called 'final' transactions such as purchases of consumer goods and services and investment goods (houses and factories, machinery and equipment) as the main components of aggregate expenditure. These expenditures will all be measured at retail or 'market' prices actually paid by the final purchasers.†

It is standard practice (and one which complies with the need

---

* Some modification is necessary for an economy with external payments (e.g. on account of exports and imports). The case of an 'open' economy, which forms part of a larger international system, is considered only in Chapter 14.
† It has generally been the case in the UK that national income and expenditure have been defined to exclude indirect taxes, yielding a concept known as the national income and expenditure 'at factor cost'. The concept of expenditure 'at factor cost' is, however, a slightly odd one since nobody ever actually buys anything at factor cost.

for consistency between income and expenditure) to include goods and services provided free by the government such as roads, schools, health facilities or defence measured in terms of their *costs* without reference to what people might have been prepared to pay for the benefits or the profits/losses which might then have accrued.

On the other hand aggregate expenditure is normally defined to exclude the produce of private gardens although it is a substantial source of food in some countries. It also excludes work carried out by housewives. Such omissions might matter if we were using the national income and expenditure accounts to make inter-country comparisons of welfare. But for the purposes of our study the inclusion of these activities would confuse matters. The income which would then have to be imputed to gardeners and housewives has no direct bearing on the uses of money and its inclusion would complicate the representation of relationships between income, financial assets and tax revenue. Therefore we ignore all employment in do-it-yourself activities; any small money payments to which these give rise may be treated as if they were gifts or transfers.

Aggregate income

Income will comprise wages, salaries and profits as well as rent, income from self-employment and the surpluses (or losses) of nationalized industries, all of which represent a division of the proceeds of aggregate expenditure. To make aggregate income equal to aggregate expenditure at market prices the definition of total income must include 'indirect' or sales taxes which are deducted by the government from the flow of expenditure and exclude subsidies, which are negative indirect taxes, which the government pays.

Timing and valuation

To maintain consistency between measurements of total income and expenditure not only the coverage but also the timing and valuation of transactions must be recorded on a uniform basis.

Imagine, for instance, an accounting system to measure expenditure on, and income from, open-cast coal. From time to time customers go up to a miner who shovels some coal into their buckets, after which they pay him for the coal. The payment is an expenditure by the customer and an income for the miner. While these are only different ways of looking at the same thing, they could be measured by two different statisticians who will not give the same answers, even if neither of them makes any mistakes, unless their concepts are completely harmonious. They would give different answers if, for instance, the statistician recording expenditure considered this to take place when payment was made, while the statistician recording ·income measured the physical operation of production in advance of cash actually being handed over. In this book the convention will be that all flows are measured as cash flows; expenditure and income will be measured when and to the extent that payments of money occur. This will facilitate precise consistency with recorded changes in stocks of money.

Imagine two lines of figures recording the money value of national income and expenditure in successive periods of time

Table 1.1 Flows of UK national income and expenditure in money terms, i.e., at 'current market prices'*

£ billion

	1975	1976	1977	1978	1979	1980
Measured from:						
Expenditure data	110.2	131.0	148.7	169.6	202.6	232.6
Income data	109.8	129.0	149.3	170.7	204.5	234.9

* Source: *National Income and Expenditure*, 1982 edition, HMSO. The estimate for gross domestic product at market prices derived from expenditure data comes from Table 1.1, line 9, *plus* stock appreciation from Table 1.2, line 9. The estimate derived from income data is constructed by subtracting the residual error (Table 1.2, line 11) derived from expenditure data.

which will be identically equal to one another if no one has made any mistakes in measurement and if concepts are harmonious. Table 1.1 above shows a time series for money national income and expenditure in one country, the UK, for the years 1975–80. Note that there are indeed significant differences between the two series because of measurement errors.

The 'time series' shown in Table 1.1 may symbolically be represented as

$$E \equiv Y \qquad\qquad (1.1)$$

where E is defined as the value of total expenditure in some period, and Y is the value of total income in the same period. The identity symbol ($\equiv$) denotes logical equivalence, an equality made true by definition.

Sectoral income

Although the definitions so far imply that the income of all individuals and institutions taken together equals their total expenditure on goods and services in each and every period, this need not be true of any particular person or institution.

Note first that the primary income of any household or business may be modified by direct taxes, social security contributions and benefits, dividends, interest payments and even gifts – all of which are termed 'transfers' in national accounts. Income after transfers is called the 'disposable' income of the household or business. Since transfers add to one person's income what they subtract from another's, disposable income in the economy as a whole adds up to the same total as primary income discussed earlier.

One important category of disposable income is the net income of government which we shall write as YG. The main components of this are direct and indirect tax revenues less grants, subsidies and interest paid on government debt. The total disposable income of all private (i.e. non-government) institutions will be written as YP. The fact that government and private income must add up to total national income, Y, in each and every period is expressed by the identity

$$YG + YP \equiv Y \tag{1.2}$$

Individual income, expenditure and money

Now let us come right down from the level of national aggregates to consider the income and spending of a single private person. The fact that any individual can choose not to spend all his or her disposable income on goods and services in any one period implies the existence of some alternative destination for the income received – specifically that he or she is able to acquire and hold money or some other 'financial' asset. Abstracting for the moment from the possibility of repaying accumulated debt,* if any individual's disposable income exceeds his or her expenditure on goods and services over a period of time, that person must have accumulated additional money or other financial assets exactly equal in value to the difference between income and expenditure. Formally this proposition will be denoted by the identity

$$\hat{Y} - \hat{E} \equiv \Delta\hat{FA} \equiv \hat{FA} - \hat{FA}_{-1} \tag{1.3}$$

This expression makes the simple statement that the excess of anybody's disposable income in any period over his or her expenditure in the same period must equal the change in their stock of financial assets in that period. In the formula 1.3 the circumflexes ('hats') mean that the identity refers to an individual or group of individuals, not (or not necessarily) to aggregates for the economy as a whole. Thus $\hat{Y}$ and $\hat{E}$ are the disposable income and the expenditure of a single person, household, business or other non-government institution. $\hat{FA}$ represents their stock of financial assets (money, bonds, securities, etc) held by the individual *at the end* of each period

---

* And from capital gains or losses, which will be discussed in Chapter 13 and 14.

of time for which accounts are being kept. $\widehat{FA}_{-1}$ represents the stock of financial assets at the end of the previous period or start of the current period. $\Delta\widehat{FA}$ represents the change in the stock of financial assets between the beginning and the end of the period.

Aggregate financial assets and debts

It is easy to understand that any one individual who does not spend all his or her income in a period will have more money left over at the end of the period. But we have chosen a system of definitions which ensures that total income in each period when summed across the whole economy equals total expenditure in the same period. It must therefore be the case that if some people or institutions are accumulating money or other financial assets, others are incurring debts on an exactly equal scale. In the economy as a whole the total increase in financial assets must always be equal in each period to the total increase in debt (financial liabilities).

Once the possibility of borrowing is included as a source of funds for spending, our formal representation of the budget constraint for any individual or institution including the government, is

$$\widehat{Y}-\widehat{E} \equiv \Delta\widehat{FA}-\Delta\widehat{D} \tag{1.4}$$

Equation 1.4 simply says that any excess of income over spending must equal the acquisition of financial assets less the acquisition of debts. As this is true for all individuals it must also be true for the economy as a whole.

But since total national income equals total national expenditure (i.e., $Y \equiv E$) it must also follow for the economy as a whole that the change in financial assets must be equal to the aggregate change in debt, i.e.,

$$\Delta FA \equiv \Delta D \tag{1.5}$$

The equivalence, which must always hold by the rules of logic, between the creation of financial assets and that of debt is something which the reader need only take note of at this stage. The mechanisms which reconcile individual decisions about accumulation of assets and increases in debt are central to our main line of argument and will be the subject of several later chapters.

Note finally that (with appropriate definitions)* the proposition that total financial assets are equal to total debt will be true not only as regards changes but also as regards levels – i.e., total values at each moment of time. Thus we may write, for total financial assets and debt at the end of each period, the identity

$$FA \equiv D \qquad\qquad (1.6)$$

Volumes of expenditure and output

The measures used so far have been expressed in actual cash values. Somewhat more hypothetically, the method can be extended to measure aggregate 'volumes' of expenditure and output.

One way of obtaining an estimate of the volume of national output is to take the full list of goods and services produced and calculate their total value at the prices obtaining in some specified base period. To revert to the open-cast coal mine, the statisticians must now perform more operations than before. The one measuring expenditure observes how much coal is purchased and calculates how much would have been paid for the purchases at a base-period price. This gives a measure of the physical quantity purchased through a period of changing prices.

Alternatively output can be measured directly. Physical quantities of production are counted and each product is 'priced' in terms of the income it would have generated in the same base period. Our mine thus has a third statistician standing by who counts bucketfuls and values them in terms of the average income per bucketful received in the base period.

* Qualifications necessary in respect of valuation changes (e.g., in the market prices of government bonds or corporate equity) and of an open economy are examined in Chapters 13 and 14).

The point of these base-period valuations is that they convert physical quantities which cannot be added up for the economy as a whole into money values which can be added up. It makes no sense to add buckets of coal to sacks of cement but there is at least some meaning in adding up the money that would have had to be spent, and the income that would have been received, if observed quantities of coal and cement had been produced and sold at constant, base-period prices.

Using lower case letters to denote the volume concepts,* we have chosen a definition of aggregate output such that

$$q \equiv e \qquad\qquad (1.7)$$

where q is output and e is the total volume of expenditure.

Estimates of national output in the UK are given in Table 1.2 below. Once again there are measurement errors so that the two estimates do not quite agree.

Table 1.2 National output at 1975 market prices†

£(1975) billion

Measured from:	1975	1976	1977	1978	1979	1980
Expenditure data	104.8	108.5	109.9	114.0	115.9	113.7
Output data	104.8	106.6	109.4	113.7	116.3	113.1

* The reader will find that in the table of symbols (page 9) and in later parts of the book we make distinctions between 'volume' measures and inflation-accounted 'real' values. Some of the lower case symbols used here will be given primes (') to distinguish them from real (inflation-accounted) values of the same variables. The essential difference is that the volume measure shows what something would cost at base-period prices; the real value measure shows what other goods and services its current money value could buy, given the *general* purchasing power of money.

† Sources: *National Income and Expenditure*, 1982 edition, HMSO. Gross domestic product (GDP) from expenditure data at 1975 market prices is given in Table 2.1, line 12. The estimate from output data has been constructed by using the ratio of indices in Table 1.11, i.e., the ratio of line 5 to line 3. Note that the estimate of GDP in 1975 from expenditure data in Table 1.2 differs from that in Table 1.1 although both are measured at 1975 market prices. This discrepancy arises because the change in inventories is treated differently in the two tables (the example in Table 1.3 below illustrates how this happens).

Inventories

An obvious question to ask is how total volumes of expenditure and output can always be equal to one another if anyone can go down to the shops whenever they feel like it and buy something off a shelf. When somebody buys a bottle of wine an extra bottle of wine is not simultaneously produced. The reconciliation is brought about by treating the fall in the stock of wine held by the retailer as negative component of aggregate expenditure. So the *net* expenditure and output, which is the instantaneous counterpart of the retail purchase of a bottle of wine, is equal to the retailer's margin on what he has sold. There will after all have been some 'output' – an output of retail service which is valued at the base-period retail margin (i.e., the difference between the retail sale price and the wholesale cost).

Similarly, suppose that there is an increase in the production of wine without any additional retail sales. The extra wine will have to go into stocks held by wine producers, wholesalers or retailers. To maintain the identity between aggregate volumes of expenditure and output it is necessary to take account of all changes in stocks or 'inventories' of goods, whether finished or in progress. The change in the aggregate volume of inventories in any accounting period will be written as

$$\Delta i \equiv i - i_{-1}$$

where i denotes the volume of inventories *at the end* of each period and i_{-1} denotes inventories at the end of the previous period or start of the current period.

The change in inventories forms part of the total volume of expenditure. The remainder, aggregate purchases in the normal sense, is termed 'final purchases' to distinguish it from changes in inventories. In symbols we write

$$q \equiv e \equiv fe + \Delta i \tag{1.8}$$

where fe represents the total volume of final purchases.

The money values of inventories

A parallel line of reasoning applies to money expenditures and income. When a distributor buys goods from a factory, the factory receives income whether or not the goods are immediately sold to a final purchaser. Nor has the distributor lost income in any meaningful sense when this happens. The same holds true for work in progress for which payments of wages and other costs are made in advance of sales. The change in the aggregate money value of inventories in each period must be included in the measure of total expenditure together with the total money value of final purchases in order to keep total expenditure exactly equal to total money income. In symbols we write

$$Y \equiv E \equiv FE + \Delta I \tag{1.9}$$

where FE represents the money value of final purchases, I, is the *end-period value* of inventories (valued at actual cost) and ΔI is the change in the value of inventories in the accounting period.

Translation of values into volumes

The construction of volume measures is in practice generally carried out by statisticians on the basis of a range of physical indicators on the one hand and, on the other, price indices which are used to convert accounts at current prices into constant-price estimates. Apart from the technical problems of doing this, the reader should be aware that there are conceptual difficulties (e.g., in allowing for 'quality' changes in goods and services produced) and that the correspondence of the two sets of accounts is beset with pitfalls for the unwary.

Table 1.3* below provides an example of valuation problems connected with inventories for the courageous reader to puzzle

---

* But although the measurement problem illustrated is important and will turn up again, it is not essential to spend much time on it at this stage.

over. The values of opening and closing inventories (rows 1 and 2) and final expenditure (row 4) are all equal to the corresponding volumes (rows 9, 10 and 12) multiplied by price indices (rows 6–8, divided by 100) which are all rising continuously. Changes in inventories (rows 3 and 11) are obtained by subtracting opening inventories from closing

Table 1.3 Example of inventory valuation effects

	'1975'	'1980'	'1981'
Values (current $)			
1. Opening inventories	200	300	400
2. Closing inventories	220	400	420
3. Change in inventories	20	100	20
4. Final expenditure	300	450	480
5. Total income (3+4)	320	550	500
Price indices (1975=100)			
6. Opening inventories	95	130	160
7. Closing inventories	105	160	170
8. Final expenditure	100	140	150
Volumes at 1975 prices			
9. Opening inventories	210	231	250
10. Closing inventories	210	250	247
11. Change in inventories	0	19	−3
12. Final expenditure	300	320	320
13. Total output (11+12)	300	339	317
14. Ratio of total income to output = (5/13)	1.07	1.62	1.58

inventories in each period. It is immediately apparent that there need not be much connection between volume changes and value changes in inventories. In '1975' the value of inventories has gone up because of inflation without any change in the volume of inventories; in '1981' the value of inventories has gone up when the volume has gone down.

The figures for national income (row 5) and national output (row 13) are obtained by adding changes in inventories (rows 3 and 11) to final expenditure (rows 4 and 12). In the base year, '1975', the money value of income is already different from the volume of output on account of inflation in the value of inventories; extra money is being paid out by businesses in advance of sales but the inflation component of this does not get into the volume measures. What is more paradoxical is that an apparent price deflator for national income (row 14), calculated by dividing money income by the volume of output, falls between '1980' and '1981' despite the fact that the price indices for inventories and for final expenditure have both risen continuously.

The paradoxes can get worse when foreign trade (exports and imports) is brought into the accounts. But we shall not pursue the problem further at this stage. The example above is mainly intended as a warning. National accounting must be handled with care!

Stocks and flows

It is essential to be clear about the difference between stock variables and flow variables.* Flows occur in certain quantities per unit of time, and measurement of them requires that the time period be designated. To say someone's income (a flow variable) is $5000 means nothing until we know whether it is his monthly,

---

* The difference is essentially that known to accountants as one between balance sheets which record stocks at points of time and appropriation accounts which record the flows during periods which link balance sheets together.

quarterly or annual income. In contrast stocks have a zero time dimension. The quantity of money (a stock variable) owned by an individual is measured not per unit of time but at a point of time and (at that point of time) has an absolute money value irrespective of the length of any accounting period.

The difference between stocks and flows and the relationship between them is illustrated by the analogy of rivers flowing into and out of a lake. The movements of water in the rivers can be measured as *flows* – i.e., quantities of water moving past a given point per designated period of time. The quantity of water in the lake is a *stock* which can be measured at any point of time. There may be a precise relationship between flows into and out of the lake and changes in the stock of water it contains. If we could be certain that there were no net movements of water into and out of the ground and air, the difference between the inflow and the outflow in any period would be exactly equal to the change in the stock between the beginning and end of that period.

In our system of definitions income, final expenditure and production are all unambiguously flow variables. We also had three stock variables, inventories, I, financial assets, FA, and debt, D. In all three cases, the stocks entered into flow identities as differences between stock levels at the beginning and end of the period in question.

Stocks, flows and time lags

To conclude this chapter, let us finally consider some implications of the relationship between stocks and flows for the speed at which things can change.

Imagine a merchant who buys objects, say sacks of wheat, and later sells them. If we could assume that things are sold in the same order as they are bought ('first in, first out') and that there is a steady flow of purchases, the length of time each sack of wheat is held by the merchant would be given by the ratio of purchases per unit of time to the total stock at each point of time. Thus suppose the merchant buys and sells a regular quantity of wheat per month and that he always holds inventories equal to twice that quantity. It necessarily follows that each sack of wheat remains in the distribution pipeline for exactly two months; each month the trader must be selling wheat which he bought two months ago.

In the case described above the time lag between the inflow of each sack and its subsequent outflow is precisely equal to the stock-flow ratio, no more and no less.

Another possibility is that the merchant does not follow a strict first in, first out rule. For instance, his sales in each period might be made up as to 20% from purchases the same period and 80% from older inventories. In such a case the same stock-output ratio would be observed (if the system were stationary) as in the 'first in, first out' case. But some sacks of wheat would pass through the system more quickly than implied by the stock-output ratio and a corresponding number would pass through more slowly.

Table 1.4 illustrates the concept of a *mean lag*. This is the *average* length of time it takes for a sack of wheat to pass through

Table 1.4 Method for calculating mean lag

Month	(1) Proportion of month 0 purchases sold in current month	(2) Time lapse between purchase and sale	(3) Calculation of mean lag (1)×(2)	(4) Stock remaining at end of current month from purchases in month 0
0	0.2	0	0	0.8
1	0.2	1	0.2	0.6
2	0.2	2	0.4	0.4
3	0.2	3	0.6	0.2
4	0.2	4	0.8	0.0
Total	1.0		2.0	

the merchant's hands. For the analysis of the aggregate relationship between flow variables in time this is likely to be the most important thing to know. The *total* lag, i.e., the longest time taken for any item to get sold, is less important since by logical implication a corresponding number of items gets sold after a time lag shorter than the mean.

In this example the mean lag between the purchase and sale by the merchant remains two months although the lag is 'distributed' and some wheat is held in stock for as long as four months.

The practical importance of stocks for making inferences about flows will be much influenced by the size of stocks relative to flows. If stocks are extremely large relative to flows, the mean lag tells us little about the relationship between outflows and recent inflows. Reverting to the water analogy, the size of flows out of Lake Ontario on any one day is unlikely to bear any close relationship to that of inflows on the same day or in the few days before. But flows into and out of a bathtub will be closely related by the hour.

Summary

This chapter has introduced some indispensable concepts and principles of measurement. Although the definitions which bind the whole system are in the last resort arbitrary, it is essential that they should be logically coherent. A sharp distinction has been made between stock variables and flow variables, and attention has been drawn to logical interrelationships between them. We have adumbrated the notion that stock-flow ratios have implications for the time lags between related flows.

2. Macroeconomic theory

Up to this point we have only discussed concepts, definitions and logical interrelationships. We have said little about how anything works. The choice of definitions could be controversial but the identities cannot be wrong.

Before proceeding to any analysis of how monetary economies work, let us reflect at this stage on what illumination about the behaviour of macroeconomic systems can possibly be achieved. What is the status of the propositions which might be made?

Economic models

According to standard practice, models of whole macroeconomic systems (or parts of them), whether theoretical or empirical, take certain variables as *exogenous* – which means that they are not themselves determined by the particular model or submodel under consideration. Then *behavioural relationships* between variables are postulated which can in principle be established as empirically plausible. Then the system of logical and behavioural relationships is 'solved' to yield the fruits of the exercise – the behaviour of the model's *endogenous* variables in response to its exogenous variables.

For instance, when considering part of the economic system one might regard the flow of personal income and the average tax rate as exogenous, and postulate a behavioural relationship between disposable personal income in one period and personal consumption in that and subsequent periods. The system could then be solved for the flow of personal consumption, giving correct answers if we know the values of the exogenous variables and have reliable estimates of the behavioural parameters.

Thus with exogenous pre-tax personal income, $\hat{Y}$, and an exogenous tax function that makes tax payments, $\hat{T}$, a proportion, τ, of pre-tax income –

$$\hat{T} = \tau\hat{Y} \qquad (2.1)$$

we might postulate, or establish, that consumption in one period, $\hat{PC}$, is always some proportion, 0.6, of disposable income in that period and another proportion, 0.25, of disposable income in the previous period –

$$\hat{PC} = 0.6(\hat{Y}-\hat{T})+0.25(\hat{Y}_{-1}-\hat{T}_{-1}) \qquad (2.2)$$

Equation 2.1 can now be solved simultaneously to obtain

$$\hat{PC} = 0.6(1-\tau)\hat{Y}+0.25(1-\tau_{-1})\hat{Y}_{-1} \qquad (2.3)$$

This equation system yields consumption, $\hat{PC}$, conditional on the exogenous variables, $\hat{Y}$ and τ, and the behavioural parameters, 0.6 and 0.25.

By extension, a model of a whole economy might regard policy variables which the government can control (like public expenditure and tax rates) as exogenous; it might also regard as exogenous variables which are not under the control of the government nor part of the system being analysed (such as changes in world trade and world commodity prices). Then a comprehensive equation system, representing direct and indirect responses to these exogenous variables, could solve for all the things we want to know about such as national income, output and prices.

It is a widespread practice, both at the theoretical and empirical level, to assemble systems of this kind which, although determinate as systems, are essentially conceived on an 'equation by equation' basis. By this we mean that each relationship is studied and evaluated largely on its own merits, often by specialists. One of the most important examples is the 'consumption function' – the study of how consumers' expenditure is determined – on which there exists an enormous self-contained theoretical and empirical literature.

Methodological problems

The methodology raises a number of well-known questions.

One extensive area of controversy concerns the so-called 'micro foundations' of macroeconomics. The view is widely held that no relationship between aggregates (between, say, total income and total expenditure) can validly be postulated which cannot be justified precisely in terms of the behaviour of individual agents. Such a view seems perilously close to a denial that macroeconomics as defined in the opening sentence of this book ('the study of how whole economic systems function') can be a valid subject at all.*

Another important area of controversy starts from the fact that any system of equations can only be as valid as its behavioural parameters. There is much difference of opinion as to the correct procedures for validation of behavioural parameters. Much of this discussion concerns the proper use and practice of econometrics – the rapidly evolving and ever more complex endeavour to obtain conclusions by statistical methods about empirical relationships between economic time series.

Yet another area of controversy, closely related to the two already mentioned, concerns the optimum size of a macroeconomic model. If the economy is better represented with four equations than three, is there any point at which further disaggregation will produce nil or negative returns?

The approach in this book

These questions are all profound ones which oblige us to question the status of our own approach.

What is put forward in the following pages is a conditional theory as to how *whole* economic systems function.

The main results are conditional on the behavioural axiom

---

* Hashem Pesaran has pointed out to us that, pushed far enough, the insistence on micro foundations is like demanding a map that has a one to one scale.

that stock variables will not change indefinitely as ratios to re-lated flow variables. If the flow of a river into a lake increases, the volume of water in the lake will not rise for ever. At some point a new water level will become established; then (and only then) the outflow will equal the inflow. In the same way, if the flow of sales by a merchant is constant, his inventory level will not rise or fall indefinitely. If the flow of income is constant, holdings of money will not change indefinitely.

This axiom has implications which turn out to be particularly important when we consider how whole economic systems function. Reverting to the water analogy, imagine a group of riv-ers flowing into a system of lakes before flowing out to the sea. If the overall rate of inflow increases it will take time for the water level to rise throughout the system. But a stage will be reached when the volume of water in each and every lake will be stable at a new level; changes in all stocks will then be zero and the total outflow will equal the total inflow.

The power of the axiom to generate theorems about the way which whole systems function, and in particular to impose constraints on the sum of individual actions, is something which will only become fully apparent as we proceed. It will be discovered that, conditional on this axiom, and a number of logical identities, the room for manoeuvre which may seem to be permitted in the 'equation by equation' approach to model building is greatly reduced. A 'system' approach also illuminates the problem of optimum disaggregation.

But what is the status of the stock-flow axiom? Is it a postulate about how groups of people actually behave? Why should the reader build anything at all on such a postulate in the absence of evidence?

The formal status of the axiom is akin to that of an *exogenous variable*. It is something which the model itself cannot explain. We admit without reservation that if stock-flow norms were to move about too wildly most of the theory set out in this book would be rendered useless, though the stability of *norms* is con-sistent with fluctuations in *actual* stock-flow ratios.

The stability of stock-flow norms

Our contentions are, first, that the stock-flow norms which are crucial to determining how actual economic systems work do, as a matter of fact, exhibit a fair degree of stability.*

Another observation is this.

The fact that a cornerstone of the model is an assumption that stock-flow norms are given does not commit us to the view that in reality the norms are entirely invariant; the model does not become useless if the norms turn out, within limits, to change or fluctuate. As adumbrated in the previous chapter, stability of stock-flow norms would enable strong conclusions to be drawn about the speed of adjustment of related flow variables. But even when the norms change, the consideration of stock-flow and flow-flow relationships and an understanding of the logical connection between them provides important diagnostics; it gives a systematic technique for analysing actual data.

By stating the conditionality of the models in this book on the stock-flow axiom we formally exonerate ourselves from the need to provide further 'microeconomic' foundations for the most important part of the analysis. This is not to deny that the study of microeconomics is a valid and relevant exercise; but it gives us the licence to demarcate a separable area of study. The assumption of constant aggregate stock-flow norms may be consistent with a large number of different patterns of individual behaviour, although it will generally require that individuals behave with some degree of consistency.

Structural change

The pattern of stock-flow norms may indeed change suddenly or

---

* We may add that anyone who calls the axiom fundamentally into question also calls into question, to an equivalent degree, the core of macroeconomics as conventionally taught and practised. For the 'IS-LM' apparatus on which the equilibrium postulated by the 'neoclassical synthesis' rests assumes, *quite unequivocally*, that equilibrium stocks of 'money' have, at given interest rates, a unique counterpart in flows of income.

gradually in a way that disturbs outcomes for the system as a whole. Reverting to the water analogy, if the conformation of the landscape is given there may be stable relationships and time lags between flows and stock levels. But the structure of the landscape itself may alter, (e.g., if a dam is built), changing the adjustment processes and steady-state relationships. This would not render the study of systems with given structure useless; indeed, the general theory of such systems would help to clarify the consequences of structural change.

Macroeconomic determinism

We must finally draw attention to the implication that if stock-flow norms are regarded as exogenous variables a large proportion of our macroeconomic results will come in the form of logically inevitable conclusions. The ratio of purely logical propositions to those which are contingent on behavioural assumptions is higher than is normal in a book on macro-economics.

This underscores our insistence on the introductory nature of this book. We do not ask the reader to believe that the way economies work can be discovered by deductive reasoning. We take the contrary view. The evolution of whole economies, like their political systems, is a highly contingent historical process. We do *not* believe that it is possible to establish precise behavioural relationships comparable with the natural laws of physical sciences by techniques of statistical inference. Few laws of economics will hold good across decades or between countries. On the other hand we must exploit logic so far as we possibly can. Every purchase implies a sale: every money flow comes from somewhere and goes somewhere: only certain configurations of transactions are mutually compatible. The aim here is to show how logic can help to organize information in a way that enables us to learn as much from it as possible. This is what we mean by macroeconomic theory and we shall point out its limitations as well as its strengths.

PART II

A money economy

3. The adjustment of expenditure flows and money stocks

This chapter and the two which follow build up a model of how expenditure and the production and distribution of goods and services might be financed in a closed economy with banks but without taxes or a government budget. The purpose of these chapters is to develop an understanding of links between credit- or debt-creation and flows of spending and income. The analysis will be entirely in terms of money values. Nothing will be said at this stage about changes in prices or volumes of production and spending. Money income and expenditure flows constrain what can happen to prices and volumes taken together, but the implications of this fact will be left until later in the book.

The overall plan of Chapters 3–5 is as follows. Chapter 3 introduces a sub-model of decisions about final expenditure and accumulation of financial assets, taking income as exogenous. Chapter 4 provides a parallel sub-model of spending on inventories, borrowing, and income generated by production, taking final expenditure as exogenous. Chapter 5 combines the two sub-models in a complete macro-model to show how income, expenditure, stocks of financial assets and debt may be determined simultaneously. To clarify the exposition a drastic simplification is made – namely that institutions undertaking final purchases (chiefly households) have no recourse to borrowing; debt is confined to businesses which hold inventories (producers and distributors). It will become clear later what consequences follow if this simplification is relaxed.

Assumptions about final expenditure and stocks of money

As pointed out in Chapter 1, our definitions for the economy as a whole are chosen so that total income always equals total expenditure. But this chapter considers only a part of the economy. Imagine a group of households whose expenditure can individually and collectively diverge from their income. Let us assume that the group receives income in the form of money (say credits with a bank), and that there exist no financial assets other than money. We also suppose that households cannot borrow money. It follows that they must either spend their income on purchases of goods and services or allow it to accumulate as money in their pockets or in the bank.

Formally we can characterize these assumptions as a budget constraint:

$$\hat{PE} + \Delta\hat{FA} \equiv \hat{YP} \tag{3.1}$$

where YP represents disposable income in each period, PE denotes purchases of goods and services and FA is the end-period stock of money. The 'hats' mean that the symbol in question refers to an individual or group, not to the economy as a whole. The identity says that any difference between a group's disposable income and its purchases of goods and services in any period must exactly equal the change during that period in the stock of money held by the group.

In this chapter we shall regard the income flow as if it were *exogenous*; that is to say we assume that it may behave arbitrarily without explaining why. We develop a sub-model to derive, as *endogenous*, flows of expenditure and stocks of money conditional on arbitrary, exogenous income flows.

The assumptions made about exogenous variables will follow a similar form throughout the book. The exposition of a model or sub-model generally starts with consideration of a steady state in which the values of exogenous variables are all constant. We then consider the implications of well-defined shocks to exogenous variables and see how the system reacts. Although the exposition is concerned with steady states and shocks, it will be apparent that the analysis can readily be adapted to deduce how the system should behave in more complex, realistic contexts where the exogenous variables behave in a thoroughly disorderly way.

The steady state

The steady state of our sub-model of final expenditure and stocks of money corresponds to a constant flow of money income. Following the general stock-flow principle discussed in Chapter 2, we assume that with constant income a steady state would be reached in which stocks of money were at unchanging levels, implying a constant flow of final expenditure on goods and services exactly equal to the income flow. In the steady state we could say that people behaved as if they spent their income with a determinate lag, equal to the ratio of their money stock to income. This statement would not mean much since cash balances held in a bank, like drops of water in a lake, are anonymous; it doesn't make any sense to say which unit of money from a bank account is spent when. But the lag between income and spending will acquire significance when we consider the response to a change in income.

A step increase in income

Chart 3.1 illustrates a possible pattern of adjustment of expenditure and money stocks when there is a shock taking the form of a step increase in the flow of income.

The figure represents the flow of income by the line $\widehat{YP}$ and a possible response of the other variables by the lines $\widehat{PE}$ and $\widehat{FA}$.

We shall make much use of diagrams with this essential structure so it is important to be clear as to their logical construction.

Sums of money are measured on the vertical axis and time on the horizontal axis.

The top two lines represent income and expenditure flows in continuous time, at rates per unit of the time designated along the horizontal axis. Thus income is stable at a rate of $600 per unit of time in the first two periods, then rises by 50% to $900 per unit of time from the beginning of the third period onwards. The income flow in each period corresponds to the *area* between the line $\widehat{YP}$ and the horizontal axis (i.e., 600×1 in the first two

Chart 3.1 A representation of changes in the expenditure flow and the stock of money in response to a step change in income

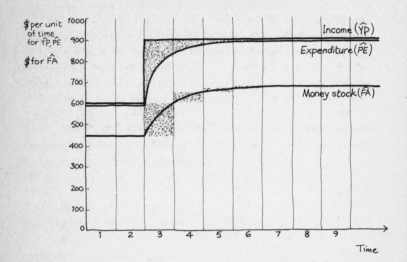

periods, 900×1 in all subsequent periods). Similarly, the expenditure flow in each period corresponds to the area between $\widehat{PE}$ and the horizontal axis. The shaded area between $\widehat{YP}$ and $\widehat{PE}$ represents the difference between income and expenditure in each period. It must consequently be equal, period by period, to the increase in the money stock (equation 3.1).

The lower line, $\widehat{FA}$, measures the money stock itself at each point of time. The size of the change in the money stock between the beginning and end of each period is equal to the difference between the closing and opening stock and is therefore equal to the shaded rectangles constructed around the line $\widehat{FA}$; the area of these is the vertical distance $\widehat{FA} - \widehat{FA}_{-1}$ times the horizontal distance given by the time unit itself. The area of each rectangle must always be identically equal, period by period, to the shaded area immediately above.

The chart shows an opening position with a stable steady state where total income equals total expenditure and the stock of money is unchanging. We have assumed that disposable income and expenditure start off at $600 per period and that the stock of money is, to begin with, constant at $450 units, implying a stock-flow ratio of 0.75.

The magnitude of the stock-flow ratio is important. If the stock of money were equal to twenty-five years' flow of income we would be in a 'Lake Ontario' situation; short-period (quarterly or annual) responses to a change in income could follow almost any pattern we care to imagine. However, the analogue to 'money'* is, in the real world, slightly above one year's flow of income (at least in the UK and in the USA). We have chosen a numerical stock-flow ratio of 0.75 so that the money stock will appear below the income and expenditure lines in the diagram; the unit of time may roughly be thought of as being a year and a half.

In period 3 income rises 'exogenously' by $300 to a new level of $900 per period and thereafter stays constant at that rate. According to the stock-flow axiom put forward in Chapter 2, a new stable steady state will eventually get established in which the stock of money is again stationary and, therefore, expenditure will have risen to exactly the same level as income. We shall suppose that the stock of money in the new steady state will again be 0.75 of the income flow. It will have risen by $0.75 \times \$300 = \$225$ to reach a new steady-state level of $675.

What happens on the way from the first steady state to the second?

One thing is certain. By the laws of logic the addition to the stock of money in each and every period must be equal to the difference between income and expenditure in the same period. And the cumulative gap between income and expenditure through the whole transitional period between the two stable steady states must exactly equal the cumulative addition to the stock of money; in the example illustrated in Chart 3.1 income must therefore exceed expenditure by exactly $225 over the transitional period taken as a whole.

* For further explanation see Chapter 8. We are asking the reader to take a good deal on trust in this sentence.

The chart was actually constructed by drawing an arbitrary, yet not obviously absurd, parabola for the path of money stock adjustment, then drawing the rectangles defined by the time units chosen, and finally drawing the implied pattern of adjustment of expenditure.*

The expenditure response is less arbitrary than might at first appear. The fact that expenditure can only fall short of income by a cumulative total of $225 over the whole period places a strong constraint on the time which it can possibly take to reach its new steady-state level.

To take one extreme, suppose that, following the rise in income, expenditure does not move at all until money stocks have risen to their new steady-state level. This may be illustrated as follows.

Chart 3.2 A very fast money adjustment

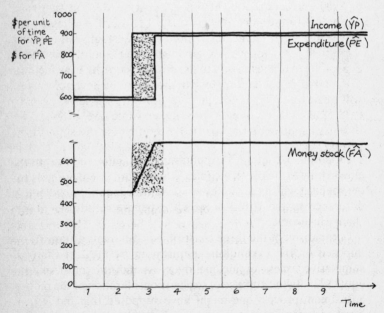

---

* Appendix 3.1 shows how examples shown here in charts may be calculated numerically.

At the other extreme, suppose that the adjustment of money stocks is very slow (much slower than in Chart 3.1). Then, after a large initial adjustment of expenditure to income, an extremely small residue of the expenditure adjustment takes place very slowly indeed. This is illustrated in the Chart 3.3.

Chart 3.3 A very slow money adjustment

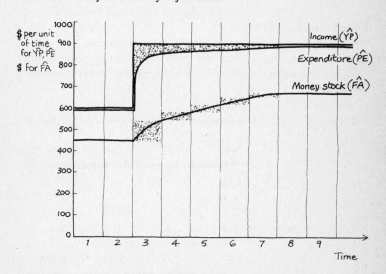

In Charts 3.2 and 3.3 expenditure has quite soon adjusted almost fully to the rise in income. What we are discovering is that the speed at which the money stock adjusts does not make much difference to the speed at which expenditure adjusts to the change in income.

Comparison of the three charts illustrates the time constraint imposed on the expenditure adjustment by the fact that the cumulative excess of income over expenditure must exactly equal $225. In the absence of explicit consideration of the money adjustment process one might have supposed that the adjustment of expenditure to income could be more or less anything – for instance it might be a straight line extending upwards to the right at an arbitrary angle. But now we find that *over the entire range of plausible assumptions* about the speed of money adjustments, and so long as the steady state ratio of money to income remains 0.75, 80% or more of the adjustment of expenditure to income must have taken place by the end of the second period after income went up.

So we come to a theorem of great importance.

The mean lag

A constant steady-state ratio of money to income is necessarily equal to the mean lag of expenditure behind income. This mean lag is *entirely independent* of the way in which the money stock adjusts to its steady-state ratio.

If the reader requires a mathematical proof of this proposition he or she should refer to Appendix 3.2.

Yet the charts are nearly sufficient to prove the proposition on their own since they all show a mean lag in the adjustment of expenditure to income of *about* three quarters of a period, which is the assumed steady-state ratio of the stock to the flow. The proposition is manifestly true in the extreme case represented in Chart 3.2 where the lag is not distributed at all and total expenditure responds with a lag of exactly three quarters of a period, no more and no less. As the asset adjustment gets slower, a larger proportion of the total expenditure adjustment takes place in less than 0.75 of a period but the balance is spread out over a correspondingly longer time.

In fact the mean lag can be given a direct graphical interpretation as the size of the shaded area between $\widehat{YP}$ and $\widehat{PE}$ relative to the size of the step increase in income, $\widehat{YP}$. This is most obvious when the adjustment of expenditure follows a straight line as illustrated in Chart 3.4 below. But whatever the shape of the adjustment path, it remains true that the area between the two lines (divided by the size of the increase in income) measures the mean lag.

In the chart above the *total* lag in the response of expenditure to income is given by the distance Y_1E_1 and the *mean* lag is half

Chart 3.4 The mean lag with a straight-line adjustment

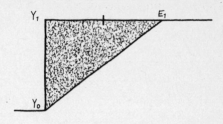

that distance. The area of the triangle in the chart is equal to the length of its base, Y_0Y_1, multiplied by half its height, Y_1E_1 – i.e., the base multiplied by the mean lag. So the mean lag is equal to the area of the triangle divided by the step increase in income, Y_0Y_1.

Now in all the charts drawn so far the shaded region between $\widehat{YP}$ and $\widehat{PE}$ has the same area. The area is equal to the increase in the steady-state stock of money, $\widehat{FA}$. It follows that the mean lag in the adjustment of expenditure to a change in income must always be equal to the ratio of the change in the steady-state stock of money to the change in income (i.e., $225 \div 300 = 0.75$). This is an entirely general proposition. If, as was assumed in the charts, the value of the steady-state money/income ratio remains constant when income changes then the mean lag must necessarily be equal to that value.

Suppose that the steady-state stock of money does *not* vary in proportion with income. We still know exactly what must happen. If it varies proportionately less than income, the ratio of changes in the steady-state money stock to changes in income will be smaller and the mean lag will be shorter. If it varies proportionately more, the mean lag will be longer.

Usually, and especially if money income is changing because of inflation, we assume that the steady-state stock of money will vary in proportion with income, so that the money/income norm remains constant when income changes.

Expectations

What would happen if people adjusted their expenditure or stock of money in anticipation of a rise in their money income? The following three charts illustrate some logical possibilities.

Chart 3.5 Unconstrained flow anticipation

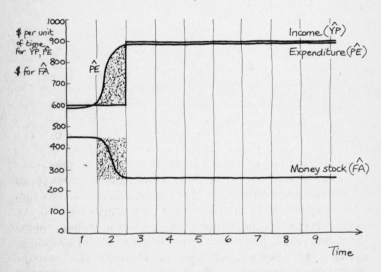

The story told in Chart 3.5 is obviously unacceptable. Expenditure moves towards its new steady state rate of flow in advance of the step increase in income. But the logical concomitant is that the stock of money falls and stays permanently lower.

To carry plausibility we must be able to end up with the same stock-flow relationship with which we started. The only flow anticipation story that could make any sense looks as follows.

Chart 3.6 Constrained flow anticipation

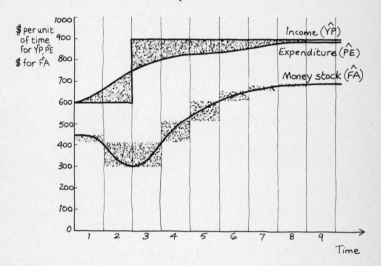

But there are two important points to be made about Chart 3.6. First, the mean lag of expenditure *behind* income is still preserved. Expenditure now starts to rise before income – there is a 'negative lag' at the beginning of the process. But this can only happen at the expense of a correspondingly slower approach to the new steady state after the rise in income has taken place. Second, while the expenditure flow starts its approach to the new norm earlier under the anticipations story, the stock-flow ratio initially moves *away* from its norm. Why should the principle of anticipations lead people to give priority to flow-flow norms over stock-flow norms? If people anticipate systematically, or at all, it is at least as likely that they will adjust their *stocks* early. We could, in other words, just as well have Chart 3.7 as Chart 3.6.

Chart 3.7 Stock anticipation

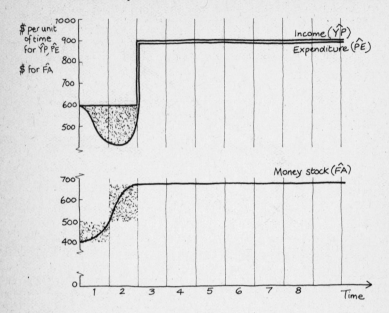

Steady growth in income

We have so far only considered the response of money stocks and expenditure flows to a step rise in income. But the same principle of adjustment towards stock-flow norms applies equally well to growing systems.

Chart 3.8 represents responses of money stocks and expenditure flows to *steadily* growing income flows.

It demonstrates that if assets are to grow as fast as income then expenditure must lag behind (i.e., be lower than) income in a growing system. The point is important because it is sometimes supposed that if the growth rate of income is accurately anticipated, then the adjustment of expenditure may be instantaneous in the sense that it will no longer lag behind income at all. Such a theoretical possibility is illustrated by the

Chart 3.8* Steady growth

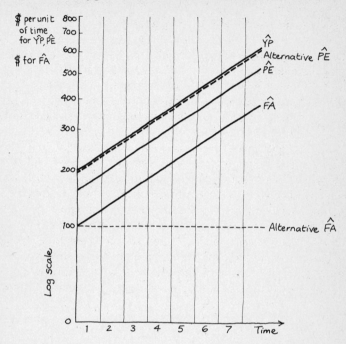

dotted lines in Chart 3.8. But the postulate that correctly anticipated income growth leads to any speeding up of the expenditure flow, most particularly if (as illustrated by the dotted lines in the chart) it rises so as to equal the income flow, implies that the stock of assets falls continuously relative to the income flow, contradicting our central axiom.

Our conclusion is that stock-flow norms make some anticipation stories impossible and most of them implausible.

---

* This chart is drawn on a log scale which has the advantage that stable growth rates of any magnitude are represented as straight lines and have the same slope whatever their absolute value – a convenience which outweighs the disadvantage that the area representing accumulation of financial assets is smaller when represented as the difference between income and expenditure than it is when represented as an increase in the assets themselves.

Measurement problems and aggregation

Macroeconomists have a limited choice of observation periods. Most aggregate data are only available on a quarterly or annual basis. We shall generally specify aggregate relationships as if decision-making periods were all the same and equal to some chosen accounting period. This inevitably introduces some lack of precision.

There is another loss of precision when we consider aggregate responses for the private sector as a whole. The money/income norms of individual households and businesses will not all be the same. We shall treat the private sector as a whole *as if* it had a unique, average money/income norm and a unique, common budgetary period even though, in reality, differences between individual norms and budgetary periods could mean that what happens to aggregate expenditure and the money stock may be influenced to some some extent by the way in which aggregate income is distributed between individual people and institutions.

Summary

This chapter has described how expenditure must respond to changes in income flows if it can be assumed that there is some normal relationship between stocks of financial assets and income flows. The main conclusion was that stock-flow norms have very strong implications for the speed at which expenditure flows respond, the mean lag of the response being necessarily equal to the norm. We pointed out that stock-flow norms also impose constraints on the extent to which expenditure decisions can be governed by expectations about future income flows.

The final sections of the chapter adopted a more technical style of exposition and explored the properties of certain specific adjustment processes. They also briefly considered other technical problems such as aggregation.

Appendix 3.1 *Calculating the sequential process – an arithmetical example*

Some people may like to work through one or more numerical examples of the adjustment processes illustrated in the charts.

The first assumption is that there is a stock-flow norm which is independent of income. Formally this can be written as

$$\widehat{FA}^\star = \alpha \widehat{YP} \qquad (A3.1.1)$$

where the star ($\star$) denotes a *normal* as opposed to actual value of the variable. The equation says that the norm for the money stock is some given proportion, α, of income.

The second assumption is that the change in the stock of money which actually takes place in any period is a certain proportion, ϕ, of the gap between the stock of money inherited from the previous period, $\widehat{FA}_{-1}$, and the stock of money warranted by the current income flow, $\widehat{FA}^\star$, This assumption can be written formally as

$$\Delta\widehat{FA} \equiv \widehat{FA} - \widehat{FA}_{-1} = \phi(FA^\star - FA_{-1}) \qquad (A3.1.2)$$

The two assumptions may be combined to yield the expression

$$\widehat{FA} = \widehat{FA}_{-1} + \alpha\phi\widehat{YP} - \phi\widehat{FA}_{-1}$$
$$= \alpha\phi\widehat{YP} + (1-\phi)\widehat{FA}_{-1} \qquad (A3.1.3)$$

This says that the money stock at the end of any period, $\widehat{FA}$, is equal to some proportion, $\alpha\phi$, of income in that period plus some other proportion, $(1-\phi)$ of the stock of money inherited at the start of the period.

Equation A3.1.3 above has a precise implication for expenditure in each period as well as representing the adjustment process for the money stock. Recall the budget constraint given at the start of this chapter (equation 3.1) which says that expenditure in any period plus accumulation of money must be equal to income in the period:

$$\widehat{PE} + \Delta\widehat{FA} \equiv \widehat{YP} \qquad (A3.1.4)$$

Combining this with A3.1.3 gives

$$\widehat{PE} = (1-\alpha\phi)\widehat{YP}+\phi\widehat{FA}_{-1} \qquad (A3.1.5)$$

This equation says that *expenditure* in any period will be equal to a proportion $(1-\alpha\phi)$ of income in that period plus a proportion, ϕ, of the inherited stock of money.

Examples may be constructed by choosing values for the money/income norm, α, and the speed of adjustment parameter, ϕ. Given starting values for income, $\widehat{YP}$, and the inherited stock of money, $\widehat{FA}_{-1}$, expenditure in each period may then be calculated from equation A3.1.5.

The end-period stock of money can be obtained by rearrangement of the budget identity (equation 3.1.4) which implies

$$\widehat{FA} \equiv \widehat{FA}_{-1}+\widehat{YP}-\widehat{PE} \qquad (A3.1.6)$$

This is sufficient to calculate sequential solutions.

There is no obstacle to exploring the implications of changes through time in α or ϕ as well as in $\widehat{YP}$. As the values of these

Table A3.1

	(1)	(2)	(3)	(4)	(5)	(6)
Period	Income $\widehat{YP}$	$(1-\alpha\phi)\widehat{YP}$ $= 0.5\widehat{YP}$	$\phi\widehat{FA}_{-1}$ $= 0.67\widehat{FA}_{-1}$	Expenditure $\widehat{PE} =$ (2)+(3)	Change in money stock $\widehat{FA}-\widehat{FA}_{-1}$ $= (1)-(4)$	End-period money stock $\widehat{FA} = (5)$ $+\widehat{FA}_{-1}$
0						450
1	600	300	300	600	0	450
2	600	300	300	600	0	450
3	900	450	300	750	150	600
4	900	450	400	850	50	650
5	900	450	433	883	17	667
6	900	450	445	895	5	672
7	900	450	448	898	2	674
8	900	450	449	899	1	675
9	900	450	450	900	0	675

parameters start to change, the effects of the changes will always feed in through the first of the equations above.

As an example of how the calculations may be set out, take the income flow series illustrated in Chart 3.1 and the same stock-flow norm ($\alpha = 0.75$). All we have to do is assign a value (say 2/3) to the asset adjustment parameter ϕ.

We start from a steady state in which income and expenditure are each \$600and the money stock is \$450. Then, as in the chart, income jumps by 50% to \$900. We can now work across the columns using the formula given above to calculate expenditure in column (4) from the sum of (2) and (3). This makes it possible to infer the change in the money stock (the difference between columns (1) and (4)) which in turn provides the end-period value of the money stock $\hat{F}A$ which will be needed to calculate the next value in column (3).

The example satisfies, as it obviously must, all the logical properties of our system. The cumulative gap between income and expenditure (\$225) is exactly equal to the difference between the two steady-state money stock levels. Note too that the mean lag in the response of expenditure to income is, indeed, 0.75. This can be checked as follows:

Table A3.2

(1) Period following income jump	(2) Expenditure adjustment in period	(3) (2) expressed as a proportion of total adjustment (i.e., (2)/300)	(4) (3) weighted (i.e., (3)×(1))
0	150	0.500	0.000
1	100	0.333	0.333
2	33	0.110	0.220
3	12	0.040	0.120
4	3	0.010	0.040
5	1	0.003	0.015
6	1	0.003	0.018
∞	300	1.000	0.750

The very enthusiastic reader could take different values of ϕ, see what differences are made and check that the mean lag is unaltered.

Appendix 3.2 *Proof that the stock-flow norm equals the mean lag*

Equation A3.1.3 gave the stock of money at the end of any period as

$$\hat{FA} = \alpha\phi YP + (1-\phi)\hat{FA}_{-1} \qquad (A3.2.1)$$

The equation can alternatively be written with the stock of money as a function of current and lagged income alone since

$$\hat{FA}_{-1} = \alpha\phi \hat{YP}_{-1} + (1-\phi)\hat{FA}_{-2} \qquad (A3.2.2)$$

$$\hat{FA}_{-2} = \alpha\phi \hat{YP}_{-2} + (1-\phi)\hat{FA}_{-3} \text{ etc.} \qquad (A3.2.3)$$

By repeated substitution of such equations into A3.2.1 and collecting terms in $\hat{YP}$ we can derive the expression

$$\hat{FA} = \alpha\phi\hat{YP} + \alpha\phi(1-\phi)\hat{YP}_{-1} + \alpha\phi(1-\phi)^2\hat{YP}_{-2} \ldots \qquad (A3.2.4)$$

This relationship between the stock of money and current and lagged income has a specific functional form. It could be written more generally as

$$\hat{FA} = \alpha_0\hat{YP} + \alpha_1\hat{YP}_{-1} + \alpha_2\hat{YP}_{-2} + \alpha_3\hat{YP}_{-3} + \ldots \qquad (A3.2.5)$$

Since, in a stable-steady state, income is constant, this general formula implies a money/income norm, α, given by

$$\alpha \equiv \alpha_0 + \alpha_1 + \alpha_2 + \alpha_3 \ldots \qquad (A3.2.6)$$

Provided the coefficients, α_0, α_1, . . . have not changed since the previous period, the opening money stock can be inferred by putting an additional lag into equation A3.2.5 above:

$$\widehat{FA}_{-1} = \alpha_0 \widehat{YP}_{-1} + \alpha_1 \widehat{YP}_{-2} + \alpha_2 \widehat{YP}_{-3} + \alpha_3 \widehat{YP}_{-4} \dots \quad (A3.2.7)$$

So, recalling the budget constraint

$$\widehat{PE} \equiv \widehat{YP} - (\widehat{FA} - \widehat{FA}_{-1}) \quad\quad\quad (A3.2.8)$$

we substitute equations A3.2.5 and A3.2.7 into A3.2.8 and collect terms:

$$\widehat{PE} = (1-\alpha_0)\widehat{YP} + (\alpha_0 - \alpha_1)\widehat{YP}_{-1} + \\ (\alpha_1 - \alpha_2)\widehat{YP}_{-2} + (\alpha_2 - \alpha_3)\widehat{YP}_{-3} + \dots \quad (A3.2.9)$$

The sum of the coefficients on current and lagged values of $\widehat{YP}$ in A3.2.9 is clearly 1. The mean lag is then given by adding successive coefficients multiplied by their associated lags in exactly the same way as Table 1.4:

$$
\begin{array}{ll}
(1-\alpha_0) \times 0 = 0 \\
(\alpha_0 - \alpha_1) \times 1 = \alpha_0 - \alpha_1 \\
(\alpha_1 - \alpha_2) \times 2 = \quad\quad 2\alpha_1 - 2\alpha_2 \\
(\alpha_2 - \alpha_3) \times 3 = \quad\quad\quad\quad 3\alpha_2 - 3\alpha_3 \\
\quad\quad \dots \quad\quad\quad\quad\quad\quad\quad \dots \\
\hline
\end{array}
$$

The mean lag $= \alpha_0 + \alpha_1 + \alpha_2 + \alpha_3 \dots$

which is the same as the money/income norm (A3.2.6).

4 The finance of working capital

This chapter examines the finance of production and trade. Entrepreneurs have to pay out money for working capital to keep production and distribution going in advance of receiving money from the sale of goods. At this stage we shall ignore fixed capital. The main result we shall prove is that profits can only become fully available as cash income to entrepreneurs if their working capital is financed by borrowing. Historically the need for borrowing to finance working capital has been a major force behind the growth of money and banking. By establishing a process whereby money can be 'created' and fed into an economic system, this chapter prepares the way for a macroeconomic analysis, presented in the following chapter, of the properties of money stocks and flows in a simple but complete economic system.

Working capital in the production process

The time needed to carry out production and distribution of goods implies the existence of work-in-progress and stocks of materials, components and finished goods which may all be classified under the general heading of 'inventories'. As in the case of money and income, the ratio of inventories to the flow of production has a precise logical connection with the length of time taken by the production and distribution process.

Let us bring some precision to these ideas.

A trader buys and sells objects (say apples), the payments he makes constituting the receipts of apple growers.

Suppose that the time period between the trader's purchases of apples and receipts from sales is *precisely* fixed. This might happen if the trader bought apples only in response to firm orders; the time lag between purchase and sale would then be governed entirely by the time needed to fetch and deliver the apples. Then, counting in numbers of apples, we could have the following, starting right from the beginning of the trader's operations.

Table 4.1 Preliminary example of inventory accumulation
(The unit of measurement is physical objects)

	(1)	(2)	(3)	(4)
Day	Purchases	Sales	Change in inventories: (1) less (2)	Level of inventories at end of period
1	100	0	100	100
2	100	0	100	200
3	100	100	0	200
4	110	100	10	210
5	121	100	21	231
6	121	110	11	242
7	121	121	0	242

In this example objects purchased on one day are always sold two days later. The trader builds up inventories for the first two days without making any sales. Then, whenever a stable steady state is established, the change in inventories is zero and the level of inventories is twice the flow of sales per day. Any increase in sales is necessarily preceded by an increase in inventories which, so long as it lasts, causes purchases from producers to exceed the current level of sales.

The relationship described in this example concerns stocks and flows of physical objects under conditions of certainty. In the actual world inventories are held, also, so that unanticipated fluctuations in sales and production can be absorbed without too much disruption. They may sometimes be held for purely speculative reasons.* The physical adjustment of inventories in

---

* But note that most speculative transactions are in 'paper' rather than physical commodities.

response to changes in the volume of sales presents problems similar to those discussed in the last chapter but more complicated because the initial effect of an unanticipated change in sales volume is to alter the level of inventories in the 'wrong' direction. For simplicity of exposition in this chapter we shall assume that producers and traders do correctly foresee changes in sales and make advance adjustments in the pipeline of production and distribution such that the time taken for goods to pass through is held constant. Failures of foresight and the corrective action then required are assumed away, although we shall return to them in the macro-model of the next chapter.

Working capital and profits

The fact that inventories have to be paid for by entrepreneurs in advance of receipts of sales revenue gives rise to the financing problem which is the main theme of this chapter. We may start with an accounting definition of profits.

$$\hat{\Pi} \equiv \hat{S} - \hat{C} + \Delta\hat{I} \tag{4.1}$$

This says that profits, $\hat{\Pi}$, in any period are equal to sales revenue, $\hat{S}$, less costs, $\hat{C}$, paid in the same period *plus* the change in the value of inventories, ΔI, between the beginning and end of the period. The last term is included because costs may have been incurred to build up inventories (or saved by running inventories down). Note that for any individual trader, sales revenue may include not only sales of final goods and services but also intermediate sales of raw materials, components, producer services, partly-finished products and finished goods at various stages in the production and distribution pipeline. Similarly costs may include not only wages but purchases of intermediate goods and services. However, when equation 4.1 is aggregated for the economy as a whole, intermediate transactions cancel out and we may write

$$\Pi \equiv FE - WB + \Delta I \tag{4.2}$$

where (net) sales are represented by total final purchases, FE, and (net) costs are represented by total wages, WB. This measure of profits is consistent with the national income identity from Chapter 1 which said that total income was equal to total expenditure, defined as the sum of final purchases and the change in inventories:

$$Y \equiv E \equiv FE + \Delta I$$

By implication, total income is the sum of wages and profits:

$$Y \equiv \Pi + WB \tag{4.3}$$

Equation 4.3 is the identity constraining the distribution of primary income between aggregate profits and aggregate wages. The measure of profits in primary income is taken here before distribution in the form of rents, interest payments, dividends, etc. and provision for depreciation (though in the simple economy now under discussion there is strictly speaking no depreciation since we have assumed away all fixed capital).*

The distinction between profits and cash flow

Although equation 4.1 provides a consistent definition of profits, it evidently does not measure the net cash available for distribution from a business. The producer or trader has to pay the whole of costs and cannot offset changes in the value of inventories against this cash requirement unless he borrows or obtains credit to finance inventories. If the cost of inventories rises rapidly (for example in a period of inflation) the entrepreneur could find that costs of inventory accumulation absorb all or more than all of the cash flow from sales. He could be making a profit on every sale but yet continuously be in the position of having to find more cash to put into the business.

For instance, consider the following business. As in Table 4.1,

---

* In later chapters we shall usually consider profits net of interest. Chapter 13 brings in questions of depreciation, dividend payments, etc.

the trader sells each object he purchases after two periods, but the figures now represent the cash value of transactions rather than physical objects. It is assumed that the trader sells each object at cost plus 10% and that (after the initial period in which the business gets established) the value of turnover expands by 10% once every two periods.

Table 4.2 Example of inventory accumulation and profits
(The unit of measurement is values in $)

Period	(1) Costs	(2) Value of sales (costs two periods ago plus 10%)	(3) Inventories valued at cost	(4) Change in (3)	(5) Profits ((2) less (1) plus (4))
1	100	0	100	100	0
2	100	0	200	100	0
3	110	110	210	10	10
4	110	110	220	10	10
5	121	121	231	11	11
6	121	121	242	11	11
Cumulative position so far	662	462	242	242	42

We start from the beginning of the trader's operations. Column (1) shows costs paid in each period. Column (2) shows the value of sales on the assumption that the trader always sells what he paid for two periods previously plus 10%. Column (3) shows inventories at the end of each period valued at cost; on the timing assumptions made, the value of inventories at the end of each period is always equal to costs in that period plus costs in the previous period. Column (4) shows the change in inventories (i.e., the change in column (3)) in each period. Finally, column (5) shows profits implied by the rest of the table on the definition given in equation 4.1, i.e., current sales less current costs plus the change in inventories valued at cost ((2) *less* (1) *plus* (4)).

Note that although from period 3 onwards the trader earns profits equal to 9% of the value of sales (column (5) divided by column (1)), the cash flow in each period is only just sufficient to meet outlays necessary to keep the business going; the trader can extract nothing at all for himself. The *cumulative* cash position is that, having invested $200 in the first two periods, the trader remains $200 out of pocket and has recovered no part of the initial outlay.

How can the trader live? His accountant will be telling him he is making a profit; but far from having money to buy bread for himself, he is out of pocket on a substantial scale. He can walk round a heap of apples and tell himself he is 'worth' $242 at the end of six periods, having only paid out $200, but this will not give him anything with which to pay his own grocery bills.

The story in table 4.2 reveals two different dimensions to the financing problem. There is first the problem of setting up the business – the situation where the need for finance is most acute. Then there is the problem of keeping the business going once it has been established. We have deliberately illustrated a rather extreme case where increases in the cost of inventories absorb the whole of the profit mark up in order to drive home the nature of the second problem.

This second aspect of the financing problem has attracted attention during the past decade in the context of the debate on 'inflation accounting' – the contentious business of how to measure profits correctly when there is rapid inflation. But the problem is more general than this. There is always a need for finance when a business is started. And if the value of sales is expanding, the need to pay out cash for higher inventories generates a need for additional finance irrespective of whether the expansion is 'real' or the result of inflation. In fact the cumulative total of cash generated by business operations always falls far short of the cumulative total of recorded profits which are therefore by no means all, *prima facie*, available as spending money to the entrepreneur. Given the production period and the profit mark-up, the faster business expands the greater will be the discrepancy between profits and the cash flow.

The finance of inventories by borrowing

If we now suppose the trader finances all his inventory accumulation by borrowing, the position is transformed.

Table 4.3 Cash flow counterpart of Table 4.2 when working capital is financed by borrowing
(The unit of measurement is values in $)

	(1)	(2)	(3)	(4)	(5)	(6)
Period	Costs	Sales	New borrowing = change in inventories	Total cash receipts (2)+(3)	Cash surplus (4)−(1)	End period assets = liabilities
1	100	0	100	100	0	100
2	100	0	100	100	0	200
3	110	110	10	120	10	210
4	110	110	10	120	10	220
5	121	121	11	131	11	231
6	121	121	11	131	11	242
Cumulative position so far	662	462	242	704	42	242

Because inventories have been financed by borrowing there is a debt at the end of each period equal to the value of inventories. But the accounting profit shown in column (5) of Table 4.2 has been turned into the cash surplus shown in column (5) of Table 4.3 above. The trader can now spend all his profits. Yet he remains solvent because his debt is matched by realizable assets.*

* This is not to say that in the event of a cessation of business remaining inventories can always be sold off at prices which cover, or more than cover, their accounting valuation.

The trader may have to pay interest on the borrowing which finances inventories, and this could generate a net cash requirement in the first two periods before any profits are realized. From the third period onwards profits will hopefully cover interest charges. To maintain a steady flow of net profits (after deduction of interest) the trader may need to vary the profit mark-up whenever interest rates change. Alternatively, inventories could be valued inclusive of interest paid over the period for which each item is held and the profit mark-up could be calculated on costs inclusive of interest charges. If the trader was able to borrow against the value of inventories inclusive of interest charges, the cash-flow problem would then be entirely solved.*

The debt in aggregate

Individual businesses may not only borrow from banks or suppliers but also extend credit to purchasers. At this stage we assume that although trade credit may be extended among producers and traders, final sales are always paid in cash. This maintains consistency with the simplifying assumption made in the previous chapter that people or institutions undertaking final expenditure have no recourse to borrowing. Given this assumption, trade credit within the production and distribution sector cancels out to zero for businesses in aggregate. If, as we assume, inventories are financed by borrowing, the total value of inventories in the economy as a whole will be matched by a corresponding debt of the production and distribution sector as a whole to financial institutions (banks). In the absence of other types of debt, total lending by the banks will be equal to the total value of inventories. We shall write this identity as

$$LI \equiv I \qquad (4.4)$$

where LI is total bank loans outstanding at the end of each period on account of inventories and trade credit.

* Again, it may be questionable whether, in the event of a cessation of business, remaining inventories could be sold off at a price which fully covers this valuation.

Chart 4.1 The value of inventories and bank lending

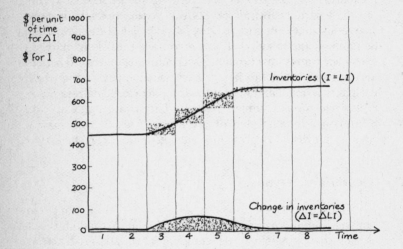

Chart 4.1 illustrates the relationship between loans outstanding, a stock concept, at successive points of time, and the change in inventories financed by loans, a flow concept, using the same principles as for the charts in Chapter 3. The shaded areas must equal one another period by period. Whenever inventory accumulation is zero there is no change in loans outstanding.

The measurement of profit mark-ups

Before leaving this discussion of business finance let us draw attention to a useful theorem about profits which is illustrated in Table 4.2.

The theorem is this. If prices are in a fixed ratio to the historic cost of producing what is sold, then profits in any period will be a constant proportion of the value of sales in that period.* This theorem is useful for the measurement of mark-ups because profits and the value of business turnover can be looked up in accounts directly, whereas the historic costs of goods sold in each period can only be inferred by indirect calculations.† The theorem holds irrespective of how prices are actually fixed. For example, if competitive market processes cause prices to settle at levels which yield a constant share of profits in the value of sales, then prices must move in exactly the same manner *as if* they had been set by adding constant percentage mark-ups to historic costs.

Summary

In this chapter we first showed how the time taken by the production process implies the existence of inventories. We then demonstrated why finance for working capital is necessary if profits are to be available as a cash flow for entrepreneurs to spend.

---

* The historic costs of goods sold in each period, $\hat{H}C$, is equal to the inherited value of inventories, $\hat{I}_{-1}$, plus current costs, $\hat{C}$, less what is left over at the end of the period, $\hat{I}$. Thus

$$\hat{H}C \equiv \hat{I}_{-1} + \hat{C} - \hat{I} \equiv \hat{C} - \Delta\hat{I}$$

Profits may then be written (equation 4.1) as

$$\hat{\Pi} \equiv \hat{S} - \hat{C} + \Delta\hat{I} \equiv \hat{S} - \hat{H}C$$

If λ is the profit mark-up on historic costs, then

$$\hat{S} \equiv (1+\lambda)\hat{H}C$$

It follows that profits are a fraction of the current value of sales:

$$\hat{\Pi} \equiv \hat{S} - \hat{H}C \equiv \frac{\lambda}{1+\lambda}\hat{S}$$

Therefore if the mark-up on historic costs, λ, is constant, the ratio of profits to the current value of sales will also be constant.

† Note to the knowledgeable reader: the accounting relationships imply that when the mark-up on historic costs is constant the ratio of profits 'including stock appreciation' (English English) or 'before inventory revaluation adjustment' (American English) will be a constant proportion of business sales. The latter concept *excludes* inventories (however valued) altogether.

5 The closed economy with credit money

We are now in a position to consider how flows of income and spending and also stocks of money could be jointly determined in a whole economic system which has banks but as yet no government budget, external trade or international financial transactions. Our model of such an economy is obtained by bringing together the sub-model of final purchases and accumulation of money discussed in Chapter 3 with that of the finance of production and distribution discussed in Chapter 4.

Commercial banks and credit money

As mentioned in the introductory paragraph to Chapter 3, it is being assumed here that the economy is closed and that there is no government budget. But there are commercial banks.

Before tracing the consequences of the identities and adjustment processes of our model it is necessary to enter briefly into a discussion of the workings of a banking system which makes a credit-money economy possible.

Banks' loans represent their assets; their corresponding liabilities are deposits and notes in circulation.* Bank deposits and notes are the normal means by which people make payments; the 'liabilities' of banks, in other words, *are* money. In the absence of other financial institutions the liabilities of banks are the *only* form of money.

In such a world there is only one way in which the stock of

---

* In the simple world postulated here we ignore coins; also we ignore the equity of banks and their reserves (there being as yet no government).

money can be changed – namely by banks increasing or decreasing the total value of their loans. We may suppose that entrepreneurs come to banks and request loans to finance working capital, offering as collateral the value of inventories which they will be purchasing (or trade credit which they will extend). Once entrepreneurs have overdraft facilities, additional money balances are created when they draw these facilities down by making payments to other people's accounts. The total stock of money only changes when, and to the extent that, the total of bank loans outstanding changes. Payments not associated with additional borrowing result in a credit balance (or banknotes) owned by one person being transferred into the name or ownership of another; such payments can therefore make no difference to the total stock of money in existence. There is no way in which owners of bank-notes and credit balances as a whole can alter the liabilities of the banking system as a whole.

Although the total value of bank deposits and notes owned by the public must always be exactly equal to the total value of bank loans outstanding, this need not be true for any individual bank. It would in practice be impossible for banks to operate, let alone provide a convenient service to the public, if they had individually to preserve a continuous equivalence between their lending to the public on the one side and deposits owned by the public and banknotes they have issued on the other. This problem is readily overcome if banks more-or-less automatically accept deposits from one another. Given a system of inter-bank credits, individual banks may specialize in deposit-taking or in lending – the 'deposit banks' relending in an 'inter-bank market' to 'loan banks' which borrow in the same market.

Once a system of inter-bank credits is in existence, there is no logical or institutional constraint on the extent to which the whole banking system can supply additional loans, thereby simultaneously expanding the stock of money held by the public by an amount exactly equal to the increase in loans. Changes in the stock of loans and money will be governed solely by demand for loans and the credit-worthiness of would-be borrowers.

This conclusion, that money is created or destroyed by

changes in borrowing from the banks, is the starting-point of our analysis of spending and income.

As yet we have made no mention at all of interest rates which are often regarded as fundamental in the regulation of money and credit. At this stage we simply assume that interest rates are determined exogenously. Interest rates on different types of loans and deposits will have an influence on the evolution of the economic system under discussion because they may affect decisions on money balances (the ratio of money stocks to income) as well as decisions on borrowing and accumulation of inventories. But we shall entirely postpone discussion of how interest rates themselves are determined until Chapter 8. Any reader who feels uncomfortable about this may for the time being assume either (i) that all interest rates are fixed by law or (ii) that there is a 'central bank' which stands ready to lend or borrow without limit on the inter-bank market at a fixed 'base' rate,* and that all other rates bear relativities to the base rate determined by competition between commercial banks.

Aggregate income determination

We are now in a position to describe how aggregate income and expenditure flows are determined as a sequential process in time.

The solution of the entire dynamic model can be apprehended by careful consideration of Chart 5.1 below as long as the analysis of Chapters 3 and 4 has been properly understood.† We cannot overestimate the importance for everything which follows in later chapters of fully mastering the process described and analysed here.

---

* Note that a central bank's total lending to commercial banks will always be exactly equal to the total of their deposits with the central bank. In other words the central bank's transactions will never create or destroy money held by the non-bank public as long as the central bank does not undertake transactions with non-bank institutions (the public or government).
† The numerical calculations underlying the chart are explained in the last part of this chapter. The Appendix provides a general algebraic formulation.

Chart 5.1 Solution for the dynamic path of a closed credit money economy with no government

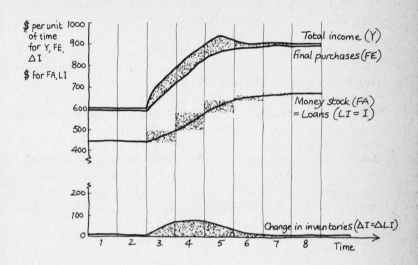

First note the *logical* structure of the chart.

The top line shows the aggregate national income flow, Y, and the second line the flow of final purchases, FE, per unit of time. The shaded area between these two lines equals the increase in money balances, ΔFA, held by recipients of income.

The third line represents, in the first instance, the *stock* of money, FA. The shaded areas constructed around it correspond to the change in the money stock in each period which must be equal, period by period, to the shaded area between the top two lines.

The bottom line represents a postulated path for inventory accumulation expressed as a flow per unit of time; the lower shaded area is equal to the flow ΔI in each time period, exactly as in Chart 4.1.

Finally, assuming that inventories are always matched by loans, we reinterpret the line in the centre of Chart 5.1 as the total of loans outstanding, LI, as well as the total value of inventories, I. The middle and lower shaded areas are again, period by period, exactly the same as in Chart 4.1, and they are both equal to the shaded area between the two top lines.

How does the whole system solve?

First recall the principle for exposition of sequential processes already enunciated in Chapter 3. We start with a steady state where changes in all stocks are zero, then administer a well-defined and finite disturbance, and finally see exactly how and with what time profile the system achieves a new steady state. We remind the reader that an analysis presented in this form does not in any way preclude solutions where shocks to the system continue indefinitely so that it is, like any real economy, in a continuous process of adjustment.

Let us for the time being take as *exogenous* the accumulation of working capital by entrepreneurs, ΔI, which, by assumption, is entirely financed by bank loans. The logical and causal relationships of our model make it possible to deduce as *endogenous*, period by period, aggregate flows of national income and expenditure and a time path for the stock of money.*

The steady state

Chart 5.1 opens with a steady state where inventory accumulation is zero. The flow of final sales equals the flow of income, and the stock of money and loans is unchanging. A unit of time has been chosen such that the money stock (as in Chapter 2) is equal to three quarters of the income flow per period.

---

* Yes! The change in loans ΔLI is *exogenous* and the change in the money stock ΔFA, though logically equivalent to ΔLI, is *endogenous*.

An exogenous disturbance

Starting at the beginning of period 3, we now go through a period of disturbance when entrepreneurs obtain finance to increase the value of their inventories. They borrow at a rate which rises to $75 per unit of time and then after six periods falls back to zero, thereby increasing the total value of inventories and bank debt by 50% from $450 to $675.

Watch carefully: this is the tricky bit.

The 'exogenous' expenditure on inventory accumulation, ΔI, in period 3 simultaneously creates an equal addition to the stock of money and to the aggregate income flow. This initial addition to income generates, with some lag, final sales which generate more income and, with a further lag, yet more final sales. The interactive process must take place on whatever scale ensures that the gap between total income and total expenditure in each period is exactly equal to the amount of money created by additional bank borrowing in the same period.

So long as the flow of bank loans can be taken as given, the whole interactive process is finite and determinate. Every change in the stock of money is always equal to the change in loans, assumed equal to inventory accumulation. At the moment when inventory accumulation, ΔI, reverts to zero at the beginning of period 8, the change in the money stock, ΔFA, must also be zero and final sales are from then on exactly equal to total income.

The transitional process

We can deduce by how much the flow of income and final sales must have risen between the old and new steady states. The increase in the income flow must have been such as to induce additional holdings of money stocks exactly equal to the increase in loans outstanding. In the case illustrated, where loans have increased by $225 and the steady-state money-income ratio is

3/4, the increase in the income flow between the old and new steady states must have been \$300 (\$225 = 3/4×\$300). During the transitional period the cumulative income flow must have exceeded the cumulative flow of final sales by the amount \$225 needed to 'pay' for the increase in the stock of money. Indeed the excess of total income over final sales must, period by period, have been equal to the increase in bank loans (and the value of inventory accumulation).

The example illustrated in Chart 5.1, which is worked through in algebra in Appendix 5.1, has the property that the system instantaneously reaches its full new steady state in period 8, the first period in which inventory accumulation returns to zero. Not only is the money stock constant from then on but the aggregate income-expenditure flow exactly reaches its new steady-state value. What is particularly remarkable is that the new steady state will be reached as soon as loans stop rising, regardless of the speed of the money adjustment process (represented by the parameter φ in our algebra) and regardless of the mean lag in the adjustment of expenditure to income (given by the money/income norm α). Under our assumptions this model must 'settle down' *immediately* the exogenous force (changes in the value of inventories) comes to a halt. The economic system as a whole is thus 'driven' with no lag at all even though there is a lag of final sales behind income.*

Money supply

We must draw attention to the fact that, under the assumptions so far made, there cannot be any problem about equating what is usually called the 'supply' of money with the 'demand' for it. Money is *created* when banks make loans. The act of money

---

* Quite strictly speaking, this property depends on the money adjustment process assumed and will not hold precisely if the adjustment process involves terms other than α and φ. In such cases, there may be simultaneous fluctuations in income and final sales beyond period 9, 'echoing' disturbances during the main period of transition. But unless the money adjustment process is quite radically different from that assumed, the instantaneous steady-state theorem must hold as a good approximation.

creation is also an act of expenditure and (therefore) of income creation. People in receipt of additional income will in an initial period either hold it or spend it. If they spend it, they create thereby aditional income for others who in turn decide whether or not to spend. The aggregate income-expenditure flow must always adjust to the point at which people collectively but voluntarily are holding whatever additional money balance has been created.

That is all there is to it. Apart from decisions to spend out of income at a certain rate, there is no separate or additional process requiring equilibration between the 'supply' and 'demand' for money. There exists in our system the analogue to the concept commonly known as 'the demand for money function'. This is the function which relates stocks of money to current and lagged flows of income. It is a function which is logically equivalent to one relating *expenditure* to current and lagged flows of income; given the budget identity, one can be derived from the other.

To summarize, the *exogenous* flow of inventory accumulation together with one behavioural axiom governing the adjustment of holdings of money has been sufficient to determine *endogenously* the evolution of the entire system of aggregate money income and expenditure flows through time.*

Steady-state income

Note that there is a formula which relates the total income flow to the stock of money in a steady state which can be derived very

---

* It is risky to draw parallels with the real world at too early a stage. Yet there are two cases where this model probably provides realistic insights. One is the historical case where development of commercial banking and the invention of bills of exchange had the effect of monetizing what were essentially barter economies using commodity money (gold or yams); such institutions greatly facilitated growth and development in economies which did not have governments with fiscal policies to manage their economies. The other case with significant similarities is the recent development of an unregulated international banking system. In the absence of a world fiscal policy, loans by this banking system are indeed providing what little engine of growth now drives the world economy.

simply. In the steady state the actual stock of money, FA, is equal to the desired stock, FA*, which is in turn equal to a proportion of the total income flow. Written formally,

$$FA = FA^\star = \alpha Y \qquad (5.1)$$

It follows that the steady-state income flow is given by the stock of money divided by the money/income norm:

$$Y = FA/\alpha \qquad (5.2)$$

Since the total stock of money equals the total stock of loans, it also follows that in the steady state total income is equal to total loans outstanding divided by the money/income norm:

$$Y = LI/\alpha \qquad (5.3)$$

Development of the model

The basic model which has just been illustrated retained certain simplifying assumptions, notably that bank loans are made exclusively to finance working capital and that inventory accumulation is determined exogenously.

This restriction on purposes for which loans are made can quite easily be relaxed without significantly modifying the essential properties of the model. Let us now suppose that there is borrowing which finances final purchases including some consumption expenditure and, more particularly, purchases of real assets such as houses, cars or fixed capital used in production. The device we now adopt is to divide total final purchases into two separate categories termed 'income-generated' expenditure, YFE, and 'loan-financed' expenditure, LFE,* thus

$$FE \equiv YFE + LFE \qquad (5.4)$$

* See Chapters 12 and 13 for a more sophisticated approach which allows for repayments of existing debt and the possible need for stocks of money associated with ongoing streams of loan-financed expenditure.

The discussion of adjustment of spending and money stocks in Chapter 3 now applies only to income-generated expenditure (determinants of loan-financed expenditure remaining unspecified). in the complete model the equation for loans must be rewritten as

$$\Delta L = \Delta I + LFE \tag{5.5}$$

i.e., new loans, ΔL, are equal to the sum of changes in the value of inventories and loan-financed final purchases. It is the combination of the two latter which 'drive' the model as a whole.

The above helps to make it clear that development of realistic forms of the model, applied to actual economies, may require descriptions of the determination of many types of loan-financed expenditure.

The process of generalization will bring in more types of financial asset (e.g., bonds and equity) and more financial institutions (e.g., those engaged in providing consumer credit or finance for real estate). This is why we have used the general notation FA (financial assets) for the stock of money discussed up to this point. Although government debt will soon be brought in, the main examination of issues raised by wider classes of financial assets and liabilities is left until Chapter 13.

One other point worth mentioning here is that some borrowing may be undertaken purely for the purpose of, or as a counterpart to, the holding of financial assets. This is broadly true of the liabilities of banks and financial institutions but it can also be true in part for private individuals and non-financial businesses. We shall always consider financial assets and liabilities to be measured net of debt of this kind.

Endogenous inventories in the simple model

Chapter 4 postulated that inventories are endogenous – their size being determined by the production period and the level of sales. Yet so far in this chapter they have been treated as exogenous.

It is important to discuss the consequences of treating loan-financed inventories as endogenous in the model now deployed because it brings out very strikingly the importance of monetary policy.

As pointed out earlier in this chapter, the adjustment of aggregate income and expenditure flows to loan financed expenditure should be instantaneous. But the amount of credit supplied to finance inventories and other loan-financed expenditure is itself likely to be sensitive to changes in income. Small changes in the desired ratio of inventories to income could alter the whole dynamic of income-expenditure flows, setting in train cumulative expansions or contractions of borrowing. One can see, for instance, that if income growth causes loans to expand faster than people want to hold the money created (in view of the corresponding aggregate income flow), an explosive growth of aggregate income could occur. Alternatively if the demand for loans was persistently weak relative to income, aggregate money income could fall continuously. These possibilities strongly suggest the need for a central monetary authority which by one means or another will regulate the aggregate flow of credit.

Stability in the very short run

In the very short run inventories play, in reality, a stabilizing role. It was pointed out in Chapter 1 that stocks of finished goods make it possible for people to buy things in shops without the need for simultaneous adjustments in the flow of production (other than 'production' involved in the act of selling itself). A sudden change in the flow of aggregate final sales will in the very short run cause an offsetting change in the value of inventories. This will be reflected in a change in bank lending and the aggregate stock of money.

Suppose, for example, that people change their idea of what constitutes a sensible value for the money/income norm. Suddenly one day they feel that their holdings of money are unnecessarily high. In the very short run two things will happen simultaneously. On the one hand they will spend more, increasing the income of retailers. On the other hand inventories of finished goods will fall; money will return to the banking system as deposits and loans are simultaneously reduced. But at the second stage, as inventories are rebuilt and production is stepped up, there will be a general rise in income inducing further increases in final sales. The end result could be that the value of inventories and stock of money returned to their original level while flows of income and final purchases had permanently increased.

This example indicates the nature of the abstraction made in the period-by-period solution of the model presented in the chapter, and in other solutions later in this book which treat the total amount of debt outstanding as exogenous or as being determined by other processes. In these solutions we are abstracting from very short periods in which the stock of inventories and associated debt vary inversely with changes in the flow of final purchases unless the latter have been precisely anticipated in advance.

Summary

This chapter has been a crucially important one. We started with a description of a simple banking system which creates money by making loans.

We then showed how to obtain a sequential solution for the aggregate income and expenditure flows of a very simple but fully interdependent economic system conditional on the accumulation of working capital by entrepreneurs. In particular we showed how loans and the associated loan-financed expenditure created money to an equal extent together with a flow of aggregate income and final purchases on whatever scale was appropriate to this money creation process. As in Chapter 3, the dynamics of the entire sequential solution are governed by stock-flow norms or, what amounts to the same thing, the rate at which money is spent. The later sections of the chapter elaborated the model to include alternative forms of debt (and therefore money) creation.

Appendix 5.1 *Formal analysis of the model*

We start from the national income identity

$$Y \equiv FE + \Delta I \tag{A5.1}$$

Next we have the banks' balance sheet which says their assets (loans) always equal their liabilities (money) and we assume that loans are always equal to the value of inventories

$$FA = LI = I \tag{A5.2}$$

Final purchases are given by the identity

$$FE \equiv Y - \Delta FA \tag{A5.3}$$

The money adjustment process was formulated in Chapter 3 as

$$FA^{\star} = \alpha Y \tag{A5.4}$$
$$\Delta FA = \phi(FA^{\star} - FA_{-1}) \tag{A5.5}$$

As in Chapter 3, we can solve for FE by putting A5.4 and A5.5 back in to A5.3

$$FE = (1 - \alpha\phi)Y + \phi FA_{-1} \tag{A5.6}$$

which, as we saw, may also be written with current and lagged income terms on the right hand side as

$$FE = (1 - \alpha\phi)Y + \alpha\phi^2 Y_{-1} + \alpha\phi^2(1 - \phi)Y_{-2} + \\ \alpha\phi^2(1 - \phi)^2 Y_{-3} + \ldots \tag{A5.7}$$

where (in accordance with the proof in Appendix 2 to Chapter 3) the sum of all the coefficients on income is unity and the mean lag of final expenditure behind income is α.

Now whereas in Chapter 3 we had to treat income as exogenous, we can now solve for aggregate income, Y, by putting A5.6 back into A5.1 to obtain the disequilibrium solution

$$Y = (\Delta I + \phi FA_{-1})/\alpha\phi \qquad (A5.8)$$

The steady-state solution of this model already noted in equation 5.2 is given by

$$Y = FA/\alpha \qquad (A5.9)$$

We can infer from the disequilibrium solution A5.8 that the steady state is reached instantaneously – i.e., it holds for all periods in which $\Delta I = 0$ and, therefore, $FA = FA_{-1}$.

The flow of final sales may be derived by virtue of A5.2, A5.3 and A5.8 as

$$FE \equiv Y - \Delta FA \equiv Y - \Delta I$$

$$= \frac{(1-\alpha\phi)}{\alpha\phi} \Delta I + \frac{1}{\alpha} FA_{-1} \qquad (A5.10)$$

Note that the period-by solutions only make sense if

$$\alpha\phi < 1 \qquad (A5.11)$$

A numerical simulation

We start with an *exogenous* time-series for the value of inventories, I, at the end of each period from which, by differencing, we can immediately calculate the change in the value of inventories in each period, ΔI. Table 5.1 below illustrates this with the value of inventories in column (1) and

Table A5.1 Example of a numerical solution of the simple model

Period	(1) End-period value of inventories = loans = stock of money	(2) Change in inventories in period = change in stock of money (from (1))	(3) Final sales in period = final purchases	(4) Total income = total expenditure = (2)+(3)
1	450	0	600	600
2	450	0	600	600
3	500	50	667	717
4	575	75	767	842
5	650	75	867	842
6	665	15	887	902
7	675	10	900	910
8	675	0	900	900
9	675	0	900	900
10	675	0	900	900

changes in the value of inventories in column (2). The numbers in the table are those from which Chart 5.1 was drawn.

How do we obtain the flows of final and total income in columns (3) and (4)? If we knew either one, it would be easy to calculate the other since total income must always be equal to total expenditure which is the sum of final sales and the change in inventories:

$$Y \equiv FE + \Delta I$$

But this does not tell us what the level of income and final sales must be.

The general principle is that the flow of income must be at the level at which people choose to hold the stock of money which in this example is equal to the value of inventories in column 1. In the initial steady state (periods 1 and 2), income will have to be $600 (if the money/income norm is 3/4) in order to be consistent with the stock of money which is \$450. And in any steady state after the value of inventories has levelled off at \$676 (period 8 onwards) income will have to be \$900. But how do we calculate the transitional path and how do we know when the new steady-state level of income will be achieved?

A sequential solution for total income may readily be calculated from equation A5.8 given an exogenous time series for ΔI, an opening value for FA, and values for α (here 3/4) and ϕ (here 4/7). Thus income in period 3 is $(50 \times 4/7 \times 450) \div (3/4 \times 4/7)$ = 717. Final sales can now be obtained as the difference between columns (4) and (2) (i.e., 667) and it should be checked that this satisfies equation A5.10, i.e., $(1 - 3/7) \div 3/7 \times 50 + 450 \div 3/4 = 667$. We then have for period 4 a new opening value for FA_{-1} (the difference between columns (4) and (3)) which makes it possible to calculate a solution for period 4 conditional on ΔI in that period.

The reader may check that the new steady state is invariably reached instantaneously when ΔI settles down to zero although final expenditure lags behind income throughout the transitional period.

A specific version of the adjustment process

Equation A5.4 and A5.5 may be combined to yield the expression

$$FA = FA_{-1} + \alpha\phi YP - \phi FA_{-1}$$
$$= \alpha\phi YP + (1 - \phi)FA_{-1} \qquad (A5.12)$$

This says that the *money stock* at the end of any period, FA, is equal to some proportion, $\alpha\phi$, of income in that period plus some other proportion $(1 - \phi)$ of the stock of money inherited at the start of the period.

Equation A5.12 above is logically equivalent to A5.6 which said that *expenditure* in any period will be equal to a proportion $(1 - \alpha\phi)$ of income in that period plus a proportion, ϕ, of the inherited stock of money.

Now the total amount of funds available for spending in any period (always assuming no borrowings) is equal to the flow of income in that period plus the stock of money inherited from the previous period (i.e., $Y+FA_{-1}$). Let us now assume that in deciding how much of the total funds available will be spent in any period, the income flow, Y, ranks one-for-one with the inherited stock of money, FA_{-1}, the latter being nothing other than the remaining balance of income received but not spent in all previous periods. For this to happen, the proportion of income in any period, $(1-\alpha\phi)$ in equation A5.6, has to equal the proportion of inherited money, ϕ, which is spent in that period. This yields a unique value for the parameter, ϕ, which governs the speed of adjustment of the money stock. The value of ϕ must be such that

$$1-\alpha\phi = \phi$$

which implies that ϕ is given by

$$\phi = \frac{1}{1+\alpha} \qquad (A5.13)$$

When ϕ takes this value, the allocation of total funds available between expenditure and the end-period stock of money is unbiassed. That is to say, the use of funds is independent of whether they derive from current income or unspent past income (the inherited money balance). This may be demonstrated formally by substituting the specific value of ϕ given in equation A5.13 into the equations for the end-period stock of money A5.12 and for expenditure A5.6. The results are

$$FA = \frac{\alpha}{1+\alpha} (Y+FA_{-1}) \qquad (A5.14)$$

and

$$FE = \frac{1}{1+\alpha} (Y+FA_{-1}) \qquad (A5.15)$$

We can relate the end-period stock of money, FA, to final purchases in a very simple form. Combining equations A5.14 and A5.15 above yields

$$FA = \alpha FE \qquad\qquad (A5.16)$$

This equation implies that in each and every period, whether in a steady state or a steady growth path or before or after a shock change in income, the ratio of the end-period stock of money to expenditure will always be exactly α, the money/income norm.

Table A5.1 revisited

When we devised Table A5.1 we chose to give a value to ϕ (4/7) which did indeed satisfy $\phi = 1/1+\alpha$, α being 3/4.

In view of this assumption the numbers in the table can be very much more simply derived than before.

In view of the equation A5.16 above

$$FA = \alpha FE$$

we can simply write down the values in column (3) as $FA \div \alpha$. FA can alternatively be obtained as the sum of the opening stock, FA_{-1}, and the change in inventories, ΔI, which is exogenous. For instance in period 3 we may now simply write down final sales as

$$(1) \div 3/4, \text{ which is } 500 \div 3/4 = 667$$

The reader may check that the adjustment of money stocks implied by the table makes sense in relation to income. For example, in period 3 the money stock norm corresponding to income of $717 is

$$0.75 \times \$717 = \$538$$

while the opening money stock is only $450. Actual holdings of money rise to $500 by the end of the period. The proportion of the gap which has been made up during the period is

$50/$88 = 0.57

It will be found that the same proportion of the gap between the current money stock norm and the opening money stock is made up in every subsequent period. This proportion is in fact the value of the speed-of-adjustment parameter, ϕ, which is equal to

$$\phi = \frac{1}{1+\alpha} = \frac{1}{1.75} = 0.57$$

The calculation of the whole solution shown in Table 5.1 is deceptively simple, although it is extremely convenient since we can more or less write down the answers. We have explained what is going on behind the figures rather carefully in order to be sure that the reader will be fully aware of the adjustment processes which underlie the numerical calculation. Once having grasped these, the reader will not be disturbed to find similar short-cuts employed in numerical examples in later chapters. So long as the specific adjustment process with $\phi = 1/(1+\alpha)$ is assumed, we shall always know that private final purchases in every period must be equal to the end-period stock of money or financial assets divided by α, from which we shall readily be able to obtain solutions for total money income.

Simple solution for national income when $\phi = 1/(1+\alpha)$

When the money adjustment process is given by equation A5.16, and given that FA $\equiv$ I (A5.2), the solution of the model is

$$FE = I/\alpha \tag{A5.17}$$

and, using the national income identity (A5.1),

$$Y \equiv FE + \Delta I = \frac{I}{\alpha} + \Delta I \tag{A5.18}$$

Instability of the model with endogenous inventories

The solution for final sales, conditional on inventories, is given by A5.10 above (putting $FA_{-1} = I_{-1}$) as

$$FE = \frac{(1-\alpha\phi)}{\alpha\phi} \Delta I + \frac{1}{\alpha} I_{-1}$$

Using g to denote the proportionate change in the value of inventories in each period we may write

$$\Delta I = gI_{-1} \tag{A5.19}$$

We can derive the ratio of opening inventories, I_{-1}, to final sales in each period as

$$\gamma \equiv \frac{I_{-1}}{FE} = \frac{\alpha\phi}{\phi + g(1-\alpha\phi)} \tag{A5.20}$$

Suppose that there is a normal or desirable level of opening inventories relative to final sales. Sales will turn out to be such that this norm is fulfilled if and only if the 'growth rate' of inventories, g, takes the particular value

$$g = \frac{(\alpha-\gamma)\phi}{\gamma(1-\alpha\phi)} \tag{A5.21}$$

where γ now represents the inventory/sales norm.

In principle the model could follow a steady growth path in which inventories, final sales and total income all grew steadily at the rate given by A5.21 and the actual inventory/sales ratio always matched the norm.

But the system would be unstable. This can be seen by considering the consequences of any disturbance to inventory accumulation decisions, represented by g. From A5.20 we can infer what would happen to the *ex post* ratio of opening inventories to final sales:

$$\frac{d\,\gamma}{dg} = \frac{\alpha\phi(1-\alpha\phi)}{(\phi+g(1-\alpha\phi))^2}$$

$$- \frac{(1-\alpha\phi)}{\alpha\phi} \cdot \gamma^2 \qquad (A5.22)$$

It was noted earlier (A5.11) that period-by-period solutions only make sense at all if

$$\alpha\phi < 1$$

Assuming that this condition is fulfilled, A5.22 tells us that the more inventories are increased in each period, the higher final sales will be relative to opening inventories. Thus once the steady growth rate given by A5.21 was exceeded, inventories would never 'catch up' with the norm no matter how fast inventories increased. The norm could only be reestablished if for some reason the growth of inventories happened to slow down again to the rate given by A5.21.

Things may not be quite so bad if the norm relates to the ratio of closing (rather than opening) inventories to sales in each period. Redefining the inventory/sales ratio γ in this sense, the outcome in each period (obtained by multiplying A5.20 by $1+g$) is now

$$\gamma = \frac{\alpha\phi(1+g)}{\phi+g(1-\alpha\phi)} \qquad (A5.23)$$

The effect of changes in g is

$$\frac{d\gamma}{dg} = \frac{(\phi(1+\alpha)-1)}{\alpha\phi} \cdot \frac{\gamma^2}{(1+g)^2} \qquad (A5.24)$$

If ϕ takes the value

$$\phi = \frac{1}{1+\alpha}$$

changes in g have no effect on the (end-period) inventory/sales ratio which must always turn out to be equal to α. If ϕ is smaller than this, A5.24 implies the same kind of instability as before. If ϕ is larger (i.e., if people adjust money stocks rapidly when income changes), it becomes possible for inventories to 'catch up' with a norm for γ.

There is little point in formulating mechanical rules to determine g and thereby close the model as a whole with inventories endogenous. Inventory accumulation must by its nature be an act of faith, prompted by anticipations of future sales which will hardly ever be fulfilled precisely. These anticipations are the one basic driving force of the very simple model examined so far. They may be influenced not only by what has actually been happening to sales but also by monetary policy (the cost and terms of credit). And in a more realistic model they will be affected by guesses about other things (e.g., fiscal decisions and external trade) which intervene in the determination of income and expenditure.

PART III

Fiscal and monetary policy in a closed economy

6 The fiscal system

This chapter and the next two are designed to show how fiscal and monetary policies work in a closed economy. The analysis is still in money terms at current prices, and to keep the model simple we shall still confine private debt to borrowing which finances inventories. In this chapter and in Chapter 7 the only financial assets will be money in the form of notes and bank deposits: the government is assumed to finance deficits in its budget by borrowings from banks on which it pays interest.* Bonds will only appear for the first time in Chapter 8.

Our plan is as follows. This chapter introduces taxation and government expenditure as such and shows how they affect aggregate income and expenditure flows in the absence of any independent monetary policy. It will be shown that the government's tax and expenditure decisions can determine steady states and that, once again, transitions from one steady state to another take a well-determined length of time. There will be a mean lag in the response of the whole system to changes in government spending which is analogous to the mean lag for private spending relative to income described in Chapter 3.

Chapter 7 examines how monetary policy can affect expenditure decisions and income determination, but without enquiring into mechanisms within the financial system itself by means of which a central bank may enforce monetary policy. The latter question is taken up in Chapter 8.

These three chapters will complete our main discussion of the monetary system. We return to look at the significance of wider classes of assets and debts in Chapter 13.

---

* The formal assumption is that interest rates and terms of credit to private borrowers are held constant (just as in Chapter 5) irrespective of the state of the government's budget.

New concepts

In order to discuss the effect of government budgets on a macroeconomic system it is necessary to expand the national income/expenditure identity. Final sales, FE, must include government expenditure, G, as well as private sector purchases, PE.

$$FE \equiv G + PE \qquad (6.1)$$

The national income identity is

$$Y \equiv E \equiv FE + \Delta I \equiv G + PE + \Delta I \qquad (6.2)$$

which puts total income, Y, in each period equal to the sum of government expenditure, private final purchases and the change in the value of inventories, ΔI.

Chart 6.1 The split of aggregate expenditure between the government and the private sector

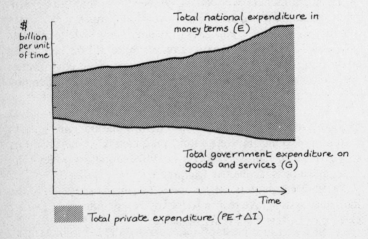

The diagram represents the path of aggregate expenditure and its main components through time. The numbers are arbitrary, the purpose being to show logical, accounting relationships not causal ones. The shaded area represents private expenditure (including inventory accumulation)* – necessarily the difference between total national expenditure and government expenditure.

Next we introduce the division of total income between the government and the private sector.

Chart 6.2 The split of primary income between the government and the private sector

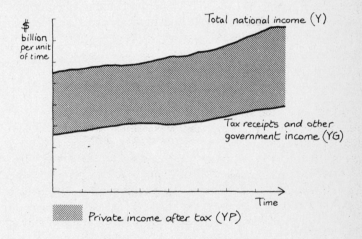

The flow of funds

Since the national income must always be equal to total national expenditure we can superimpose Charts 6.1 and 6.2 to illustrate what is called *the flow of funds identity*.

* It is assumed that there is no accumulation of inventories by the government.

Chart 6.3 The flow of funds identity

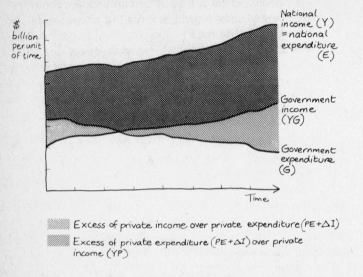

Excess of private income over private expenditure $(PE + \Delta I)$

Excess of private expenditure $(PE + \Delta I)$ over private income (YP)

In Chart 6.3 the single hatched areas are *simultaneously* the difference between government expenditure and tax receipts, and the difference between private income less tax and total private expenditure. Thus any budget deficit of the government *must* always, by the laws of logic, be matched by a private sector financial surplus (vice versa if the government has a budget surplus).

Let us derive this result algebraically from national accounting identities.

Chapter 1 introduced the division of aggregate money income, Y, between private disposable income, YP, and net government income, YG:

$$Y \equiv YP + YG \tag{6.3}$$

Net government income in fact depends on other things beside tax receipts. It also includes on the credit side social security contributions and profits of government-owned enterprises. But from these must be deducted payments of social security benefits, subsidies and interest on the government's debt.

Now recall the national income identity (6.2 above).

$$Y \equiv G + PE + \Delta I$$

and subtract net government income from both sides. This gives

$$YP \equiv Y - YG \equiv G - YG + PE + \Delta I$$

and, rearranging,

$$YP - (PE + \Delta I) \equiv G - YG \qquad (6.4)$$

The left-hand side represents the excess of private disposable income over private expenditure including inventory accumulation, which is the private sector financial surplus. The right-hand side represents the excess of government spending on goods and services over net government income which is the government's budget deficit. The identity 6.4 says that the private sector surplus must be equal to the government's deficit.

Money creation

The government budget makes a fundamental difference to the money creation process.

In Chapter 5 changes in the stock of money were always exactly equal to changes in bank lending to the private sector. Now, with a government budget, changes in the stock of money are equal to changes in bank lending to the private sector *plus* changes in bank lending to the government.

The budget deficit in each period (G−YG in equation 6.4) must be financed by government borrowing in the same period:

$$G - YG \equiv \Delta GD \qquad (6.5)$$

where in our very simple financial system GD, end-period

government debt, takes the form of bank lending to the government.

The private financial surplus in each period – the excess of disposable income over expenditure by the private sector (the left-hand side of equation 6.4) – is equal to the change in the stock of money, ΔFA, less private borrowing in the same period:

$$YP - (PE + \Delta I) \equiv \Delta FA - \Delta PD \qquad (6.6)$$

where PD, end-period private debt, takes the form of bank lending to the private sector.

The flow-of-funds identity (6.4) may therefore be rewritten entirely in terms of changes in stock variables

$$\Delta FA - \Delta PD \equiv \Delta GD$$

or, rearranging,

$$\Delta FA \equiv \Delta GD + \Delta PD \qquad (6.7)$$

The equation says that the change in the stock of money is always equal to the change in bank lending to the government plus the change in bank lending to the private sector.

It provides the identity ruling the money creation process when there is a government budget (and, of course, when money is still the only financial asset).

The balance sheet of the banking system

What we have just discussed is the equivalence between *changes* in stocks of money and *changes* in bank lending to the government and private sector. The same equivalence holds for *levels*, as can be seen from the balance sheets of the banking system which, when consolidated, can be written as

$$GD + PD \equiv FA \qquad (6.8)$$

Banks' assets comprise lending to the government and to the private sector; their total assets are equal to their liabilities which consist of deposits and notes held by the non-bank public. If the government itself holds money balances, these are implicitly to be offset against government debt. Thus, properly speaking, GD is a net concept representing bank lending to the government less money balances held by the government. In this chapter we shall assume that government debt has no special status and that transactions of banks with the private sector are subject to no form of regulation other than exogenous determination of interest rates (as in Chapter 5). Discussion of the possible role of government debt as a 'reserve asset' of the banks will be deferred to Chapter 8.

Further assumptions to complete the model

In what follows we take the flow of government expenditure as exogenous.

Next imagine that the government can in each period determine the share, θ, of the aggregate income flow it desires (by its choice of tax rates etc).* Net government income will be equal to aggregate income multiplied by this 'tax rate' or income share:

$$YG \equiv \theta Y \tag{6.9}$$

---

* Many indirect taxes as well as direct taxes have yields which are broadly proportionate to national income. But in real life there may be problems of fiscal management arising from non-proportionality of the yield of the tax system as a whole relative to money national income, particularly when what matters, as here, is the net proceeds of taxes less grants and subsidies paid out. Payments of interest by the government introduce a further real-life complication especially when (for whatever reason) rates of interest change rapidly. Perhaps the biggest difficulty of all, which is not discussed in this book, is that the overall 'tax rate', θ (net of grants, subsidies and interest payments), often cannot readily be adjusted, especially upwards, because of political and/ or administrative limitations on the government's power to raise revenue. When government spending also has a dynamic of its own, use of the fiscal system as a policy instrument to influence the processes we are now going to discuss may be fraught with practical difficulties. In the extreme case it would

To make inventory accumulation endogenous, let us assume that producers and traders sufficiently foresee changes in expenditure to keep their inventories at the end of each period at a normal level relative to the flow of final sales in the previous period.*

In formal terms this may be written

$$I = \gamma FE_{-1} \tag{6.10}$$

where I is the end-period value of inventories, γ is the normal inventory/sales ratio, and FE_{-1} is the flow of final sales in the previous period.

Finally, just as in Chapter 5, let private debt, PD, be confined to borrowing on inventories, LI,

$$PD \equiv LI \equiv I \tag{6.11}$$

and as before we postulate norms for the asset/income ratio, α, and the money adjustment process, ϕ.

be necessary to regard the tax rate and government spending simply as exogenous variables without any connotation that they could be used as deliberate policy instruments for macroeconomic regulation.

* This might be the case, for example, if they have enough foresight and flexibility to avoid a fall in inventories in a period when sales rise (however rapid the increase in sales) and if they manage to 'catch up' with a past change in the flow of sales by the end of the period after the one in which the flow of sales changed. We shall need to reconsider changes in the money value of inventories in later chapters when the distinction between inflation (price changes) and volume changes is made explicit.

How does the whole system work?

We now have a model which determines a unique sequential path for national income and expenditure, the aggregate stock of money, the government's budget deficit and private income and spending conditional on five *exogenous* variables. Of these, government expenditure on goods and services, G, and the government's income share, θ, represent fiscal decisions governed by politics and administrative policy. The other three exogenous variables are the three proportions defining private sector behaviour: the inventory/sales norm, γ; the money/income norm, α; and the ratio governing the speed-of-adjustment of assets towards a norm represented by ϕ.

Formally, given these policy and behavioural variables and the simplifying assumptions which have been made, the model is entirely composed of identities. The Appendix shows how to calculate numerical solutions, period by period, for national income and all the other endogenous variabes. But the most important thing is to understand qualitatively how the system works.

We shall now use charts to examine how the system responds to government expenditure decisions when the other exogenous variables are held fixed. This will adequately demonstrate the main properties of our closed monetary economy with a government which is able to make autonomous or independent fiscal decisions.*

The same expositional device will be used as before. Starting from a steady state, a once-for-all shock is administered to one exogenous variable (government expenditure) and all ensuing processes are tracked to the point where a new steady state is achieved.

---

* Note that, as will be shown in Chapter 7, the government may not be able to choose its spending and tax policies independently if it (and/or the central bank) is committed to targets for monetary aggregates such as the level of government debt or the stock of money.

The steady state

The easiest way into the analysis is to consider first what steady states *must* look like. From our general axiom that steady states imply zero changes in all stock variables it can be inferred immediately and precisely what the aggregate national income flow has to be. If changes in all financial assets and liabilities are zero, this logically implies, by the flow of funds identity (equations 6.4 and 6.7), that total government expenditure is equal to net government income; the budget is exactly balanced. Given the rate of government expenditure, G, and its income share, θ, there is only one value for the national income flow which results in a balanced budget – the value which generates net government income equal to government expenditure.

Chart 6.4 Flow properties of a steady state

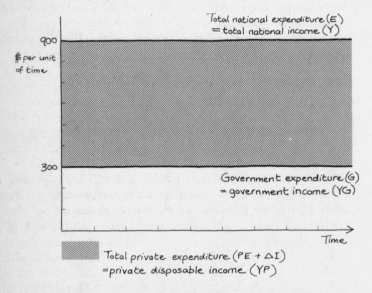

Chart 6.4 assumes that government expenditure is stable at

$300 and the income share, θ, is 1/3. The national income then has to be $900 if net government income is to equal government expenditure.

Formally, if $\quad\quad\quad\quad\quad G = YG$
and if, as we have assumed, $YG = \theta Y$
then, by substitution $\quad\quad G = \theta Y$
and $\quad\quad\quad\quad\quad\quad\quad Y = G/\theta$ $\quad\quad\quad\quad$ (6.12)

Let us call G/θ (the ratio of government expenditure to its income share) the *fiscal stance*. The equation shows that under the assumption that in a steady state when stocks of money and debt neither rise nor fall, then national income must be *equal* to the fiscal stance.

The concept of fiscal stance is of fundamental importance because in the general case it is a representation of the government's fiscal policy instruments – the levers, so to speak, which the government is actually able to pull.* And we shall go on to show that by pulling these levers the government can closely determine what the aggregate national income will be in the short run as well as in the long run.

What is the meaning of the steady state solution?

$\quad\quad Y = G/\theta$

The expression is not just a hypothetical 'equilibrium' state in the sense of being some timeless intersection of two curves. It is a prediction of the flow of national income which will actually become established in historical time if the government adopts a particular fiscal stance and does not thereafter change it. this level of income will be maintained continuously by flows between the government and the private sector as in Chart 6.4.

Recall that in the steady state the budget must balance whatever the fiscal stance. There has to be some mechanism which gets the flow of national income up or down to he level which equals the fiscal stance, thereby generating a balanced budget.

* Subject to the reservations noted in the footnote on page 107 above.

The reader may legitimately wonder at this stage just what the mechanism is and how long it takes, and we shall shortly answer these questions.

Steady-state balance sheets

Before considering how the national income moves from one steady state to another it is important to note that we have the material to infer the precise counterpart of Chart 6.4 in terms of stocks of financial assets and liabilities. These are shown in Chart 6.5.

Chart 6.5 Stock properties of the steady state

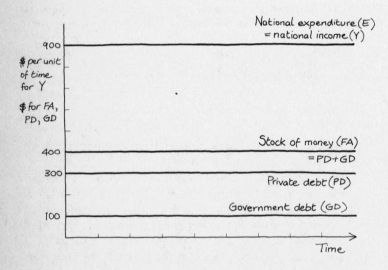

We have postulated that in the steady state the stock of money is in some proportion, α, to private disposable income:

$$FA = \alpha YP = \alpha(1-\theta)Y \qquad (6.13)$$

Assuming that α is 2/3 and that (as in Chart 6.4) θ is 1/3, the stock of money must be

$$2/3 \times (1-1/3) \times \$900 = 4/9 \times \$900 = £400.$$

We also know that private debt, PD, is equal to the value of inventories whch in the steady state are some proportion, γ, of aggregate income:

$$PD = I = \gamma FE_{-1} = \gamma FE = \gamma Y \qquad (6.14)$$

Assuming that γ is 1/3, the level of private debt must be

$$1/3 \times \$900 = \$300$$

We can derive government debt, GD, in the steady state from the balance sheet of the banking system (identity 6.8) and the results already obtained for the stock of money and private debt. Thus

$$GD+PD \equiv FA$$
$$= \$100+\$300 = \$400$$

We now have, by the identity 6.8 written out above, that the stock of money always equals government debt plus private debt. We also have (by 6.13 above) that in the steady-state money is in its normal relationship to disposable income. We therefore now have (combining 6.8 with 6.13) that in the steady state government and private debt combined are in a known ratio to income

$$FA \equiv GD+PD = \alpha(1-\theta)Y \qquad (6.15)$$

Accordingly we can now write the steady state for income in two different ways. In terms of stock variables by rearrangement of 6.15 income is given by

$$Y = \frac{GD+PD}{\alpha(1-\theta)} \qquad (6.16)$$

while in terms of flow variables steady-state income is given by 6.12

$$Y = G/\theta$$

The equivalence, in the steady state, of the right-hand side of 6.16 and 6.12

$$\frac{GD+PD}{\alpha(1-\theta)} = \frac{G}{\theta}$$

may seem a little surprising at this stage since it has the powerful implication that fiscal stance (G/θ) will somehow or other ultimately generate the same aggregate income flow *irrespective of the amount of private debt creation (PD) and also independent of the money income norm* (α). So it must be implying that more or less private debt, so long as fiscal stance is given, must give rise to a change of equal and opposite size in the total of government debt. We shall shortly be showing exactly the mechanics of this displacement (our version of 'crowding out') but it is already possible to see that such a process must occur.

We should finally draw attention to the relationship between the 'stock' version of the steady state we now have (6.16 above) and that which we reached in Chapter 5 (5.3) when there was no fiscal system. It is apparent that our new expression

$$Y = \frac{PD+GD}{\alpha(1-\theta)}$$

will converge to the earlier steady state

$$Y = \frac{PD}{\alpha}$$

as the government's debt GD and its income share θ shrink to zero. (In Chapter 5 debt was generated by inventories, i.e., PD = LI.)

The consequence of a step change in government expenditure

Chart 6.6 illustrates an economy in two steady states. To avoid congestion, stock variables shown in the upper half have been separated from flow variables shown in the lower half.

The opening steady state is exactly the same as that illustrated in Charts 6.4 and 6.5. Government expenditure is $300 per period and the government's income share is 1/3. The aggregate income flow is $900 per period. This is the only solution consistent with zero changes in all stocks.

$$Y = G/\theta = \$300 \div 1/3 = \$900$$

The stock of money FA represented in the upper half of the table is

$$FA = \alpha(1-\theta)Y = 2/3 \times 2/3 \times \$900 = \$400$$

The stock of private sector debt PD is

$$PD = \gamma Y = 1/3 \times \$900 = \$300$$

Government debt, GD, is the difference between the stock of money, FA, and private sector debt, PD:

$$GD = FA - PD = \$400 - \$300 = \$100$$

We next postulate a 50% step increase in government expenditure and can immediately infer that the value of all stocks and flows in the new steady state will also be 50% higher (the reader may check this by repeating the calculations above with G equal to $450).

Knowing that the two steady states must be determined in this way, we can ascertain from the various stock-flow relationships to a close degree of accuracy what has to be the nature and duration of the intervening period. The dynamics of the whole system are pinned down because we know:

Chart 6.6 Steady-state solutions with no characterization of the time path between them

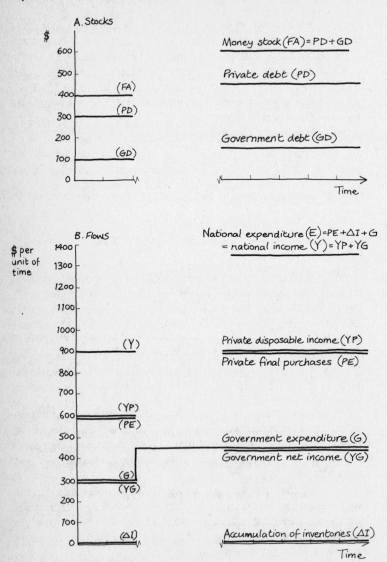

(1) The excess of the flow of private disposable income, YP, over the flow of private final expenditure, PE, over the transitional period as a whole must be equal to the difference between the initial and final steady-state stocks of money ($600−$400 = $200).

(2) The cumulative flow of inventory accumulation in the transitional period must be equal to the difference between the initial and final steady-state value of inventories ($450−$300 = $150).

(3) The flow of net government income must fulfil two conditions simultaneously. It must constitute a proportion, θ, of the aggregate income flow. But it also must be such as to generate a cumulative budget deficit equal to the difference between the initial and final steady-state stock of government debt ($150−$100 = $50).

The whole sequential solution is represented in Chart 6.7.

The causal story

Exposition of the sequential process in the form of a transition between two stable steady states is, as in Chapter 5, a purely expositional device. The reader should always keep in mind that real economies are never in stable steady states. They are wobbling round in response to a host of current and previous shocks of many kinds. The dynamics of the system are being illustrated by the sequential process *through* the transitional period. It is a feature of the analysis to which we attach paramount importance that it yields answers for the progress of stocks and flows in what are often called 'disequilibrium' states: *the time paths are pinned down by structure of the model.*

Those who prefer to work these things out formally may refer at each stage to the analytic solution for any 'disequilibrium' period which is given in the appendix.

The sequential process illustrated in Chart 6.7 will be easy to follow so long as the simpler process described in Chapter 5 has already been fully understood.

In Chapter 5 we had as the exogenous variable the change in the value of inventories which itself constituted an expenditure

Chart 6.7 Characterization of the transition between steady states

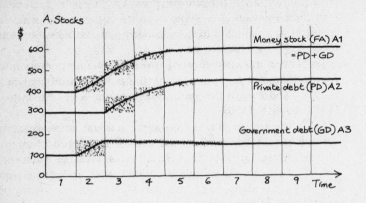

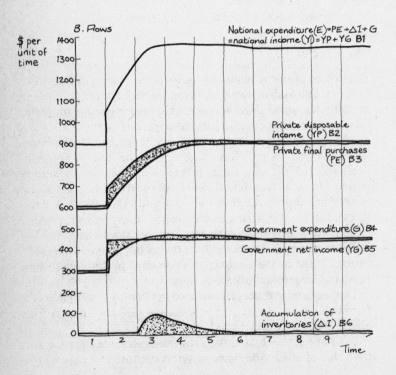

Chart 6.7 illustrates the following:

Line A1   The stock of financial assets, FA, with rectangles representing changes in the stock in each period – areas which must equal the difference between lines B2 and B3, period by period.

Line A2   The stock of private sector debt, PD, with rectangles representing increases in the debt period by period. These must be equal in area to the areas below line B6.

Line A3   The stock of government debt, GD. The rectangles must equal the areas between lines B4 and B5 period by period. They must also equal the difference between the rectangles constructed around A1 and A2.

Line B1   The flow of aggregate national income and expenditure, Y, also equal to B2+B4+B6.

Line B2   The flow of private disposable income, YP, also equal to B1 less B5.

Line B3   The flow of final purchases by the private sector, PE.

Line B4   Exogenous flows of government expenditure, G, which drive the whole system along.

Line B5   Net government income, YG, assumed to be one third of the aggregate income flow B1.

Line B6   Accumulation of inventories, ΔI, financed by borrowing.

flow but also created additions to the stock of money.

There are three important differences here compared with Chapter 5.

First, we have a different exogenous variable, government expenditure, which we take to be a policy instrument under the control of the central authority. Inventory accumulation and therefore (by assumption) bank loans to the private sector are endogenously determined by the need to increase production.*

---

* By making this assumption we are for the time being assuming away ways in which banking systems themselves may constrain macroeconomic developments. Financial institutions and their control will be discussed in Chapters 7 and 8.

Second, we now have two kinds of loan-financed expenditure, government and private (instead of the latter only); both of these have instantaneous counterparts in the form of increases in the stock of money.

Third, we have taxation of income and other transfers which mean that additions to the stock of money and to the flow of disposable income to the private sector are reduced by the amount of the net 'flow back', of income to government. It is this 'leak' of income into taxation which introduces a stabilizing process forcing the entire system to converge towards a steady state in which national income is equal to the fiscal stance.

The process illustrated in Chart 6.7

What happens is that government expenditure, rising in one step, generates an instantaneous and equivalent increase in the aggregate national income/expenditure flow. But the simultaneous addition to the stock of money and to private *disposable* income is only equal to the rise in government expenditure less the increase in the tax 'flow back'.

The private sector proceeds to spend the addition to its disposable income exactly as in Chapter 5, thereby instituting an income-expenditure-income flow process. Additions to the whole national income flow are created on a scale and at a rate which satisfies the condition that the stock of money is in an appropriate relationship at the end of each period with the collective decision to spend out of disposable income at some defined rate.

In Chapter 5 the amount of money created was equal to the flow of inventory accumulation. Under our new assumptions, the additional amount of money created in each period is equal to the flow of government expenditure, G, *plus* inventory accumulation, ΔI, *less* the flow of net government income, YG generated by the aggregate national income flow.

The speed of adjustment

The speed at which the whole process illustrated in Chart 6.7 takes place is governed by, and can be precisely derived from, three factors taken together.

First there is the speed at which the flow of private final purchases, PE, responds to disposable income; as before the mean lag of this response is equal to the steady-state ratio of money to disposable income per unit of time (two-thirds of a period in the present example).

Second, there is the scale of the response of inventories to growth of national income. If this were very large (e.g., because the normal ratio of inventories to sales was large) this would greatly speed up the response of the whole sysem without altering its steady-state values (since the change in inventories in the steady state is nil).

The third influence on the time response of the system is the rate of taxation. This point can be conveyed by considering two extreme cases. If tax rates were very high then the response of the system would be virtually instantaneous, because the addition to expenditure would take place with very little addition to disposable income. At the other extreme, if there were no taxation at all (and government expenditure were maintained indefinitely at its new level) the response of total national income would be infinite; national income would grow indefinitely because the *constant* flow of government expenditure would be generating indefinitely *rising* stocks of money and flows of private income.

The mean lag

With these observations in mind it is quite easy to infer from the model's parameters the mean lag of the adjustment of the entire system to the increase in government expenditure.

First note that the net government income, YG, has been

assumed to adjust in strict proportion to national income as a whole. So we will know the mean lag in the response of national income to the rise in government expenditure as soon as we know the mean lag in the response of government income to the rise in government expenditure.

Next recall how in Chapter 3 we were able to infer a mean lag by geometry. We did this by using Chart 3.4, by dividing the area representing the total acquisition of money by the step increase in income.

We can carry out an exactly comparable operation on the model presented in this chapter. The response of government income to the shock from government expenditure may be schematically represented as follows.

Chart 6.8 The mean lag in the response of government income

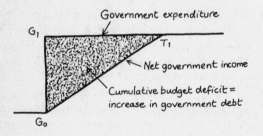

The mean lag will be the area of the triangle $G_0 G_1 T_1$ divided by its base, the length $G_0 G_1$. The area of the triangle is the increase in government debt between the two steady states which

we already know to be $50. The length G_0G_1 is the step increase in government expenditure, $150. So the mean lag must be

$50/$150 = 1/3 of a period.

The general formula for this calculation can be derived as follows.

Defining the symbol d to represent the *total* change in a variable from one steady state to another we start with the identity relating the change in government debt to the private acquisition of financial assets less debts

$$dGD \equiv dFA - dPD \qquad (6.17)$$

The change in private financial assets between steady states is given by

$$dFA = \alpha(1-\theta)dY \qquad (6.18)$$

The change in private debt between steady states is given by

$$dPD = \gamma dFE = \gamma dY \qquad (6.19)$$

Combining 6.17, 6.18 and 6.19 we can infer the addition to government debt as

$$dGD = dFA - dPD = \{\alpha(1-\theta)-\gamma\}dY \qquad (6.20)$$

Now, the change in national debt between steady states is given by

$$dY = dG/\theta \qquad (6.21)$$

The ratio of the change in government debt to the increase in government spending determines the mean lag, putting 6.21 into 6.20, as

$$\frac{dGD}{dG} = \{\alpha(1-\theta)-\gamma\}/\theta \qquad (6.22)$$

In our numerical example we have the mean lag

$$= \{2/3 \times 2/3 - 1/3\} \div 1/3$$
$$= 1/9 \div 1/3$$
$$= 1/3$$

The argument generalizes perfectly well when there are other forms of private debt in addition to loans which finance inventories. The only change which needs to be made is that the inventory/sales ratio, γ, in equation 6.22 must be replaced by the steady-state ratio of private debt as a whole to national income.

We attach great importance to this result. It demonstrates how, once we have a fully interdependent system where all stocks and flows are consistently represented, the dynamic of the response to policy changes of the whole economy through historical time is powerfully constrained by stock flow norms.

The distribution of the lag

The distribution of the lag, i.e., the precise sequence of changes in national income, is influenced by the speed at which inventories (and any other private loan-financed expenditure) adjust towards their new steady-state levels. The example in Chart 6.7 above shows traces of a possible 'inventory cycle' in the sense that national income slightly overshoots its steady-state level in the periods when inventory accumulation is positive.

In an economy with extensive private debt it is quite possible that the steady-state level of net government debt would be zero or even negative (government deposits with financial institutions would exceed its borrowing). The 'mean lag' in the response of national income to changes in government expenditure would then have to be zero or negative. What this means is that the level of national income would substantially overshoot the steady state before returning to it, or cycling around it, as illustrated in the following diagrams.

Chart 6.9 Zero or negative mean lags

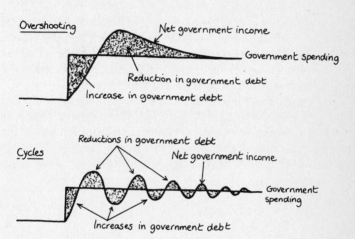

Although the fiscal stance may determine steady states with short or negligible mean lags, the responses of private borrowing to changes in sales and income can still present stabilization problems!

Supply of and demand for money again

We conclude this chapter by reiterating a point made in the last chapter (page 83). We have described a process in which the stock of money is governed determinately and inexorably by five exogenous variables of the system. The government makes decisions about expenditure and taxation. People spend their disposable income at some rate congenial to them. Entrepreneurs build up stocks (and borrow to finance these) to whatever extent is necessary to build up the production flow. That, once more, is the beginning and end of it. There cannot *in addition* be any discrepancy between the amount of money created and the amount of money which people in some sense want to hold. *Adjustments to the flow of aggregate income will always integrate what the government wants to do with what the private sector wants to do.* It cannot even be said that the government by its fiscal actions is determining the quantity of money except in a very indirect sense since the flow of tax receipts (which destroy money) and the flow of bank loans (which create it) are both endogenous to the model.

Appendix 6.1 *Formal analysis of the closed economy with a fiscal system*

Period-by-period solutions of the complete model can be conceived in terms of the following three steps:

(i)   postulate exogenous expenditures and the amount of the addition to the stock of money;
(ii) infer private spending;
(iii) add the various categories of expenditure to determine total national income.

Private spending and money adjustment revisited

The answer for private spending (step two) depends on what we assume about the money adjustment process. For an arbitrary value of ϕ (the speed-of-adjustment parameter) the increase in holdings of money in each period is

$$\Delta FA = \phi(FA^{\star} - FA_{-1})$$
$$= \phi(\alpha YP - FA_{-1}) \qquad (A6.1)$$

where YP is private disposable income, α is the money/income norm and FA_{-1} is the stock of money at the start of the period.

Private final purchases are given by the budget constraint as

$$PE \equiv YP - \Delta FA$$

Substituting A6.1 in terms of the end-period FA and rearranging, this yields

$$PE = \frac{FA}{\alpha} + \frac{(1 - \phi - \alpha\phi)}{\alpha\phi} \Delta FA \qquad (A6.2)$$

So for an arbitrary value of ϕ, private final purchases in any period can be determined once we know the end-period stock of money, FA, and the increase in the stock of money during the period, ΔFA.

When ϕ takes the particular value

$$\phi = \frac{1}{1 + \alpha}$$

the second term on the right-hand side of A6.2 falls out and we are left with

$$PE = FA/\alpha \qquad (A6.3)$$

This is the specific money adjustment process discussed in the appendix to Chapter 5.

To keep the algebra as simple as possible we shall from now on assume that this specific adjustment process is in operation. More general results could be obtained by any very keen reader using A6.2 instead of A6.3. It is clear that the effects of using one rather than the other will usually be small. The second term on the right-hand side of A6.2 is the product of a one-period change, ΔFA, and a coefficient

$$\frac{(1 - \phi - \alpha\phi)}{\alpha\phi}$$

which only differs from zero to the extent that ϕ differs from the specific value $1/(1+\alpha)$. The term will usually be the product of two small numbers.

But there is an instructive case in which A6.2 and A6.3 are significantly different. This is the case in which ϕ is very small. Indeed, as ϕ tends towards zero (no adjustment of holdings of money) the coefficient on ΔFA in A6.2 tends towards infinity. If the model as a whole is to have a solution there must then be some other mechanism which prevents the system from exploding. Given a fiscal system, this function will be performed (if necessary and by default) by taxation which can always offset disturbances to the stock of money (financial assets) held by the private sector if income and expenditure rise or fall far enough.

Solution of the whole model

Let us now follow the three steps proposed at the outset.

(i) Taking government spending, G, as exogenous, inventory accumulation, ΔI, may be regarded as predetermined, if, as proposed in the preceding chapter, it is assumed to depend only on lagged values of other variables. In equation 6.10 the end-period value of inventories was assumed to be

$$I = \gamma FE_{-1}$$

where FE_{-1} is final sales, lagged one period, and γ is the inventory/sales norm. The accumulation of inventories is therefore

$$\Delta I \equiv I - I_{-1} = \gamma FE_{-1} - I_{-1} \tag{A6.4}$$

The addition to the stock of money in each period is equal to the increase in government debt, GD, plus private borrowing to finance inventory accumulation:

$$\Delta FA \equiv \Delta GD + \Delta I \tag{A6.5}$$

The increase in government debt is itself equal to the government's budget deficit:

$$\Delta GD \equiv G - YG \equiv G - \theta Y \qquad (A6.6)$$

where YG is net government income and θ is the government's share of national income, Y. The income share, θ, is regarded as exogenous (see page 109 above). The presence of national income, Y, in A6.6 means that we shall have to go all the way to step three before any endogenous variables in this model can be calculated.

(ii) Private final purchases are inferred from the end-period stock of money (A6.3 above) as

$$PE = FA/\alpha \qquad (A6.7)$$

(iii) National income is determined by the identity

$$Y \equiv E \equiv FE + \Delta I \equiv G + PE + \Delta I \qquad (A6.8)$$

The above equations determine the solution of the model. Thus

$$Y \equiv G + PE + \Delta I \qquad \text{from A6.8}$$

$$= G + \frac{FA}{\alpha} + \Delta I \qquad \text{from A6.7}$$

$$= G + (1 + \frac{1}{\alpha})\Delta I + \frac{\Delta GD}{\alpha} + \frac{FA_{-1}}{\alpha} \qquad \text{from A6.5}$$

$$= (1 + \frac{1}{\alpha})(G + \Delta I) + \frac{FA_{-1}}{\alpha} - \frac{\theta Y}{\alpha} \qquad \text{from A6.6}$$

The disequilibrium solution for national income may therefore be calculated from

$$(1 + \frac{\theta}{\alpha})Y = (1 + \frac{1}{\alpha})(G + \Delta I) + \frac{FA_{-1}}{\alpha} \qquad (A6.9)$$

Then A6.6 gives net government income and the government budget deficit, A6.5 gives the change in the stock of money, and A6.7 gives private final purchases. Total final sales (FE = PE+G) will determine inventory accumulation in the *next* period (A6.4). Private disposable income in each period is

$$YP \equiv Y - YG \qquad\qquad (A6.10)$$

The numerical example in Chart 6.7

To illustrate the calculation of period-by-period solutions, Table A6.1 below gives the numbers from which Chart 6.7 was drawn. The following parameter values were assumed:

$$\alpha = 2/3 \ (\text{with } \phi = 1/(1+\alpha) = 0.6)$$
$$\gamma = 1/3$$
$$\theta = 1/3$$

So $\qquad 1+\dfrac{\theta}{\alpha} = 3/2, \qquad 1+\dfrac{1}{\alpha} = \dfrac{5}{2}$

and A6.9 becomes

$$Y = \frac{5}{3} (G+\Delta I) + FA_{-1} \qquad\qquad (A6.11)$$

Table A6.1 Numerical solution for a step increase in government spending

				($ values)				
period:	1	2	3	4	5	6 ...	∞
1. Government spending G	300	450	450	450	450	450 ...	450
2. End-period value of inventories $I = 1/3\,FE_{-1}$	300	300	383	424	442	449 ...	450
3. Inventory accumulation ΔI	0	0	83	41	18	7 ...	0
4. Opening stock of money FA_{-1}	400	400	467	548	584	597 ...	600
5. National income $Y = 5/3(G+\Delta I)+FA_{-1}$	900	1150	1355	1366	1364	1359 ...	1350
6. Net government income $YG = 1/3\,Y$	300	383	452	455	455	453 ...	450
7. Government budget deficit $\Delta GD = G-YG$	0	67	−2	−5	−5	−3 ...	0
8. Increase in stock of money $\Delta FA = \Delta GD+\Delta I$	0	67	81	36	13	4 ...	0
9. End-period stock of money $FA = FA_{-1}+\Delta FA$	400	467	548	584	597	601 ...	600
10. Private final purchases $PE = 3/2\,FA$	600	700	822	875	896	902 ...	900
11. Total final sales $FE = PE+G$	900	1150	1272	1325	1346	1352 ...	1350
12. Private disposable income $YP = Y-YG$	600	767	903	911	909	906 ...	900
13. End-period government debt $GD = FA-I$	100	167	165	160	155	152 ...	150

The first column of the table (period 1) shows the initial steady state. The first row shows the exogenous step increase in government spending from $300 to $450 (period 2 onwards). Now consider the sequence of calculations for period 2 going down the column. The end-period value of inventories (row 2) is calculated from *previous* period final sales (row 11); in period 2 it remains $300 so that there is zero inventory accumulation (row 3). The opening stock of money (row 4) comes straight from the previous end-period value (row 9). The solution for national income in row 5, $1150, is obtained by applying the formula A6.11 using rows 1, 3 and 4.

The rest is easy. Once row 11 for the value of final sales has been reached, we can go back to the start and do the calculations for the next period. To check that no mistake has been made it is as well to verify that national income (row 5) is the sum of inventory accumulation (row 3) and final sales (row 11). The difference between private income (row 12) and final purchases (row 10) should come out to the increase in the stock of money (row 8). And the change in the stock of government debt (row 13) should be consistent with the budget deficit (row 7).

Balance sheets

It is important continuously to keep in mind the balance sheet implications of what we are doing.

We now have a sector, the government, which has increased its debt by running a budget deficit in the early part of the transitional period. In accordance with the observation at the end of Chapter 6, the government cannot have experienced any difficulty with regard to 'financing' this deficit. It has created more money by running the deficit; money has also been created by bank lending to finance increases in inventories. The national income has expanded to the point at which the increase in the money stock is the counterpart of peoples' decisions to spend income at a certain rate: the private sector has continuously, although unwittingly, 'financed' the government's budget deficit.

But the government deficit does have an important implication for the system of balance sheets. It implies that the banks have acquired assets in the form of loans to the government. They may have done this directly or by making deposits with a central bank which in turn lent to the government.

The following system of balance sheets shows, for each sector, assets and liabilities at the end of each of the first three periods in Table A6.1 above.

Table A6.2 End-period balance sheets

| | Government | | | | | | Banks | | | | | | Non-bank public | | | | | |
| | Liabilities | | | Assets | | | Liabilities | | | Assets | | | Liabilities | | | Assets | | |
	1	2	3	1	2	3	1	2	3	1	2	3	1	2	3	1	2	3
	Debt, GD	100 167 165		Nil	— — —		Notes and deposits, FA	400 467 548		Loans to government, GD	100 167 165		Debt, PD	300 300 383		Notes and deposits, FA	400 467 548	
										Loans to private sector, PD	300 300 383					Inventories, I	300 300 383	
	100 167 165			— — —			400 467 548			400 467 548			300 300 383			700 767 931	

7 Monetary policy

The preceding chapter established a framework for analysing flows of money income and expenditure in a credit-money economy with a government budget. The assumptions about financial institutions were kept as simple as possible; the only financial assets were banknotes and bank deposits; interest rates were predetermined at fixed rates (e.g., by a central bank); and the banking system responded freely to demands for credit by the non-bank private sector and the government.

In this chapter we shall consider monetary policy, concentrating on two issues in particular. What difference is made to the national income flow if the availability, in one sense or another, of loans to the private sector changes? And what happens when the government (or central bank) adopts measures to secure a particular rate of growth in the total stock of money.

We shall defer to Chapter 8 consideration of *institutions* of monetary control, that is, the arrangements through which a central bank or government can regulate interest rates or growth in the stock of money.

Monetary policy

Note first that in the absence of monetary policy the general or average rate of interest is formally indeterminate even if interest rates influence money or debt norms relative to income. This proposition follows from the analysis in Chapter 5 where it was shown that any norm for holdings of *money* relative to income can be made compatible with any norm for *loans* relative to income (i.e., any process generating loans) through changes in the aggregate national income flow.

At a constant level of interest rates, money creation may not be very stable, especially if there is no government budget (a proposition which emerged at the end of Chapter 5 and in Appendix 5.1 where inventory accumulation was treated as endogenous). Even with a fiscal system there may still be inventory cycles (see Chapter 6, page 126). The economy could be all the more unstable if interest rates themselves were to fluctuate in some arbitrary manner (for example, in response to changes of mood in financial institutions).

Given the importance of money creation and interest rates to the economy as a whole and to actual or would-be borrowers, it is hardly surprising that in virtually all countries there is a central bank responsible for monetary policy, whether it acts under the direction of the government or quasi-independently.

There are, in principle, several ways in which monetary policy can be operated.

One is to procure adjustment of interest rates to influence the money creation process in such a way that it becomes compatible with stable income-expenditure flows.

A second option involves direct rationing of credit. The central bank fixes interest rates low enough to make sure that there is always a certain excess demand for credit, and gives instructions to financial institutions as to how fast they may expand their lending. By this means the stock of debt (and therefore the supply of financial assets) may be expanded at a steady rate without the need for changes in interest rates. So long as loans are taken up to finance expenditure (inventories, real estate, consumer durables, etc.) rather than to finance purchases of financial assets, the central bank would then directly control the growth of loan-financed private expenditure and, if the limits applied to the government, the budget deficit as well. The defects of such a scheme are that financial institutions would be disbarred from competition on the lending side (possibly resulting in new types of financial intermediary which evaded the control) and that the rationing of credit might discriminate in undesirable ways between clients of the financial system (e.g., against new businesses).

From the point of view of the public and the macroeconomy

it does not matter exactly how the trick is performed. This is why institutional arrangements within the financial system have been left to the next chapter. What does matter is interest rates and terms of credit since it is these which influence demand for money and the level of debt relative to income.

Monetary policy with a fiscal system

To study the likely effects of different monetary policies in a closed economy without a government we would need to develop the model in Chapter 5, extending the discussion of motivations for private borrowing and bringing in the influence of interest rates on the money/income norm and on demand for loans. But the exercise would have little relevance to modern economies since, as was shown in Chapter 6, the fiscal system has such important effects on money creation and the aggregate income flow.

It will therefore be more useful to examine the interaction of fiscal and monetary policy, building on the model of Chapter 6. Even this involves a major abstraction since we have left out external transactions which influence money creation in any open economy.*

As Chapter 6 has shown, the government and central bank may decide to treat the fiscal stance as the main instrument for control of money stocks and flows, adopting a passive or permissive monetary policy. The alternative course is to regard aggregate credit creation as the primary target and regulate the fiscal stance so that it remains consistent with monetary objectives. What is inadvisable and indeed potentially catastrophic, as we shall show, is to pursue independent fiscal and monetary objectives simultaneously. Let us consider these possibilities in turn.

Fiscal control with permissive monetary policy
This is the case already examined in Chapter 6 where it was

---

* This is discussed in Chapter 14.

assumed that interest rates remain fixed at levels determined once and for all by the central bank while the government's fiscal stance varies. A step change in fiscal stance induces changes in income-expenditure flows and in aggregate public and private debt without any response from the central bank in the form of credit rationing or changes in interest rates.

Fiscal control with an active interest-rate policy

The fiscal system has powerful stabilizing properties when the economy is 'shocked' by changes in interest rates or terms of credit. Let us consider what happens when, with a given fiscal stance, there is a rise in interest rates or a tightening of credit rules or any other disturbance causing private loan-financed expenditure to fall until some lower private loans/income ratio is reached.

A once-for-all change in interest rates may influence private borrowing and the money/income norm but (acording to our central axiom) it will not cause stock-flow norms to go on changing indefinitely . Sooner or later the money/income and debt/income ratios will settle down again. Neither logic nor theory can tell us much about the scale or speed of changes in such norms – these are things which empirical investigation alone may reveal. But so long as the norms do eventually settle down, we can infer something very important about the response of the macroeconomic system as a whole. For it follows that stocks and flows will eventually settle in a new steady state* and, given that there has been no change in the fiscal stance, the new steady state must have the same aggregate income/expenditure flow as the old one – equal to the fiscal stance.

$$G/\theta$$

where G denotes government expenditure and θ is the government's share of national income (net of interest payments).

An example

Assume that there is a rise in interest rates while the fiscal stance

---

* Provided, that is, that it does not 'blow up' or collapse on the way.

remains unchanged. We know from the outset that there will be no *permanent* change in the level of national income. What we have to examine is a transition from one steady state to another in which national income is the same as it was at the start. In fact *all* the flows must be the same if government expenditure, G, and the government's income share, θ, are both unchanged. Private disposable income and private final purchases must return to their original levels; inventory accumulation will, as always in the steady state, be zero.* But it is possible that the steady-state *stocks* will have changed. Private debt will probably have fallen on account of the rise in interest rates. Holdings of financial assets (money) *may* have gone up as bank deposits yield a better return. And (as we know from Chapter 6) any changes in steady-state private debt and holdings of money will have resulted in counterpart changes in the stock of government debt.

Chart 7.1 below illustrates the effect of a rise in interest rates, displaying the transition between steady states before and after interest rates went up. The opening steady state is the same as in the preceding chapter (Charts 6.6 and 6.7). This time we have had to make *arbitrary* assumptions about changes in the money/income norm and the debt/income norm. The chart assumes that the money/income norm has not changed and that the inventory/sales norm falls from 1/3 to 1/5 in two periods before settling at its new level.

The logical structure of the chart should by now hardly need explanation.† We have not considered it necessary any longer to draw rectangles around the stock variables to emphasize the equivalence between changes in stocks and counterpart flow variables period by period.

Note that in the top half of the chart the stock of money, FA, is by identity equal to government debt, GD, plus private debt, PD. Similarly, in the bottom half of the chart there is an equivalence between the budget deficit in each and every period plus changes in private debt and changes in private holdings of

---

* Any other forms of private loan-financed expenditure, net of repayments of loans, will also be zero in the steady state. Replacement investment must normally be financed out of income (in the form of depreciation provisions).
† The underlying numerical calculations are shown in the appendix, Table A7.1.

Chart 7.1 The effect of a fall in private debt relative to income

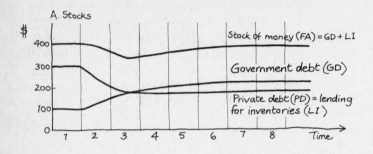

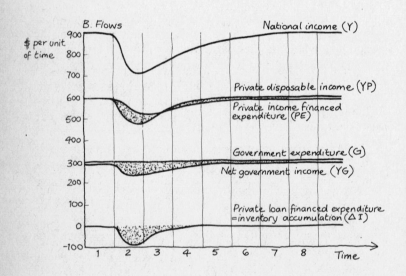

money (i.e., the difference between disposable income and expenditure).

The sequential story starts with the value of inventories being reduced towards some new norm relative to sales. The resulting fall in loans simultaneously reduces the stock of money and the flow of national income. Private income-financed expenditure consequently falls too, though with some lag so that for a time it exceeds the flow of disposable income.

When the fall in inventories tails off, inventory accumulation rises from its maximum negative value towards zero. Aggregate income and income-generated expenditure rise again, ultimately achieving the same steady-state level as existed in the first place.

Note that so long as the stock of money does not change between the two steady states, the first shaded region for private flows in the chart, where expenditure exceeds disposable income and the stock of financial assets falls, is exactly equal in area to the second shaded region where income exceeds expenditure. Also, since the net change in the stock of money is nil taking the period as a whole, it necessarily follows that the total shaded region representing the government's budget deficit must be equal in area to the total shaded region at the bottom of the chart which represents net repayment of private debt. Between the beginning and end of the transitional period the rise in government debt must have been exactly equal to the fall in private debt.

This latter result is not the outcome of any particular assumption about fiscal policy through the transitional period. So long as the original fiscal stance is eventually restored, *any* fiscal policy – for instance, one operated in such a way as to keep the national income flow constant – would necessarily have produced the same result. *So long as the cumulative change in the stock of money is nil* (which is to say that the money/income norm is constant), cumulative changes in private debt outstanding must *by identity* be matched by an equal and opposite change in government debt over the adjustment period as a whole.

Interim fiscal adjustment

The case where fiscal policy is conducted in such a way as to keep

Chart 7.2 A rise in private debt with offsetting fiscal policy

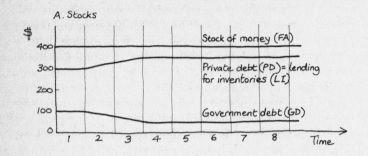

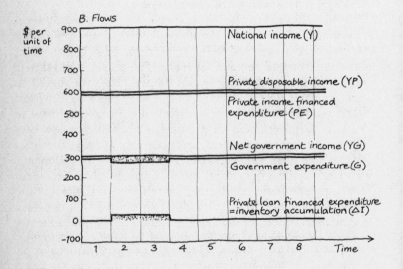

the national income constant through the transition is sufficiently interesting to merit an illustration of its own. It is simple so long as the fiscal adjustment is made entirely on the expenditure side.

In the case illustrated in Chart 7.2 it has been assumed that interest rates have fallen causing a *rise* in private debt, both absolutely and relative to disposable income. Private loan-financed expenditure is assumed to have been exactly neutralized by a reduction in government expenditure which keeps national income, net government income, private disposable income, and income-generated expenditure all exactly constant. As the chart illustrates, the change in loans to the private sector (as in the case illustrated in Chart 7.1 when fiscal policy did not change) is then exactly matched by a fall in government debt.

The fiscal system as an instrument of monetary control
The charts have illustrated how, with a stabilizing fiscal stance, government debt will be the accommodating variable in the balance sheet of the financial system, rising or falling to offset changes in private demand for loans. The reader could devise further examples to illustrate the same point with regard to changes in private demand for financial assets. With a given fiscal stance, a rise in the money-income norm will call forth an increase in government debt, supplying the higher stock of money through a temporary reduction in aggregate money income and government revenue. Provided the government's share of income is quite high, these adjustments of government debt can take place rapidly and with modest variations in the aggregate income flow.

The fiscal system affords the opportunity to put the monetary system on automatic pilot, acommodating shocks and longer-term trend changes in private behaviour without the need for credit rationing or fine tuning of interest rates. This does not preclude deliberate changes in interest rates designed to encourage or discourage private borrowing whenever such action is judged to be desirable. So long as the fiscal stance itself is set to achieve an appropriate rate of expansion of the aggregate income-expenditure flow, problems of monetary management in a closed economy will then be fairly easily resolved.

Quantitative monetary targets in the presence of a fiscal system

Suppose the government and central bank desire to maintain growth in the stock of money at a given target rate. One way of doing this, without the need for credit rationing, would be to rely on fiscal expansion to maintain whatever steady growth of the income-expenditure flow resulted in expansion of the stock of money at the desired rate. With the appropriate, steadily expanding fiscal stance the income-expenditure flow and private demand for money should grow as required. By implication the credit-creation process itself would be conforming to the target; government borrowing would supplement private borrowing to just the degree necessary to keep the stock of money growing at the target rate.

Given a consistent fiscal stance, therefore, a target for the overall rate of expansion of credit should be achieved without difficulty except in the short run when shocks or disturbances affecting private demand for loans or financial assets may cause the aggregate money stock and income flow to depart temporarily from the target path. Conceivably the central bank could improve the precision with which the monetary target was fulfilled by securing short-run variations in interest rates to counteract such disturbances. Alternatively there could be 'fine tuning' of the fiscal stance designed to achieve the same end. The problems of short-run stabilization policy (fine tuning), whether through interest rates or through the fiscal stance, are practical rather than conceptual. If there are lags in the response of private decisions and if the authorities make adjustments after the event or in the light of inaccurate forecasts, there is the obvious danger that fine tuning could itself be destabilizing.

Altogether more fundamental problems arise when the fiscal stance is *inconsistent* with the target for aggregate credit creation. This situation may formally be defined as one where at given interest rates the total stock of money would diverge progressively and cumulatively from the target path. When the fiscal stance is inconsistent with the credit creation target in the sense defined above, it *may* be possible to reconcile the two by systematic changes in interest rates. But not always.

An example of inconsistent policies

Chart 7.3 illustrates a case where fiscal policy and monetary targets are inconsistent. To keep things simple we again assume that the only effect of interest rate changes is on private demand for loans (i.e., the money/income norm is insensitive to interest rates).

Starting from a steady state the government increases its spending, G, at a fixed rate in excess of the target rate for expansion of the stock of money, FA. Private disposable income must be constrained to grow more or less in proportion to the target for the stock of financial assets since the money/income norm is, by assumption, not open to manipulation by the monetary authorities. With a constant government share of income, θ, this implies that aggregate income must somehow be constrained to grow at about the same rate as the target for the stock of money. Net government income, too, will have to grow at the same rate which by assumption is lower than the rate of increase in government spending. It necessarily follows that the government budget must move into ever-increasing deficit. If the target for the aggregate money stock is to be met, it is private debt which will have to be constrained. As the government deficit rises, private debt must eventually be forced to contract at an increasing rate. To achieve this, the rate of interest will have to rise more and more rapidly. The ultimate logical impasse is reached when government debt cumulates to the point at which it absorbs the whole of the permitted supply of credit and private debt has to shrink to zero.

If the money/income norm is sensitive to interest rates, breakdown may well occur the more rapidly. At any given point along the path higher interest rates may imply a higher money/income ratio and therefore (given the money target) a lower level of money income, a larger government deficit and a greater requirement for displacement of private borrowing.

If the fiscal stance implies credit creation in excess of the target, an eventual breakdown appears inevitable. Either the

Chart 7.3 Inconsistent fiscal and monetary policies

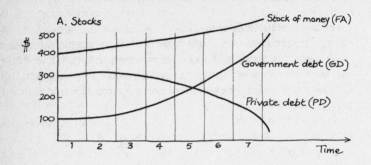

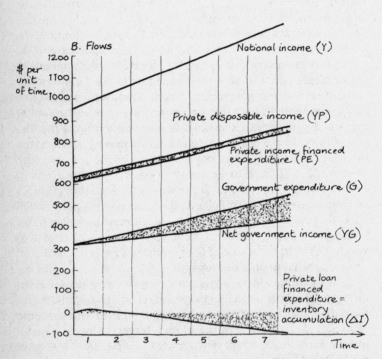

fiscal stance will have to be made less expansionary or the credit creation target will have to be relaxed. It is less clear what are the limits to the extent to which private borrowing can be expanded to compensate for a fiscal stance which is *less* expansionary than the credit target. The government's budget will move into surplus and the government may eventually become a net lender to the financial system. But with very low interest rates it might in principle be possible to sustain a more or less indefinite expansion of private borrowing* to offset the budget surplus.

Conclusion

The general conclusion is that fiscal policy by itself determines the aggregate income flow and that monetary policy only has transitory effects. In the absence of an explicit credit target, the fiscal stance needs to be such as to imply a steady expansion of the money income-expenditure flow at whatever is judged to be an appropriate rate.† If a credit target must, for whatever reason, be adhered to, there is little choice but to keep the fiscal stance broadly consistent with the credit target.

Appendix 7.1 *The effects of changes in money/income and debt/ income norms*

The algebraic model in Appendix 6.1 is sufficient to generate examples of the effects of changes in the money/income norm, α, and in the inventory/sales norm, γ. Calculations for the numerical example illustrated in Chart 7.1 in the preceding

* Especially if, in the presence of inflation, real interest rates are negative (see below, page 178).
† The question of what is the appropriate rate depends on links between monetary expansion, inflation and growth of the volume of output, discussed later in this book (Chapter 12).

chapter are set out in Table A7.1 below, following exactly the same steps as in Appendix 6.1.

Table A7.1 The effect of a fall in private debt relative to income*

					($ values)			
period:	1	2	3	4	5	6		∞
1. Government spending G	300	300	300	300	300	300	...	300
2a. Inventory/sales norm γ	.333	.25	.20	.20	.20	.20	...	.20
2b. End-period inventories $I = \gamma FE_{-1}$	300	225	170	166	170	174	...	180
3. Change in inventories ΔI	0	−75	−55	−4	4	4	...	0
4. Opening stock of money FA_{-1}	400	400	367	354	368	380	...	400
5. National income $Y = 5/3(G+\Delta I)+FA_{-1}$	900	775	775	847	875	887	...	900
6. Net government income $YG = 1/3Y$	300	258	258	282	292	296	...	300
7. Government budget deficit $\Delta GD = G-YG$	0	42	42	18	8	4	...	0
8. Change in stock of money $\Delta FA = \Delta I+\Delta GD$	0	−33	−13	14	12	8	...	0
9. End-period stock of money FA	400	367	354	368	380	388	...	400
10. Private final purchases $PE = 3/2\,FA$	600	551	531	552	570	582	...	600
11. Total final sales (900) $FE = G+PE$	900	851	831	852	870	882	...	900
12. Private disposable income $YP = Y-YG$	600	517	517	565	583	591	...	600

13. End-period
   government debt
   $GD = FA-PD$
	100	142	184	202	210	214	...	220

* The figures in this table correspond with those illustrated in Chart 7.1.

Generalization of the model

The model may most easily be generalized by substituting 'income-financed expenditure', YFE, for private final purchases, PE, and (net) 'loan-financed expenditure', LFE, for inventory accumulation, ΔI. The assumption will be that loan-financed expenditure inclusive of changes in inventories but *net* of debt repayments is equal to changes in total private debt, ΔPD, in each period. The only important modification which has to be made to the model in Appendix 6.1 is to replace the equation determining end-period inventories (A6.4) by some other equation determining end-period private debt (including debt on inventories), PD: for example,

$$PD = \beta YP \tag{A7.1}$$

where β is some debt/income norm.

To solve the model at given interest rates (i.e., for given values of α and β) it is only necessary to substitute A7.1 into the solution for national income in Appendix 6.1 (A6.8). We replace ΔI in A6.8 by

$$\Delta PD = \beta YP - PD_{-1} = \beta(1-\theta)Y - PD_{-1}$$

This yields the solution

$$\{1+\frac{\theta}{\alpha}-(1+\frac{1}{\alpha})\,\beta(1-\theta)\}Y = (1+\frac{1}{\alpha})\,(G-PD_{-1})+\frac{FA_{-1}}{\alpha} \tag{A7.2}$$

If α and β can be specified as functions of rates of interest, numerical solutions can readily be generated for any exogenous path of interest rates by calculating values of α and β in each period and feeding the results into A7.2.

Solutions with monetary targets

If both α and β are influenced by interest rates, solutions corresponding to a target path for the stock of money will in general have to be found by numerical approximation. A 'trial value' for the base interest rate will have to be used to generate trial values for α and β in A7.2; the implied stock of money, FA, can then be derived and the value for the base interest rate modified until the calculated stock of money matches the target.

But if only one of the two norms (say β) is influenced by interest rates, the solution can be found more directly. The target for the stock of money, FA, tells us what private income-financed expenditure must be (PE in A6.2 or A6.3) and hence private income (YP = PE+ΔFA). So national income must satisfy

$$(1-\theta)Y \equiv YP = \frac{FA}{\alpha} + \Delta FA \qquad (A7.3)$$

If, for example, the simple money-adjustment process (A6.3) is assumed, everything else then follows. Private debt, PD, is obtained as the residual of the money-stock target, FA, and government debt, GD. This tells us the debt/income ratio:

$$\beta \equiv \frac{PD}{YP} \equiv \frac{FA-GD}{YP} \qquad (A7.4)$$

If we knew how β is influenced by the base interest rate, we could infer from A7.4 what value the latter must take in each period in order that the money-stock target should be fulfilled.

Chart 7.3 was based on calculations using A7.3 above. We leave the derivation of numbers underlying the chart as an exercise for the reader.

Appendix 7.2 *The balance sheet of the banking system*

It should be noted that the consolidated balance sheet of the banking system is always precisely implied by the system of relationships we have postulated.

Start with the flow of funds identity

$$G - YG \equiv YP - PE \qquad (A7.2.1)$$

The stock counterpart of the flow transactions on the left-hand side of A7.2.1 is

$$G - YG \equiv \Delta RA + \Delta BB + \Delta BP \qquad (A7.2.2)$$

A7.2.2 says that the budget deficit in any period is equal to changes in banks' reserve assets plus banks' holdings of bonds plus private holdings of bonds.

The stock counterpart of the right-hand side of A7.2.1 is

$$YP - PE \equiv \Delta BD + \Delta BP - \Delta PL \qquad (A7.2.3)$$

A7.2.3 says that the private financial surplus in any period is equal to the change in bank deposits plus the change in private holdings of bonds less any increase in bank loans.

The flow of funds identity can now be expressed as an identity between the right-hand side of equations A7.2.2 and A7.2.3

$$\Delta RA + \Delta BB + \Delta BP \equiv \Delta BD + \Delta BP - \Delta PL$$

which may be simplified and rearranged to yield

$$\Delta RA + \Delta BB + \Delta PL \equiv \Delta BD \qquad (A7.2.4)$$

which represents, on the left-hand side, changes in banks' assets (reserve assets, bonds and loans) and, on the right-hand side, changes in their liabilities (bank deposits).

8 Monetary institutions

Up to this point we have discussed how fiscal and monetary policy affect aggregate income/expenditure flows and money creation with little reference to financial institutions or to financial assets other than notes and bank deposits. We have done this deliberately in order to avoid logical confusion between problems of monetary policy which are inherent in the general nature of a credit-money economy and problems which may arise because of particular institutional arrangements.

Of course the institutional structure of the financial system matters in practice – it may make some types of monetary policy easy to operate and others more or less impossible. The study of financial institutions is a specialized subject, beyond the scope of this book. Here we shall sketch out a simplified financial system to show how a central bank may implement monetary policy through the classical mechanism of 'open market operations'.* This is sufficient to illustrate the general character of problems associated with policies designed to control the stocks of money.

There is one matter of terminology which must be clarified at the start. In previous chapters we have assumed that the stock of private financial assets, FA, was the same thing as the stock of money (notes in circulation and bank deposits). This chapter introduces an additional type of asset – bonds.† So from now on the stock of financial assets, FA, will be larger than the stock of money proper.

The plan of the chapter is as follows. First we describe the

---

* For a definition of open market operations, see page 000.
† Chapter 13 will bring in corporate equity. The implications of capital gains or losses on bonds, ignored in this chapter, are also demonstrated in Chapter 13.

institutions of a simple financial system in terms of the contents of its balance sheets. Then, as in previous chapters, we consider properties of the whole system in a steady state. Finally the role of monetary policy will be examined by seeing how the system responds to exogenous shocks administered by 'open market operations' – purchases and sales of bonds by the government.

The financial system is fully interdependent with income/expenditure processes (including fiscal policy) which have been discussed in previous chapters. *We shall endeavour to keep the flows as well as the stocks of the system in mind all the time, although flows do not appear in balance sheets.* In discussion of steady states, at least, this is not difficult since steady-state income and expenditure flows are uniquely determined by the government's fiscal stance (as explained in Chapter 6).

Outline of a simple financial system

The balance sheets of a simple financial system are illustrated in Table 8.1 below. These are statements which describe the financial assets and liabilities of the three sectors in the system (government, commercial banks and the rest of the private sector) at a point in time. The stock aggregates which affect the flow system discussed in earlier chapters are to be found in the bottom line of the table. In the example shown they take the following values:

total private financial assets, FA	$1000
total private debt, PD	$500
total government debt, GD	$500

Previously, total assets and liabilities of banks have been assumed to be the same as total financial assets of the non-bank private sector, FA. In an expanded financial system they are less ($700 in the table). The stock of financial assets, FA, is now larger than the stock of money (i.e., assets and liabilities of the banking system) since it now comprises bonds as well as money.

Now let us introduce institutional features of the financial system and explain the meaning of the various balance sheet entries.

Table 8.1 Financial balance sheets in a simple financial system

($ values)

Government (central bank)		Commercial banks				Non-bank private sector		
Liabilities		Assets		Liabilities		Assets		Liabilities
Reserve assets of banks	70	Reserve assets	70	Deposits by private sector 700		Bank deposits 700		
Gov't bonds	430	Gov't bonds	130			Gov't bonds 300		Bank loans 500
		Loans to private sector	500					
Total (GD)	500	Total	700	Total 700		Total (FA) 1000		Total (PD) 500

Government bonds

First we introduce the concept of government bonds which the public and also banks can buy or sell from one another or from the government. The government pays interest on bonds but the interest payable on a bond is fixed whereas its price may go up or down, depending on supply and demand in the 'bond market'. The effective return or *yield* on bonds depends on their prices; when bond prices go up, yields fall, and vice versa.*

In Table 8.1 the value of bonds held by the general public ($300) and by banks ($130) is shown as being equal to the government's bond liabilities ($430). To make this identity hold true it is necessary that bonds should be valued at the same prices by all three sectors (government, banks and the public).

The non-bank private sector

The non-bank private sector freely chooses how to divide its total financial assets, FA ($1000 in Table 8.1), between bank deposits ($700) and government bonds ($300).† This 'portfolio choice' is made by individuals in the light of interest rates offered by banks (e.g., on time deposits) and prices and yields in the bond

---

* The 'yield' of a bond may be defined as the return to an investor buying the bond at its current market price. If a bond sells in the market for less than its face value, the yield is higher than the interest rate which the bond pays (e.g., the yield on a $100 bond which formally pays 8½% or $8.50 p.a. will be *more* than 8½% p.a. if the bond is bought at a market price of, say, $70). If a bond sells for more than its face value, the yield is correspondingly *less* than the notional interest rate. See Chapter 13 for further discussion of bond prices and yields. We shall not go into the organization of the bond market itself.

† Notes and coins have been left out. In this very simple account *everything* which is not indispensable for explaining basic principles will be left out – including non-bank financial intermediaries, corporate bonds and equities.

market.* We assume that the public borrows exclusively from banks at whatever interest rates the latter decide to charge. Bank loans to the private sector ($500 in the table) are the same thing as total private debt, PD.

Commercial banks

The balance sheet for commercial banks will always be discussed on a 'consolidated' basis – i.e., it excludes accounts which banks hold with one another (these cancel out in a closed economy as a whole). The liabilities of banks are the deposits which the public has chosen to place with them ($700) rather than buying bonds. Banks lend to the private sector and government and may also buy government bonds. Their loans to the government are termed 'reserve assets'. They are obliged (e.g., by law) to hold a minimum percentage of total assets (say 10%) in the form of reserve assets. But the government only pays a low or zero interest rate on reserve assets. So banks will never want to hold much more than the minimum they are required to hold. In Table 8.1 the banks' reserve assets are $70 – i.e., 10% of $700. These reserves, together with bank holdings of government bonds ($130) and loans to the private sector ($500), add up to the total of deposits placed with banks by the public ($700).

Note that banks have a 'portfolio choice' just like the non-bank private sector. Assuming that they never want to hold excess reserves, their choice lies between lending to the private sector and holding government bonds. This portfolio choice will be made by individual banks in the light of a comparison between what they can charge for loans to the private sector and yields they can obtain by owning bonds.

---

* The assessment of bond yields by an individual person or institution may involve a judgement about whether the market has got bond prices right – i.e., whether market prices and yields of bonds are likely to rise or fall in the short term. So the choice involves an element of speculation.

The government and central bank

The government's total debt ($500 in Table 8.1) comprises reserve assets of banks ($70) and bonds held by banks and the general public ($430).

Our closed economy has a 'central bank' with two principle functions – to manage the government's debt and to administer monetary policy.* The only instrument of monetary policy available to the central bank in our simple system is the buying and selling of government bonds in the bond market. These transactions are called 'open market operations'. We assume that the central bank does *not* have the right to intervene directly in the affairs of commercial banks (e.g., to prescribe interest rates or quantitative lending limits) or to change the 10% minimum reserve requirement. But the central bank is in a very strong position in the bond market since it can sell or buy back bonds virtually without limit. This gives it the power, if it chooses, to fix bond prices and yields unilaterally at any level† and thereby (as we shall soon see) determine the general level of interest rates in the commercial banking system.

The system in a steady state

Having described the institutions, let us consider what the entire system must look like when everything is in a steady state with constant interest rates, bond yields, stocks of assets and liabilities, and income/expenditure flows. We shall take the flows first, then the aggregate stocks of assets and debt, and finally the breakdown of balance sheets in the financial system.

---

* The central bank has to fund the government's operations but this in itself presents no problems. Government cheques are universally accepted. When deposited with commercial banks the cheques become 'reserve assets' in the first instance; banks may immediately get rid of excess reserve assets by buying bonds.
† But speculation based on expectations of future yields may oblige the central bank to deal on a very large scale to achieve this objective.

Something must be said in advance about the bond market and interest rates. Throughout this section we assume that the central bank conducts its open market operations with the sole aim of keeping bond prices and yields at some arbitrary level; so these are exogenous to our solution just as government expenditure and tax rates are exogenous to it. We shall discuss below how the (endogenous) level of bank interest rates is determined.

Income/expenditure flows

In a steady state the government's budget will be in balance; the aggregate national income flow will be equal to the fiscal stance (see Chapter 6). For example, if government spending, G, is \$833 per period and the government's share of national income, θ, is one third, the steady-state flow of national income will be

$$G/\theta = \$833 \div 1/3 = \$2500$$

Of this, \$833 will represent net government income. The remainder, \$1667, will be private income, and private spending will be equal to private income.

Financial aggregates

The steady-state stock of private financial assets depends on the private sector's norm for financial assets/income, α. The norm, α, is not entirely exogenous since it may be affected by bond yields and bank interest rates. Suppose that it takes the value of 2/3. Then the stock of financial assets, FA, is

$$2/3 \times \$1667 = \$1000$$

The total amount of private debt will depend on norms for inventories/sales and debt/income which also are influenced by bank lending rates. Suppose the overall private debt/income norm is 30%. The steady-state stock of private debt, PD, is then

$$0.30 \times \$1667 = \$500$$

The total value of government debt, GD, has to be equal to the difference

$$GD \equiv FA - PD = \$1000 - \$500 = \$500$$

Portfolio choice and interest rates

Now we come to a novel aspect of the steady state, introduced by the existence of bonds. The system will only be in a steady state if both the non-bank private sector and commercial banks regard the composition of their portfolios of assets as appropriate or sensible, given bank interest rates and bond yields. Given bond yields, this determines what the level of bank rates must be. Thus bank lending rates must be higher than bond yields (otherwise banks would not want to lend to the private sector) and rates on interest-bearing bank deposits must be lower than bond yields (otherwise neither the public nor banks would want to hold bonds).

The constraint on bank interest rates in a competitive system can be understood by considering what happens if bank interest rates are too low or too high, respectively, relative to bond yields. When bank rates are too low, deposits will be insufficient to enable banks to meet the private sector's demand for loans. Any bank which puts up its deposit and lending rates together will attract more deposits, maintain its margins and still find willing borrowers.

On the other hand if bank interest rates are too high relative to bond yields, bank deposits will exceed bank loans to the private sector (plus reserve requirements); they must perforce invest the excess funds in bonds which by assumption are now relatively unprofitable. Any bank which undercuts loan rates charged by others will be able to exchange unwanted bonds for more profitable loans to the private sector. And if competition in the loan market obliges banks to cut loan rate, they will also have to cut deposit rates to maintain their margins.

In effect, therefore, the general level of banks' loan and deposit rates are more or less dictated by bond yields.

The steady-state balance sheets

In principle the entire structure of steady-state balance sheets is now determinate, conditional on fiscal policy (the fiscal stance) and monetary policy (bond yields). To summarize in a logical order:

(1)   the fiscal stance determines income and expenditure flows;

(2)   bond yields determine the level of bank loan and deposit rates;

(3)   bond yields and bank loan and deposit rates determine private asset/income and debt/income norms, hence aggregate assets and debt of the private sector (since income is given by (1)), and hence also the stock of government debt (since this is equal to aggregate private assets less debt);

(4)   private sector portfolio choice (conditional on bank deposit rates relative to bond yields) determines the amount of bank deposits and bonds held by the non-bank public;

(5)   the balance sheet of banks is already fully defined by (3) and (4) above and will be satisfactory to banks by virtue of (2).

Monetary policy

In the system described above, the central bank has been represented as conducting its open market operations so as to determine bond prices and yields. This is not the only possible criterion for open market operations. Nowadays emphasis is more often given to quantitative targets for the monetary base (reserve assets) or the stock of money (in our system, bank deposits). But the implications of such targets are tricky to analyse for reasons which will soon become apparent. Before discussing them we shall examine the much simpler case of a shock to the system administered by open market operations designed to secure a deliberate and permanent change in bond yields while the fiscal stance remains unchanged.

A fall in bond yields

Let us assume that the policy decision has been that the central bank should push up prices of existing bonds and cut bond yields. One immediate consequence will be cuts in bank interest rates to keep them consistent with bond yields (as discussed earlier above). The other immediate consequence is that there will be capital gains to existing holders of government bonds, increasing the market value of government debt.

Now consider stock-flow relationships. The fall in interest rates will stimulate additions to private borrowing. This will set in train an expansion of income and expenditure flows. Government tax revenue will rise, putting the government's budget into surplus, causing government debt to fall. But sooner or later private debt will stop rising relative to income. Just as in the examples discussed in Chapter 7, income/expenditure flows will then return to their original steady-state levels and the government's budget surplus will vanish again. But there will have been a change in aggregate stocks of assets and liabilities.

Balance-sheet changes

What will have been happening to the balance sheets of the financial system through the stock-flow process? We know that total government debt will have been falling. Private debt will have been rising. In broad terms the banks, lending more to the private sector, will have expanded their balance sheets while

holdings of bonds by banks and the public must have contracted.
The eventual change in steady-state balance sheets is illustrated in Table 8.2 below.

Table 8.2 A change in private debt with an equal and opposite change in government debt

| | ($ values) | | |
	Original balance sheets	Change	New balance sheets
Non-bank private sector			
Assets	1000	0	1000
bank deposits	700	+80	780
government bonds	300	−80	220
Liabilities: bank loans	500	+100	600
Commercial banks			
Assets	700	+80	780
loans to private sector	500	+100	600
government bonds	130	−28	102
reserve assets	70	+8	78
Liabilities: deposits by private sector	700	+80	780
Central bank/government			
Liabilities	500	−100	400
government bonds	430	−108	322
reserve assets of banks	70	+8	78

First consider the three financial aggregates, remembering that income/expenditure flows will have returned to their original levels. Given the fall in yields and interest rates, the private sector is unlikely to want to hold more financial assets (in the table the total is assumed unchanged at $1000). Private debt will certainly have increased (in the table it has gone up from $500 to $600). So government debt must have fallen by a corresponding amount (e.g., from $500 to $400).

Since reserve assets are such a small part of banks' assets and government debt, the value of government bonds held by banks and the public combined will have fallen by about the same amount as the total value of government debt. But the rest is more uncertain. *Probably* the banks will not have had many bonds to sell (or will not have wanted to reduce their bond holdings much). In this event bank deposit rates will have been kept high enough to induce the private sector to sell bonds and switch into bank deposits, providing banks with the additional funds required by private borrowers.

Although it is probable the steady-state stock of money will have increased as illustrated in Table 8.2 , it is not certain. The banks *might* have had quite large holdings of bonds originally and they might have been content to hold very few bonds after yields had fallen. In this case they could have accommodated the fall in government debt and rise in private debt themselves without needing to attract more deposits. The stock of money (bank deposits) might not have risen at all.

Monetary targets

We can now finally infer why it is difficult to conduct open market operations so as to keep the stock of money close to quantitative targets. First, the effects of general changes in the level of interest rates on the *size* of financial aggregates can only roughly be predicted. Second, the relationship between bond yields and bank interest rates is as much up to the commercial banks, as the central bank, to decide. So changes in portfolio *composition* are not easily predictable. Yet the outcome for the stock of money depends *both* on what happens to financial aggregates *and* on portfolio composition.

Note that if the central bank tries to keep ahead of commercial banks so as to ensure a certain pattern of portfolio shifts, there may be a cumulative spiral of bond yields and bank rates. For example, suppose the central bank raises bond yields to attract the non-bank public to buy bonds and reduce bank deposits. Commercial banks may raise interest rates so as to retain deposits. If the central bank goes further, so can they. The certain consequence is that private borrowing will be 'crowded out' (discouraged by high interest rates) and this by virtue not of fiscal policy but monetary policy.

Conclusion

The most important point for macroeconomic analysis is that the central bank can regulate the general level of yields and interest rates at any desired level, regardless of fiscal policy. By varying interest rates it can influence financial aggregates, notably the ratio of private to government debt, to a degree which should at least be roughly predictable. This, too, can be done independently of fiscal policy. What is far more problematic is whether the central bank can keep the stock of money (defined quite conventionally as bank deposits) near to some target path, how far it will have to vary interest rates in trying to do so and, therefore, what will be the cost to private borrowers or savers.

It seems entirely pointless to make a target for the stock of money the criterion for monetary policy unless the stock of money is a crucial determinant of inflation (or something else which really matters). The next part of this book proceeds to examine costs, prices and inflation but we shall not find the stock of money playing any evident role.

PART IV

Inflation

9 Costs and prices

This chapter and the next show how inflation can be analysed as a sequential process. Once again our main concern is with logical accounting relationships which constrain what *can* happen without fully determining what *will* happen. In previous chapters we supplemented accounting identities with a general behavioural axiom (that stock-flow ratios do not change indefinitely). For inflation, too, we shall adopt a general behavioural axiom – that none of the main categories of income (wages, interest, profits, tax revenue) is indefinitely altered as a share of the total by general inflation of prices. Just as principles of asset creation have been illustrated by examples using specific versions of the stock-flow axiom, so principles of inflation will now be illustrated using specific assumptions about the adjustment of wages, interest, profits and tax revenue when prices rise.

But there is an important difference. In the case of financial stocks and flows we were able to suggest what, specifically, determines steady-state values. We cannot do the same for rates of inflation. On the contrary, although we can show in general how inflation must be transmitted, the analysis itself suggests that steady-state rates of inflation in a closed economy can change rather capriciously.

Plan of the two chapters

This chapter presents accounting relationships and points out the consequences of certain norms for prices and interest rates. Basic principles of inflation accounting are introduced.* The main result of the chapter is to show precisely how costs must add up.

* A more complete discussion of inflation accounting will be found in Chapter 11.

Chapter 10 introduces a general axiom about adjustment of wages, profits, interest rates and tax revenue which enables us to analyse inflation as a determinate, sequential process. The rate of inflation will be solved endogenously for specific cases which illustrate the general axiom.

Costs, interest and profits

Let us start the analysis of how costs add up by considering once again the accounts of a single business. In Chapter 4 we set out a model in which a business holds inventories of goods and work-in-progress. This was used to illustrate the cash-flow problems which are one important motive for borrowing.

This time we are not interested in cash flow but in costs and prices. We must now distinguish explicitly between changes in volumes of transactions and changes in unit costs and selling prices. To keep the examples as simple as possible we assume throughout this chapter that the volume of goods and services produced and sold, and the volume of inventories, remain constant through time. All changes in money values will then represent changes in unit costs or prices. The appendix provides an algebraic treatment which demonstrates that the results hold equally well when volumes change at the same time as prices.

A rise in unit costs

First suppose that there is a rise in unit costs of production and consider how prices must rise if profits are to be maintained. Table 9.1 below provides a specific example.

The time periods have been chosen such that inputs purchased and work undertaken in one period emerge as sales in the next period – i.e., the time periods are equal in length to the period of production. Inventories at the start of each period are sold in that period; inventories at the end of the period represent costs incurred during the period.* The starting-point of the table is

---

* The algebra in the appendix allows accounting periods to differ from the period of production.

Table 9.1   A rise in costs with a constant volume of sales turnover and inventories

Period	(1) Unit cost index (period 1 = 1.00)	(2) Costs in period = end-period value of inventories	(3) Interest charge on opening value of inventories	(4) Profits net of interest	(5) Value of sales in period	(6) Price index of goods and services sold (period 1 = 1.00)
		($)	($)	($)	($)	
1	1.00	700	35	265	1000	1.00
2	1.00	700	35	265	1000	1.00
3	1.10	770	35	265	1000	1.00
4	1.21	847	39	291	1100	1.10
5	1.33	932	42	321	1210	1.21
6	1.46	1025	47	352	1331	1.33
7	1.46	1025	51	388	1464	1.46
8	1.46	1025	51	388	1464	1.46

that unit costs of production, having been constant in periods 1 and 2, rise by 10% in each of periods 3 to 6 and then remain constant in periods 7 and 8. Column (1) shows the unit cost index, and column (2) shows amounts of money paid out as costs in each period.

From now on we shall need to distinguish interest charges on inventories from profits proper. Column (3) of the table shows interest charges calculated at the rate of 5% per period on the value of inventories at the start of each period (end of the previous period). The reader may imagine that the business is financing its inventories entirely by borrowing and therefore actually has to pay the interest charges shown in column (3) to its creditors. Alternatively, whatever part of the value of inventories is not financed by borrowing represents money locked up in the business which could otherwise have earned interest. Either way, it is meaningful to separate out interest on money invested in inventories from profits of the business as such.

Columns (4), (5) and (6) of the table give the answer to the problem posed at the outset – how selling prices must be increased in order that profits are maintained as costs rise. To be precise, profits *net of interest* have been maintained constant *in real terms* – measured by their purchasing power relative to the average price of goods and services sold (column (6)). The reader may verify this by dividing the price index into the profit figure for each period (the answer always comes out as $265). To confirm that profits have been calculated correctly, let us refer back to Chapter 4 where profits (before deducting interest) were defined as sales revenue, $\hat{S}$, less costs, $\hat{C}$, plus the change in the value of inventories, $\Delta\hat{I}$. Here we have profits net of interest given by

$$\hat{\Pi} = \hat{S} + \Delta\hat{I} - \hat{C} - R.\hat{I}_{-1} \qquad (9.1)$$

where R is the rate of interest per period and $\hat{I}_{-1}$ is the opening value of inventories. In the table, column (4) is equal to column (5) plus the change in column (2), *less* columns (2) and (3).

The solution for the price index (column (6)) should not surprise the reader if he or she recalls that sales lag one period behind the purchase of inputs and the activity of production. The price index rises by 10% in each of periods 4 to 7 – i.e., by the same amount as the unit cost index (column (1)), but one period later.

The adding-up property

Note that the value of sales in each period is equal to costs incurred in the *previous* period plus interest and profits in the *current* period. Moreover profits and interest are both constant proportions of sales revenue. We may therefore say that prices have risen *as if* historic costs of production were being passed into selling prices with the addition of interest charges and a constant average profit mark-up. We can write this formally as

$$\hat{S} \equiv \hat{C}_{-1}(1+R)\,(1+\hat{\lambda}) \qquad (9.2)$$

where $\hat{C}_{-1}$ represents historic costs, R is the rate of interest charged on costs, and $\hat{\lambda}$ is the proportionate mark-up for profits net of interest. This represents the adding-up property of costs, interest, profits and prices.

To be absolutely clear that the equation is an *identity* which does not rely on any particular assumption about how prices are determined, consider the example of period 4 in the table above. Lagged costs, $\hat{C}_{-1}$, are $770. The rate of interest, R, is 5%, so interest charges are 5% × $770 = $39, bringing costs plus interest up to $809. Profits are $291, making the total value of sales $809 + $291 = $1100. The profit mark-up on costs plus interest is

$$\hat{\lambda} = \$291/\$809 = 36\%$$

Whatever the level of profits and the value of sales, we can always calculate the profit mark-up, λ, in this manner.*

At first sight the adding-up identity (9.2) may not appear to be very revealing. We still have some way to go before its precise significance will emerge. But it is obvious already that we can convert the identity into a statement about the price index, $\hat{p}$, relative to lagged unit costs, $\hat{UC}_{-1}$. The price index is defined as sales value divided by sales volume,

$$\hat{p} \equiv \hat{S}/\hat{s} \qquad (9.3)$$

where $\hat{s}$ is the volume of sales in the current period. The volume of sales is equal by assumption to the volume of production in the previous period. So lagged costs per unit of output, $\hat{UC}_{-1}$, must be equal to

$$\hat{C}_{-1}/\hat{s}$$

---

* If prices were low enough relative to costs, the mark-up might come out negative.

Therefore if we divide the adding-up identity (9.2) by the volume of sales, s, we get

$$\hat{p} = \widehat{UC}_{-1}(1+R)\ (1+\hat{\lambda}) \tag{9.4}$$

This says that the ratio of prices to lagged unit costs depends on the rate of interest and the profit mark-up. In our example the volume of sales at period 1 prices is $1000 (the volume of sales is constant throughout). So, for example, the price index in period 4 is

$$\$1100/\$1000 = 1.10$$

Lagged unit costs are

$$\$770/\$1000 = 0.77$$

The reader may verify that

$$1.10 = 0.77\,(1+0.05)\ (1+0.36)$$

i.e., lagged unit costs plus the interest charge (5%) plus the profit mark-up (36%) are indeed equal to the price index.

We want to obtain an expression for real wage costs, interest and profits as shares of output. But we cannot do this meaningfully by dividing the identity 9.4 by the price index since the resulting unit-cost term

$$\widehat{UC}_{-1}/\hat{p}$$

describes a sum of money paid out in the previous period divided by the price index in the current period. We shall not get any further until we have looked more carefully at the question of inflation accounting.

Inflation accounting – a paradox

The behaviour of costs, interest payments and profits in Table 9.1 above is at first sight paradoxical when expressed in 'real' terms. Suppose that we divide the various payments in each period by the price index so as to get a measure of their purchasing power in terms of the goods and services actually produced. The result is as follows.

Table 9.2 Payments from Table 9.1 divided by the price index (period 1 purchasing power, $)

Period	Costs in period = real value of end-period inventories = end-period real capital invested	Interest charge	Profits	Total
1	700	35	265	1000
2	700	35	265	1000
3	770	35	265	1000
4	770	35	265	1000
5	770	35	265	1000
6	770	35	265	1000
7	700	35	265	1000
8	700	35	265	1000

Total receipts from sales are constant in real terms. The flow of interest payments is constant in real terms. Profits (after payment of interest charges) are constant in real terms; moreover according to the principle set out in Chapter 4 (page 72), if inventories are wholly financed from borrowing the whole of profits is available as a cash flow to the owners of the business. Yet, because money costs rise before prices, real costs (money costs divided by the price index) are 10% higher throughout the period of rising costs (i.e., periods 3 to 7). Where have the resources to pay for the higher real costs 'come from'?

Inflation and the real value of money debt

The resolution of this paradox is illustrated in Table 9.3 below. It is now best to treat all money invested in finance of inventories as if it was a debt of the business so that we can clearly distinguish what happens to the money invested. The first column of the table corresponds to the end-period value of inventories in Table 9.1. The second column shows changes in the first column which determine the amount of new money the business has had to borrow in each period. The third column reproduces the price index from Table 9.1 which we use to measure the real value of transactions in each period and the real value of end-period debt.*

Table 9.3 The fall in real value of existing debt of the business

	(1)	(2)	(3)	(4)	(5)	(6)
Period	End-period money value of debt	New money lent in period (change in (1))	Price index (period 1 = 1.00)	Real value of end-period debt	Real value of new money lent in period ((2)÷(3))	Change in real value of existing debt in period
	($ values)			(period 1 purchasing power $)		
1	700	0	1.00	700	0	0
2	700	0	1.00	700	0	0
3	770	70	1.00	770	70	0
4	847	77	1.10	770	70	−70
5	932	85	1.21	770	70	−70
6	1025	93	1.33	770	70	−70
7	1025	0	1.46	700	0	−70
8	1025	0	1.46	700	0	0

* Note that, until we aggregate, this price index may not be a good measure of the general purchasing power of money. For discussion of the implications of deflating *end-period* debt by the average price index for sales in the period see Chapter 11, page 224.

Columns (4) and (5) of the table are obtained by dividing the first two columns by the price index. They show that in period 2 there was no change in the real value of debt and no borrowing of new money. The rise in the real value of debt in period 3 was exactly equal to the real value of new borrowing. But when prices rose in periods 4 to 6 the real value of debt remained constant despite the fact that borrowing of $70 in real terms was taking place each period. Existing creditors of the business were in fact losing out to the tune of $70 each period as inflation eroded the real value of debts fixed in money terms. This continued in period 7 (when prices rose for the last time) although the flow of new borrowing had by then come to an end.

The 'inflation loss' shown in column (6) of the table broadly resolves the paradox noted at the outset. It is existing creditors of the business who have 'paid for' higher real wage costs through erosion of the real value of the money they have invested.*

Real interest

The main point which emerges is that when there is inflation, interest actually paid on money debt is an inappropriate measure of the return to creditors and, for that matter, the cost to debtors. The proper measure of real interest in each period is given by interest paid (deflated by the price index) *less* the real capital loss caused by inflation.†

---

* There is still a small timing problem because extra real costs (Table 9.1) occurred in periods 3 to 6 when unit costs were rising, while the 'inflation loss' to creditors occurred in periods 4 to 7 when prices were rising. Note that the identity between additional real costs and inflation losses to creditors could be made precise, period by period, if we measured the real value of debt in terms of the unit cost index instead of the price index.

† The precise formula for the real interest rate, r, is

$$1+r = (1+R)/(1+\%p)$$

where r is the nominal interest rate and %p denotes the rate of inflation (see the appendix).

In our example the real interest rate has been negative, approximately

$$5\% - 10\% = -5\%$$

from period 4 to period 7. In each of these periods creditors of the business have received interest payments worth $35 (period 1 purchasing power) but have suffered a $70 inflation loss. They have received negative *real interest* of $35 per period. The exact value of the real interest rate in periods 4 to 7 is real interest divided by the *opening* real debt, i.e.,

$$-\$35/\$770 = -4\tfrac{1}{2}\%$$

Inflation-adjusted accounts

Inflation-adjusted accounts of the business can now be set out.

Table 9.4 Inflation-adjusted accounts of the business (period 1 purchasing power, $)

Period	(1) Costs = end-period value of inventories = end-period debt	(2) Change in inventories = change in debt	(3) Sales	(4) Real interest	(5) Profits
1	700	0	1000	35	265
2	700	0	1000	35	265
3	770	+70	1000	35	265
4	770	0	1000	−35	265
5	770	0	1000	−35	265
6	770	0	1000	−35	265
7	700	−70	1000	−35	265
8	700	0	1000	35	265

These accounts satisfy the same identities as the accounts in current prices shown in Table 9.1. Profits (column (5)) are equal to sales *less* costs and real interest *plus* the change in the value of inventories. Profits turn out to be a constant percentage of sales and a constant percentage (36%) of historic costs plus real interest (which always comes out at $735).

Real profits of the *business* (column (5)) have been constant. But for *creditors* of the business the fall in the value of money has implied a loss of real wealth. The reason why creditors have received negative real interest of $35 in four periods is that the nominal interest rate has been held constant at 5%, regardless of inflation.

Cost inflation from period 3 to period 6 has increased the real incomes of employees and suppliers of the business at the expense of the creditors.*

Adjustment of nominal interest rates

If nominal interest rates had kept up with inflation the story would have been different. To illustrate this the episode of cost inflation is now re-run with a constant *real* interest rate. This is done by raising the nominal interest rate to 15½% from period 3 to period 6 inclusive.†

---

* In period 3 the extra real costs were paid out of an increase in real debt (column (2)) but this was recovered from creditors in period 7.
† The calculation is

$$(1+0.05)\times(1+0.10)-1 = 0.155$$

(see the formula in the footnote on page 177 above). Observant readers may wonder why the nominal interest rate has gone up in period 3 since in the preceding example real interest only went negative in period 4. It will be found that the only way to preserve the *real* interest rate at 5% in period 4 is to start the higher *nominal* interest rate from period 3. When the profit mark-up is constant, nominal interest rates must adjust simultaneously with changes in *cost* inflation if real interest rates are to be preserved, period by period (see appendix).

Table 9.5 A rise in costs accompanied by a rise in the nominal interest rate

Period	(1) Unit cost index (period 1 = 1.00)	(2) Costs in period = end-period inventories ($)	(3) Interest charged on inventories ($)	(4) Profits net of interest ($)	(5) Value of sales in period ($)	(6) Price index of sales (period 1 = 1.00)
1	1.00	700	35	265	1000	1.00
2	1.00	700	35	265	1000	1.00
3	1.10	770	109	291	1100	1.10
4	1.21	847	119	321	1210	1.21
5	1.33	932	131	353	1331	1.33
6	1.46	1025	144	388	1464	1.46
7	1.46	1025	51	388	1464	1.46
8	1.46	1025	51	388	1464	1.46

As before, the value of inventories at the end of each period is equal to costs incurred in the period. Goods and services are sold with a constant 36% mark-up on historic costs plus current interest charges.

It emerges that the rise in the nominal interest rate from 5% in periods 1 and 2 to 15½% in period 3 is sufficient by itself to raise the price of sales in period 3 by 10% (in this period unit costs have started to rise but have not yet fed through into sales). The consequence is that real costs in period 3 (measured in period 1 purchasing power) remain constant at $700; the simultaneous rise in the nominal interest rate has prevented them from getting ahead of prices. Since the higher nominal interest rate has been passed through into prices, the purchasing power of money has fallen; the inflation loss leaves the real interest rate at 5%.

From period 4 to period 6 costs and prices rise together at a rate of 10% per period with the nominal interest rate held constant at its new level of 15½%, maintaining the real interest rate at 5%. Then in period 7 when unit costs stop rising, we have put the nominal interest rate back to 5% which has the effect of halting the inflation of prices; the cut in the nominal interest rate exactly offsets the remaining cost increase still coming through and the system settles into a new steady state at a permanently higher level of money prices and costs.

The reader may check that our various identities for profits hold in each period in this example as in previous examples. If the inflation-accounting procedures applied before are worked through again it will be found that *nothing at all changes in real terms through the inflation episode*. The volume of sales is, by assumption, always equal to $1000 at period 1 prices. Real costs and the value of the end-period inventory are always $700 (period 1 purchasing power). Real interest is $35 in every period and real profits are $265. In fact the process of inflation has left no trace whatsoever on inflation-adjusted accounts for the business.

Inflation neutrality

We have come to an exceedingly important and quite general conclusion.* If the nominal interest rate varies in line with inflation of costs, and if, in addition, percentage profits are a constant mark-up on historic costs plus interest, then prices will change simultaneously and in proportion to unit costs. General changes in the level of money costs and prices will have no effect at all on the real income of employees and suppliers, the owner of the business, or its creditors.

What we have found is the set of assumptions under which inflation is strictly 'neutral', having no effect on any category of real income per unit of production and sales.

---

* The appendix gives an algebraic demonstration.

Steady states

When the results are inflation-neutral in the sense just described, we shall say that the cost-price system is in a 'steady state'. In other words, we define an inflation steady state as a situation in which the real interest rate (measured relative to cost inflation) *and* the profit mark-up are both constant. As has just been shown, real costs per unit of output will then also be constant. But the rate of inflation is not determinate from the characteristics of these steady states. It could be anything and it could change instantaneously (as it did in periods 3 and 7 in the example just discussed).

It is intuitively obvious what will happen when neutral or steady-state assumptions do not hold. Given the volume of sales, an increase in any one category of real income is at the expense of others. If nominal interest rates get ahead of inflation, real costs and/or real profits must fall. If costs get ahead, real interest and/or real profits must fall. If profit mark-ups rise, real costs and/or real interest rates must fall.

But we must be careful. The price index which has been used for inflation accounting so far has been the average price of the products of the business in question. This may not be a very relevant measure of purchasing power for the incomes being measured. This defect of the approach will only disappear if the results are aggregated for the economy as a whole.

Aggregation

It was explained in Chapter 4 that when business accounts are added up for a closed economy, purchases and sales of 'intermediate' goods and services can be netted out. What is left on the sales side is final sales, FE, defined in Chapter 1 as sales to consumers and government and sales to businesses in their role as purchasers of durable capital goods (e.g., factories and equipment). If rent is regarded as a part of aggregate profits, the only item left on the cost side is money wages and salaries. The *average* profit mark-up, λ, is defined by the ratio of aggregate profits to aggregate costs plus interest charges. The aggregate price index, p, representing the average price of all final sales in the economy as a whole, is a reasonable general measure of the purchasing power of money.*

It is high time that we introduced taxes as a further element of costs. Taxation will here be represented formally as a percentage charged on the value of final sales.

An example of aggregate costs and profits

The following table adapts the example for a single business in Table 9.1 to provide a hypothetical set of accounts for a whole economy. It is *aggregate* volumes of output, final sales and inventories which are now assumed to be constant.

Table 9.6 provides a description *not* of disposable income but of primary income generated by production. Several forms of income transfer are left out – notably taxes on income, interest on government debt, interest on private debt other than that which finances inventories and grants like social security benefits which have no direct bearing on incomes earned in production. But note that if wages, profits and interest on inventories were shown after tax, the column for taxes should include direct taxes on these incomes and social security contributions paid by businesses and employees.

There is one other important point of interpretation. The table says nothing about the average wage *per employee*. Column (2) provides figures for the aggregate wage bill but the table does not

---

* It is obviously unrealistic to assume a unique, common period of production for all businesses. The appendix shows that this is unnecessary since our results hold equally well when the accounting period differs from the period of production. Strictly, one modification is required – the interest-rate term in adding-up identities must be multiplied by a ratio representing the share of lagged costs in the total cost of current sales. But to keep the examples as simple as possible this will be ignored here; we assume a unique, aggregate period of production and continue to use this as the accounting period.

Table 9.6 Accounts for a whole economy

Period	(1) Wage cost per unit of output (period 1 = 1.00)	(2) Aggregate wage bill = end-period value of inventories	(3) Interest charged on opening inventories	(4) Profits net of interest	(5) Sales taxes	(6) Value of final sales in period	(7) Price index of final sales (period 1 = 1.00)
		($)	($)	($)	($)	($)	
1	1.00	700	35	265	250	1250	1.00
2	1.00	700	35	265	250	1250	1.00
3	1.10	770	35	265	250	1250	1.00
4	1.21	847	39	291	275	1375	1.10

say how many people are employed. Column (1) provides an index of wage cost per unit of output. This would only give us an index of the average wage per employee if labour productivity (defined as the average volume of output per person) was constant.

Real incomes and inflation-neutrality

The same inflation-accounting procedures as before can be applied to the aggregate accounts.

Table 9.7 Inflation-adjusted accounts for a whole economy (period 1 purchasing power, $)

Period	Wage bill = end-period value of inventories	Interest on inventories	Profits net of interest	Sales taxes	Volume of final sales
1	700	35	265	250	1250
2	700	35	265	250	1250
3	770	35	265	250	1250
4	770	−35	265	250	1250

These aggregate accounts have essentially the same properties as those for a single business discussed earlier.

The adding-up property is now that lagged real wage costs per unit of output plus the real interest charge on inventories plus the profit mark-up and the tax mark-up must be equal to the volume of final sales.

There are now three conditions for 'neutrality' of the inflation-accounted results. Not only must the real interest rate (relative to *cost* inflation) and the profit mark-up remain constant, but also the average rate of sales tax must not change. The first of these conditions is infringed in the example above from period

3 onwards. This is why the real wage bill has changed in period 3 and real interest has gone negative in period 4.

Just as before, we define an inflation steady state as a situation in which the three conditions for neutrality are met, comparing one period with the next. Again, real wage costs per unit of output are necessarily constant in a steady state. This implies that money wage costs *cannot* get ahead of prices provided nominal interest rates are adjusted immediately and profit and tax mark-ups are maintained.

Finally, recall that in steady states the rate of inflation is indeterminate and may change instantaneously from one period to another.

Appendix 9.1 Inflation and incomes from production

This appendix provides an algebraic treatment of costs, prices and the distribution of income when volumes of output, sales and inventories are changing and the length of accounting periods differs from the period of production. The presentation here is for a closed economy as a whole.

The definition of profits and the adding-up identity

Our starting-point is the definition of profits net of interest charged on the value of inventories:

$$\Pi \equiv FE + \Delta I - WB - T - R.I_{-1} \qquad (A9.1)$$

Here Π denotes profits, FE is the value of final sales, ΔI is the change in the value of inventories during the accounting period, WB is the wage bill, T is sales taxes (net of subsidies), R is the rate of interest and I_{-1} is the opening value of inventories on which interest is charged.

The historic cost of current-period sales, HC, is equal to the current wage bill less the change in the value of inventories:

$$HC \equiv WB - \Delta I \qquad (A9.2)$$

The proportion of historic costs of sales in each period which has been carried over from earlier periods, κ, is measured by the opening value of inventories:

$$\kappa \equiv I_{-1}/HC \qquad (A9.3)$$

We may now write historic costs plus interest charges as

$$HC + R.I_{-1} = (1 + \kappa R)HC$$

The profit mark-up on historic costs plus interest charges is defined as

$$\lambda \equiv \Pi/(HC + R.I_{-1}) \qquad (A9.4)$$

So the sum of historic costs, interest and profits may be written as

$$HC + R.I_{-1} + \Pi = (1 + \lambda)(1 + \kappa R)HC$$

Finally let us define an average sales tax rate, τ, as a percentage of the costs of sales including interest and profits:

$$\tau \equiv T/(HC + R.I_{-1} + \Pi) \qquad (A9.5)$$

We may now rewrite the definition of profits (A9.1) in two alternative forms:

$$FE \equiv HC + R.I_{-1} + \Pi + T \qquad (A9.6)$$
$$FE \equiv (1 + \tau)(1 + \lambda)(1 + \kappa R)HC \qquad (A9.7)$$

Volumes and wage costs

The basic volume measures are

    fe   the volume of sales at base-period market prices, and
    i′   the end period volume of inventories at base-period cost

It will be convenient to define the volume of output at base-period cost so that the wage bill in each period can be expressed accurately as the volume of output at cost multiplied by an index of wage costs per unit of output.

The historic cost of final sales in the base period,

$$HC_0 \equiv WB_0 - \Delta I_0$$

includes an element of costs carried over from earlier periods. We can correct for this by revaluing opening base-period inventories at base-period cost to measure what final sales in that period would have cost at base-period wages per unit of output:

$$fe'_0 \equiv WB_0 - \Delta i'_0$$

A general measure of the volume of final sales at base-period cost is then given by

$$fe' \equiv fe/\sigma \qquad\qquad (A9.8)$$

where σ is the ratio of base-period market prices to base-period cost:

$$\sigma \equiv fe_0/fe'_0$$

The volume of output at base-period cost may now be defined as

$$q' \equiv fe' + \Delta i' \qquad\qquad (A9.9)$$

and the index of wages per unit of output at cost as

$$W' \equiv WB/q' \qquad (A9.10)$$

The above definitions imply that in the base period the volume of output at cost is equal to the wage bill –

$$q'_0 = WB_0$$

so the index of wages per unit of output at cost takes the value of unity in the base period:

$$W'_0 = 1$$

We shall assume* that the end-period value of inventories depends only on current wage costs per unit of output and on the volume of inventories:

$$I = W'i' \qquad (A9.11)$$

The change in the value of inventories in each period may be divided into two components:

$$\begin{aligned}
\Delta I &\equiv I - I_{-1} \\
&= W'i' - W'_{-1}i'_{-1} \\
&= W'\Delta i' + (W' - W'_{-1})i'_{-1} \qquad (A9.12)
\end{aligned}$$

The first component represents the volume change in inventories valued at current cost: the second component represents a

---

* A more general formulation would have to allow for the possibility that the unit cost of end-period inventories may diverge slightly from current wage costs per unit of output. This would considerably complicate the formulae which follow by introducing 'relative inventory valuation adjustments' of the form

$$I - W'i'$$

which would usually in practice be very small. Note that the problem is confined to shifts in the relative unit cost of inventories compared with the base period; we have just shown that $W'_0 = 1$, which implies that A9.11 will always be consistent with

$$I_0 = i'_0$$

valuation change due to changes in money wage costs per unit of output.

Historic costs in each period may now be derived as a function of current and lagged unit wage costs. Using A9.2, A9.9, A9.10 and A9.12

$$
\begin{aligned}
HC &= WB - \Delta I \\
&= W'(fe' + \Delta i') - W'\Delta i' - (W' - W'_{-1})i'_{-1} \\
&= W'.fe' - (W' - W'_{-1})i'_{-1} \qquad (A9.13)
\end{aligned}
$$

This says that the historic cost of current sales is equal to sales valued at current cost less the valuation change on inventories.

Now let us define the proportion of final sales volume deriving from the opening volume of inventories:

$$
\kappa' = i'_{-1}/fe' \qquad (A9.14)
$$

The historic cost of sales may be expressed (using A9.13 and A9.14) as

$$
\frac{HC}{fe'} = (1 - \kappa')W' + \kappa'W'_{-1} \qquad (A9.15)
$$

This says that the unit cost of current sales is a weighted average of current and lagged wage costs per unit of output.

Costs and prices

It is now convenient to scale the index of wage costs by defining

$$
W \equiv W'/\sigma \qquad (A9.16)
$$

so that W' and fe' in equation A9.15 above can be replaced by market-price measures, W and fe. Noting that the interest charge on inventories can similarly be expressed in terms of lagged wage costs and the opening inventory/sales ratio, κ', the result for historic costs (A9.15 above) can be expanded to include the interest charge as

$$HC + R.I_{-1} = \{(1-\kappa')W + \kappa'(1+R)W_{-1}\}fe$$

and, including profit and tax mark-ups, the value of final sales is

$$FE = (1+\tau)(1+\lambda)\{(1-\kappa')W + \kappa'(1+R)W_{-1}\}fe \quad (A9.17)$$

Finally, defining the price index for final sales as

$$p \equiv FE/fe \quad (A9.18)$$

we arrive at a relationship between unit wage costs and prices:

$$p = (1+\tau)(1+\lambda)\{(1-\kappa')W + \kappa'(1+R)W_{-1}\} \quad (A9.19)$$

Real interest

Consider a stock of money, MON, and define its end-period real value as

$$mon \equiv MON/p \quad (A9.20)$$

The real value of the same stock of money at the end of the previous period was

$$mon_{-1} = MON/p_{-1}$$

and the change in real purchasing power due to the change in prices between the previous period and the current period is

$$\Delta mon \equiv MON/p - MON/p_{-1}$$

If the rate of inflation is defined as

$$\%p \equiv p/p_{-1} - 1 \quad (A9.21)$$

the change in real purchasing power reduces to

$$\Delta \text{mon} = -\%\text{p. mon} \qquad\qquad \text{(A9.22)}$$

Interest earned on the stock of money at the rate R per period is in real terms worth

$$\text{R.MON}/\text{p} = \text{R.mon} \qquad\qquad \text{(A9.23)}$$

Adding A9.22 and A9.23, we obtain the real return on the stock of money as

$$(\text{R}-\%\text{p}).\text{mon} = \frac{(\text{R}-\%\text{p})}{(1+\%\text{p})} . \text{mon}_{-1}$$

$$= \{\frac{1+\text{R}}{1+\%\text{p}} -1\} .\text{mon}_{-1} \qquad \text{(A9.24)}$$

The real rate of interest, r, may therefore be defined relative to the end-of-previous-period real value of the stock of money as

$$r \equiv \frac{1+\text{R}}{1+\%\text{p}} -1 \qquad\qquad \text{(A9.25)}$$

To maintain a constant real interest rate as inflation varies, the nominal interest rate must be adjusted so as to satisfy

$$(1+\text{R}) = (1+\text{r}).(1+\%\text{p})$$

Costs and prices again

We now return to the price formula (A9.19 above). Cost inflation may be defined in the same way as price inflation by

$$\%\text{W} \equiv \text{W}/\text{W}_{-1}-1 \qquad\qquad \text{(A9.26)}$$

The real interest rate measured in terms of cost inflation, is, by analogy with A9.25 above,

$$r' \equiv \frac{1+R}{1+\%W} - 1 \qquad (A9.27)$$

This definition can be substituted in A9.19 to simplify the term for unit wage costs and interest. First note that

$$(1+R)W_{-1} = \frac{(1+R)}{(1+\%W)} \cdot W$$

$$= (1+r') \cdot W$$

It follows that A9.19 can be rewritten as

$$p = (1+\tau)(1+\lambda)(1+\kappa' \cdot r')W \qquad (A9.28)$$

Now, finally, defining the index of real wage cost per unit of output as

$$w \equiv W/p$$

we derive the constraint on real incomes generated in production as

$$w(1+\tau)(1+\lambda)(1+\kappa' \cdot r') = 1 \qquad (A9.29)$$

For inflation-neutrality of the distribution of real incomes from production, it is evidently sufficient that any three of the four terms w, τ, λ and $\kappa' r'$ in A9.29 should remain constant.

Note that when real unit wage cost, w, is constant from one period to the next, the rates of cost and price inflation must be equal:

$$\%W = \%p$$

In this case r' in A9.29 can be replaced by r (the real rate of interest measured in terms of price rather than cost inflation).

Inflation-accounted incomes from production

Using lower-case letters without primes to denote variables measured in terms of real purchasing power, historic real costs can be defined by analogy with A9.2 as

$$hc \equiv wb - \Delta i \tag{A9.30}$$

Note that the real value of end-period inventories, i, is *not* the same as the volume of inventories except in periods when the unit wage cost index, W', and the price index, p, happen to coincide. In general

$$i \equiv I/p = W'.i'/p$$
$$= w'.i' \tag{A9.31}$$

where $w' \equiv W'/p$.

The change in the real value of inventories can be decomposed, by analogy with A9.12, as

$$\Delta i = w'.\Delta i' + (w' - w'_{-1}).i'_{-1} \tag{A9.32}$$

where the first term is the volume change and the second term is the real valuation change.

Following identical steps to those employed for money costs, interest, profits and taxes, the real unit cost of sales may be expressed as a weighted average of current and lagged real wage costs per unit of output (see A9.15),

$$\frac{hc}{fe} = (1 - \kappa')w + \kappa'.w_{-1} \tag{A9.33}$$

and the summation of wage costs and other incomes may be expressed in the alternative forms (see A9.6 and A9.7)

$$fe \equiv hc + r.i_{-1} + \pi + t \tag{A9.34}$$

and

$$fe \equiv (1+\tau)\ (1+\lambda)(1+\kappa''.r)hc \qquad (A9.35)$$

where κ'' is the share of the opening real value of inventories in the historic real cost of sales:

$$\kappa'' \equiv i_{-1}/hc \qquad (A9.36)$$

The problem noted in this chapter about the timing of adjustments to the nominal interest rate can be understood from A9.33 and A9.35. In the chapter we had a period of production exactly equal to the accounting period so that by assumption

$$\kappa = \kappa' = \kappa'' = 1$$

and

$$hc = w_{-1}.fe$$

The real cost of sales in each period was entirely predetermined by wages and prices in the previous period. Thus in A9.35 the product

$$(1+\tau)\ (1+\lambda)(1+\kappa''.r) = fe/hc = 1/w_{-1}$$

was predetermined. Given a zero tax rate and a fixed profit mark-up, the real interest rate measured in terms of price inflation, r, was also predetermined. This result would not hold if the acounting periods were longer than the period of production since the real cost of sales would no longer be entirely predetermined by what had happened in earlier periods. But the element of predetermination is a genuine phenomenon (not just a product of the way in which we have carved up time periods) which arises because in the sequence of production, wage costs must generally be incurred before interest, profits etc. can arise.

10 Inflation processes

The previous chapter has shown how wages, interest charges, profits and taxes feed into the average price of final goods and services in a closed economy. This chapter proceeds to analyse inflation as a sequential process. Our general hypothesis is that none of the various components of final prices will fall behind progressively or indefinitely in the course of a sustained inflation; they are protected by a variety of adjustment mechanisms which tend to keep costs and prices rising together.

The general hypothesis

In a modern economy there are tendencies for stabilization of most individual categories of income in real terms or relative to one another or as a share of national income. For example, taxes are usually assessed as percentage rates applied to money incomes and expenditures. This sustains tax revenue in real terms and as a share of national income when money prices and incomes rise. Similarly there is a tendency for nominal interest rates to adjust in response to changes in the rate of inflation so as to reduce the variations in the real return to owners of financial assets which would occur if nominal interest rates remained fixed.

Again, although profit shares generally go up and down between booms and recessions of *real* output, the share of profits usually does not alter so drastically in response to changed inflation rates.*

* Note that this statement refers to profits as defined in Chapters 4 and 9. It is not true as regards another frequently used measure – profits *less* inventory revaluation (stock appreciation).

There is also in most countries a fairly pronounced tendency for the rate of increase in money wages to vary in response to the rate of inflation of prices, helping to keep the share of wages in national income reasonably stable. Since wages form a large part of national income, the observation of a correlation between movements of the average money wage in the economy as a whole and movements of a general price does not necessarily prove much; there is a chicken-and-egg question about which moves first. But most individual money wages, as well as the average for the economy as a whole, do broadly keep up.

Our objective is now to analyse the cumulative or continuing inflation processes which arise when most categories of real income are capable of being defended, to a greater or lesser degree, against erosion of their purchasing power. The instruments through which each income category may be adjusted are fairly self-evident – profits through revision of prices in the light of rising costs, tax revenue through proportionate tax rates, real interest on financial assets through changes in nominal interest rates, and real wages through increases in money wages.

The overall constraint

As emphasized in the preceding chapter, the components of prices add up in a well-defined way. This constrains the combined value of wages, interest, profits and taxes in real terms, as illustrated in Chart 10.1 based on figures from Table 9.7.*

Through time, the shares of different components of prices may change, as is illustrated in Chart 10.2. But nothing can be inferred directly from observed changes in shares about whether inflation has accelerated or decelerated and why. Readers may

---

* When unit wage costs rise at a different rate from prices, the adding-up property for real incomes requires, strictly speaking, that real interest should be measured relative to the rate of inflation of unit wage costs rather than prices (see Appendix 9.1)

Chart 10.1 The constraint on components of prices as shares of the real value of sales

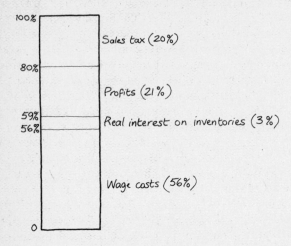

ask themselves whether, in Chart 10.2, wage inflation has accelerated with profits lagging behind or whether, on the contrary, profit margins have fallen, slowing down inflation to the benefit of real wages. There is no way of telling.

Assumptions are required about the specific manner in which components of prices adjust before we can infer anything about the rate of inflation. In the remainder of this chapter we shall usually treat the shares of taxes and profits as being determined exogenously, independent of the rate of inflation, on the assumption that taxes are determined as percentage rates and that in a closed economy there is nothing to prevent prices from being revised so as to preserve the average profit mark-up.*

The next part of the chapter considers the adjustment of wages

* But note the qualifications at the end of this paragraph and the remarks about how the share of profits may be sensitive to the *volume* of output and sales on pages 204 and 252 below.

Chart 10.2 A change in the shares of different components of prices

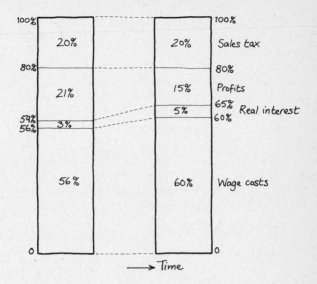

and its implications for inflation. A similar treatment is then provided for interest. Finally we note the case, which may be important in practice, where the profit mark-up is calculated without proper allowance for interest charges.

Money wages are nearly always adjusted at discrete intervals of time. It is a fairly common practice, for instance, for the money wages of any given group of workers to be adjusted once a year. But different arrangements obtain at different times and in different places. Sometimes wage indexing arrangements are made according to which money wages are put up almost instantaneously to compensate for rises in prices. At the other extreme a significant number of workers may be covered by long-term contracts which predetermine money wages for as much as three years at a time.

No theory of the long-term determinants of wages in modern economies will be presented here. Our discussion is strictly limited to the question of how money wages react to rising prices in the short run. There are certainly few topics in contemporary economics which are more vexed than the theory of wage determination; we and several of our colleagues have made reasonably plain our views about how the process operates in our own country.*

To show how an analysis of short-run money wage determination can be developed, we postulate that money wage bargains are made with reference to the purchasing power of money at the time contracts are negotiated. We call the real value of the agreed money wage at the time when the contract is made the *real wage settlement*. This will differ from the real wage actually received (unless there is no inflation) because in the period up to the next wage settlement price inflation will erode the real value of the money wage. The average level of the real wage settlement may be affected by a great variety of factors including the extent to which unemployment is feared, or by the government exercising some kind of incomes policy. We shall here regard it as an exogenous variable.

Given the real value of wage settlements, we can determine how inflation affects the real value of wages paid.

To keep things very simple, suppose that money wages in each period are the outcome of contracts made with reference to prices in the previous period. In this case the *real* value of money wages paid and received in any period will be proportionately lower, the *higher* is the rise in prices since the previous period.

Chart 10.3† illustrates what will happen following a real settlement of $770 (measured in purchasing power in some base period), depending on the rate of inflation and the degree to which the wage contract provides for indexation. With *no* indexation and 20% inflation per period, wages subsequently paid out would only be worth $642 in real terms at the time of payment.

* See in particular Coutts, Tarling and Wilkinson, 'Wage bargaining and the inflation process', *Economic Policy Review*, March 1976, Department of Applied Economics, Cambridge.
† Up to now all the charts in this book have represented time on the horizontal axis. Chart 10.3 and all the remaining charts in Chapter 10 represent *inflation rates per unit of time* on the horizontal axis.

Chart 10.3 The real value of wages, given the real wage settlement, at different rates of inflation

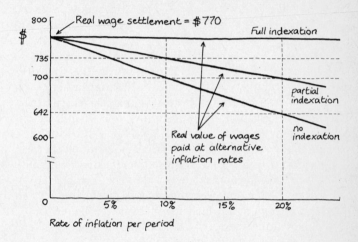

The effect of inflation on real wages (given real wage settlements) illustrated in Chart 10.3 may alternatively be represented as a process taking place in time. In Table 10.1 it is postulated that inflation moves from zero in periods 1 and 2 to 5% in the following two periods, thence to 10% and 20%. The real wage settlement (shown in column (5)) is assumed to remain constant throughout, implying the money wage settlements shown in column (3) obtained by multiplying the real wage settement by the price index. Money wages actually paid (column (4)) are assumed to be equal to settlements in the previous period and these have been divided by prices to yield real wages (in column (6)). The values for real wages corresponding to each rate of inflation are exactly equal to those shown in Chart 10.1

Partial or full indexation can be achieved if the wage contract provides for automatic adjustment of money wage payments whenever prices rise. Contracts of short duration frequently

Table 10.1 Real wage settlements and the real value of wages paid

Period	(1) Price index (period 1 = 1.00)	(2) Increase in prices over previous period (per cent)	(3) Money wage settlement (5) × (1)	(4) Money wages paid in period = settlement in previous period	(5) Real wage at settlement	(6) Real value of wages paid in period = (4)/(1)
			(current $)		($, period 1 purchasing power)	
1	1.000	0	770	770	770	770
2	1.000	0	770	770	770	770
3	1.050	5	808	770	770	733
4	1.102	5	849	808	770	733
5	1.213	10	934	849	770	700
6	1.334	10	1027	934	770	700
7	1.601	20	1233	1027	770	642
8	1.921	20	1479	1233	770	642

renegotiated would have much the same effect. In general, wage contracts suffer less erosion, the more up-to-date the price information on which they are based. At the extreme, settlements which incorporate an accurate expectation about inflation to come can have the same effect as full indexation.

Taking account of possibilities like these, it is likely that in a real-life economy outcomes for average real wages will be more like the one sketched in Chart 10.4 than any of the lines in Chart 10.3. At high rates of inflation, particularly if they persist for long, indexation by one device or another will become increasingly pervasive and effective.

Chart 10.4 Indexation varying with the rate of inflation

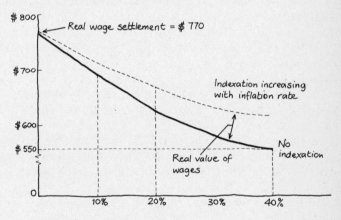

Note that it is only possible to make an empirical study of the adjustment of wages in the terms discussed above if there are data which measure the level and timing of contractual wage *settlements* as well as flows of money wage *payments*. Unfortunately macroeconomic series for wages and salaries are generally confined to data on wage payments or on average rates of pay in force. Aggregate data on settlements scarcely exist.*

Unit wage costs

The relevant wage component of costs is wage costs per unit of output, not wages paid per employee. When wage contracts specify 'piece' rates of pay (i.e., payments per unit of output), the preceding discussion carries through directly to wages per unit of output. But it is more common for wages and salaries to be specified per hour, week or month ('time' rates) with little or no automatic adjustment for changes in output per employee during the period of the contract. Employers then bear the costs and benefits of short-run variations in the volume of turnover or output per employee unless they pass these through into prices. This practice is one reason (possibly the main reason) why the share of profits usually fluctuates quite sharply with the volume of business turnover. In such cases real wage cost per unit of output will be varying inversely with the share of profits. Purely cyclical fluctuations in the relative shares of profits and unit wage costs will, however, be ignored in what follows because they have little or no effect on prices.

Another point to bear in mind is that wages are subject to income tax deductions and social security contributions. For this reason wage costs to employers are usually much higher than cash payments to workers. To the extent that contracts are motivated by consideration of the real value of what workers actually receive, our model of the interaction between prices, taxes and wage costs is formally deficient. However, it would be easy to reorganize accounts for components of prices to show unit wage costs (and, for that matter, interest and profits) on a net-of-tax or 'take-home' basis. What we have termed a 'sales tax' would then have to be expanded to include income taxes and social security contributions.

* Estimates for the UK have, however, been compiled by Coutts, Tarling and Wilkinson, *op. cit.*

Inflation when interest rates are indexed and the profit mark-up is constant

Let us now put assumptions about the adjustment of real wage costs into the identity (Chart 10.1 above) which shows how shares of real wages, real interest, profits and sales taxes in final sales must add up.

The chart below shows how real wage costs per unit of final sales depends on the level of real settlements and the rate of price inflation per period. To keep the lines as steep as possible wage indexation has been assumed away altogether (in real life the lines may be more nearly horizontal). The dotted lines indicate, for example, that a 56% wage share could be achieved with 'low' settlements and 10% inflation per period or 'high' settlements and 20% inflation per period.

Chart 10.5 Outcome for the share of wages in total costs at different levels of settlement and rates of inflation

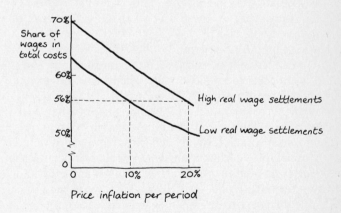

Price inflation per period

From the previous chapter we know that there are well-defined circumstances in which the wage share would *have* to be 56% (or some other number) irrespective of the level of real wage settlements. This would be the case if the shares of sales tax, profits and *real* interest charges in final sales were all fixed, independent of the rate of inflation. We might well assume a given percentage rate of sales tax and a given profit mark-up. To keep the share of real interest fixed we should also have to suppose that the nominal interest rate rises or falls in line with changes in the rate of inflation.

The case when the wage share is fixed, irrespective of the level of wage settlements, is illustrated in Chart 10.6 below. Starting from the bottom line for wage costs (corresponding to 'low' settlements in the previous chart above), we add on real interest

Chart 10.6 Inflation with a given wage settlement

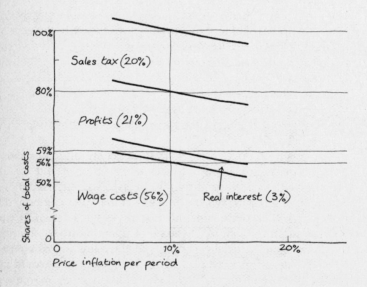

at a fixed 3% rate, a profit mark-up of 36% on wage costs plus interest, and sales tax at 25%. The result has to add up to 100%, but it does so only at one unique rate of inflation – 10% per period.

It is not difficult to imagine an inflation steady state in which wage negotiators have to put up money wage rates per unit of output by 10% each period to maintain the real value of wage settlements. A nominal interest rate of 15½% would be providing an effective 5% real rate of interest. With constant percentage profit and tax mark-ups, prices would be rising by 10%. So long as the level of real wage settlements did not change, the 10% rate of inflation would continue indefinitely.

The steady state illustrated in the chart above could very easily be disturbed. If we had put in the 'high' settlements wage curve (Chart 10.5) instead of the 'low' one, the rate of inflation would have been 20%, not 10%. Note that a transition from one steady state to the other could be very rapid if nominal interest rates were adjusted as soon as wage settlements started to escalate.*

It is not only a change in the average level of real wage settlements (expressed per unit of output) which can alter the rate of inflation. Higher real interest, profit mark-ups or sales taxes could all equally well push the rate of inflation up. This is illustrated in Chart 10.7 below which is exactly the same as the preceding chart except that a new line has been added at the top to represent a rise in the rate of sales tax from 25% to 36%. This, too, is sufficient to increase the steady-state rate of inflation from 10% to 20%.

The effects on prices of a rise in sales tax are often discussed as if the tax increase caused prices to go up once and for all (possibly with some 'second-round' effects). Note that under our assumptions a rise in sales tax or in any of the other components of prices will increase not only the price level but also the ongoing rate of inflation. The scale of the addition to ongoing inflation depends crucially on the slope of the lines in our charts. If wage indexation were pervasive, the bottom line would be almost flat. The rate of inflation would then be extremely

---

* See the numerical examples in Chapter 9 where inflation jumps from zero in one period to 10% in the next and a few periods later suddenly returns to zero.

Chart 10.7 Effects of an increase in sales tax

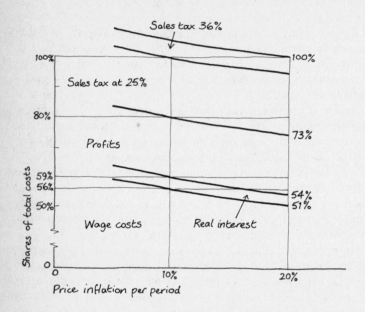

sensitive to upward or downward shifts in any or all of the different components of prices.

The effect of an increase in the rate of sales tax on the inflation rate illustrated in Chart 10.7 may alternatively be represented as a sequential process taking place in time.

Table 10.2 illustrates two inflation steady states, the first (period 1 to 4) at a rate of 10% per period, the second (periods 5 to 8) at a rate of 20% per period. The transition between the two is caused by a once for all rise in the rate of sales tax in period 5 from 25% to 36%.

The first (10%) inflation steady state can be traced through starting with the postulated real wage settlement (column (9)) together with the price index (column (7)), and inferring the money wage settlement. Everything else then follows inevitably from the assumptions given at the head of each column. The stability of the real cost components shown in the lower half of the table imply that the inflation is in a steady state, and the 10% rate of inflation can be considered as a resolution of the fact that the sum of the cost claims exceeds 100%; the inflation turns the real wage settlement per unit of output worth 62 (column (9)) into real wages actually paid per unit of output worth 56 (column (10)).

In period 5 sales taxes are assumed to rise from 25% to 36%. The new inflation rate of 20% per period then follows inevitably from the same set of assumptions about real cost claims. In the top half of the table a heavy line has been drawn for each series at the point when its rate of change alters from 10% to 20%. The new (20%) rate of inflation resolves the unaltered real cost claims partly by reducing the real value of wages per unit of output from 56 to 51 (column (10)) and partly by reducing the share of real profits per unit of output (column (12)) since this is determined as a constant mark-up on *costs* (column (5)) which are now, because of the higher tax rate, a smaller proportion of the total value of sales.

The logical steps displayed in the table can be used to explore the consequences of making alternative assumptions about real cost claims. For instance one could enter a higher figure than 62 for real wage settlements per unit of output on the assumption that with a higher rate of inflation real wage settlements are raised in an attempt to recover the lost ground. In this case the new inflation rate will be more than 20%. Alternatively one could assume that the nominal rate of interest remains constant at 15½%, in which case (everything else being equal) the new rate of inflation will be significantly less than 20%. This case is illustrated in Chart 10.9.

In the light of this observation the reader may begin to wonder not why inflation occurs but why it is usually not, after all, so very unstable. The only stabilizing element in the charts above is the downward slope of the line for wage costs (but for this, all the lines would be flat since the upper lines are defined by percentage mark-ups). However, the charts have so far assumed that the

Table 10.2 An inflation process showing the effects of an increase in sales tax

(cents per unit; the volume unit is an assortment of goods and services costing $1.00 at period 1 selling prices)

Period	(1) Money wage settlement per unit of output: rises of 10% | 20%	(2) Money wages paid per unit of output = (1) lagged	(3) Unit wage cost of goods & services sold in period = (2) lagged	(4) Interest charge = (3) × interest rate at 15½% | 26%	(5) Profit per unit of sales = ((3)+(4)) × mark-up of 36%	(6) Tax per unit of sales = ((3)+(4)+(5)) × tax rate at 25% | 36%	(7) Average price of sales = ((3)+(5)+(4)+(6))	(8) Increase in price over previous period (per cent)
1	62	56	51	8	21	20	1.00	10
2	68	62	56	9	23	22	110	10
3	75	68	62	9	26	24	121	10
4	82	75	68	10	28	27	133	10
5	98	82	75	12	31	43	160	20
6	118	98	82	21	37	51	192	20
7	142	118	98	26	45	61	230	20
8	170	142	118	31	54	73	276	20

(real values; cents, period 1 purchasing power)

	(9) Real wage at settlement per unit of output = (1)/(7)	(10) Real value of wages paid per unit of output = (2)/(7)	(11) Real interest charge = (10) lagged × real interest rate	(12) Real profit per unit of sales = (5)/(7)	(13) Real tax per unit of sales = (6)/(7)	(14) total real income per unit of sales = (10)+(11)+ (12)+(13)
1	62	56	3	21	20	100
2	62	56	3	21	20	100
3	62	56	3	21	20	100
4	62	56	3	21	20	100
5	62	51	−2 (3)*	19	27	95 (100)
6	62	51	3	19	27	100
7	62	51	3	19	27	100
8	62	51	3	19	27	100

* Figure in brackets is for real interest measured relative to *cost* inflation (see Chapter 9)

real interest rate is independent of inflation, which is not in practice very realistic. We shall now show that failure to index interest rates to inflation can contribute an additional, surprisingly important, stabilizing element.

The role of interest rates

First consider how the real interest rate depends on the nominal interest rate and the rate of inflation. This is illustrated in Chart 10.8. When there is no inflation, the real interest rate is the same as the nominal rate (e.g., 5% on the lower line in the chart). Inflation makes the real interest rate lower than the nominal rate (see Chapter 9, page 178). When the rate of inflation reaches the nominal interest rate (e.g., 5%) the real interest is zero. And when inflation exceeds the nominal interest rate, real interest is negative. In the most extreme case shown in the chart, with nominal interest of 5% per period and 20% inflation, the real interest rate is *minus* 12½%.*

Now in earlier charts the real interest charge on inventories

Chart 10.8 Outcome for the real interest rate at different nominal interest rates and rates of inflation

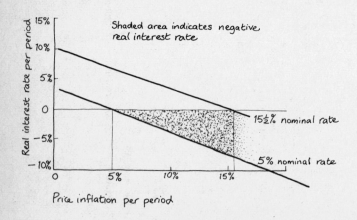

has always been shown as an addition to wage costs. But if the real interest rate is zero or negative, this will no longer be the case. With negative real interest the sum of real wage costs and real interest is *lower* than real wage costs alone. Whoever lends money to businesses is in effect subsidizing the process of production by lending for a negative real return.

Chart 10.9 above has exactly the same form as earlier charts except that we have now assumed a fixed 15½% nominal rate of interest, regardless of inflation. This, like nil indexation of

Chart 10.9 Inflation with a given wage settlement and a given nominal interest rate

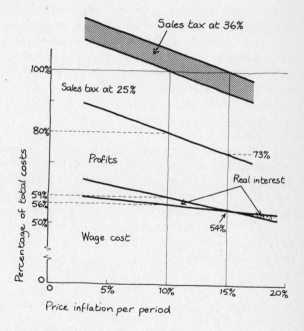

* The calculation is

$$0.125 = (1+0.05)/(1+0.2)-1$$

(see Appendix 9.1).

wages, is an extreme assumption which makes the lines in the charts as steep as they possibly can be.*

The chart once again illustrates the effect of a rise in sales tax from 25% to 36%. The effect on ongoing inflation is smaller than in Chart 10.7 because real interest falls when inflation accelerates.

Profit mark-ups and interest

Nominal interest rates are not in practice invariant with respect to the rate of inflation. But Chart 10.9 above may not be unrealistic in its representation of profits and interest taken together. Up to now we have assumed that profit mark-ups are calculated on costs plus interest. But in practice many businesses which fix their own selling prices may fail to allow properly for changes in nominal interest rates. If prices are set by marking up costs excluding interest, the share of real interest and profits combined will behave *as if* there were a constant nominal interest rate. (The mark-up can be decomposed into a notional nominal interest charge calculated at some fixed rate of interest and a *notional* residual profit.)

Imagine that interest rates are indexed but that businesses ignore changes in interest rates when they set prices. In this case the share of profits after deducting actual interest payments will fall when there is an increase in the rate of inflation. the consequences could be illustrated by redrawing the real interest line in Chart 10.9 while leaving the profit line where it is. The gap between the two lines (profits net of interest) would narrow as the rate of inflation rises.

---

* The numbers used for interest rates and inflation rates will have invited most readers to think of time periods as years. Note that the magnitude of interest charges (positive or negative) is unrealistically high if the time period is taken to be a year, since the calculations assume an average period of production equal to the accounting period whereas in real-life economies it is less than a year.

Conclusions

Each component of prices can be regarded as a claim on real income. We have portrayed inflation as a self-perpetuating process of adjustment which occurs when these real claims are mutually inconsistent. No single component – wages, interest, profits or taxes – can be regarded as causing the inconsistency by itself.

We have given no theory at all about what determines the various real claims. Instead we have concentrated on the process by which they are reconciled. If all components of prices were fully protected against this process (fully indexed) inflation would be totally unstable, accelerating rapidly and indefinitely whenever the real claims were inconsistent. The fact is that inflation is not so unstable from year to year despite substantial exogenous shocks from changes in tax rates, government incomes policies, interest rates and – in open economies – prices of imports and exports. The observed element of stability in inflation tells us that indexation is by no means complete and therefore that at least some real incomes are vulnerable to inflation.

We have seen that the rate of inflation is likely to be quite sensitive to exogenous pressures affecting real claims in the longer run. The level of unemployment and the pressure of demand on productive capacity may have an important influence. In an open economy the rate of exchange for the national currency and prices in world markets may be important. Political and social factors also come in because they influence wages and tax rates. We very much doubt whether any purely economic theory can 'explain' the rate of inflation or indeed whether it is fruitful to seek any general explanation.

PART V

Inflation accounting

11 National accounts in real terms

The purpose of this chapter is to show how a full set of national accounts* comprising all expenditure and disposable income flows together with the stock variables which relate to them can be converted into real terms. The 'real' counterparts of the whole money stock-flow system described in the early part of this book have a great intrinsic interest since they reveal the changes in real assets and liabilities which are occurring. They may, for instance, show that the real government debt is falling in periods when there is large-scale public borrowing; in other words, it may be the case that public expenditure exceeds the tax yield measured in money terms but falls short of it in real terms. In addition, a comprehensive and consistent system of information relating to real stocks and flows will, as we shall show in Chapter 12, help us to analyse the dynamics and determination of the whole system in real terms.

Estimates of real variables provided in official statistics are normally confined to expenditure and output flows and real stocks of capital goods and inventories. Estimates of real disposable income and financial assets and liabilities do not generally exist.

The measurement procedures in this chapter are an indispensable part of the logic of this book but may be tedious for readers who are not interested in accounting. Readers may skip through quickly if they are prepared to take it on trust that we can measure money stocks and flows in real terms in such a manner that everything adds up. They should then refer back to this chapter if they are baffled by some of the more remarkable results about money and the 'real economy' in the next chapter.

* Chapters 9 and 10 were only concerned to convert *business* accounts into 'real' or inflation-adjusted terms in order to measure how increases in money costs and prices interact.

Outline of the method with a numerical illustration

The main objective of inflation accounting is to adjust series measured in money terms for changes through time in the general purchasing power of a unit of money (e.g., a dollar). Values of stocks and income/expenditure flows are expressed in terms of purchasing power in some base period. These 'real' values measured in base-period purchasing power are not the same as *volumes*. For example, when the price of oil increases more than the average price of goods and services in general, an oil producer could sell a constant volume of oil but secure a rising real income. Note also that real values as defined in this book make no allowance for differences in the assortment of goods and services typically purchased by particular groups or sectors within the economy. The aim is to measure the general purchasing power of financial stocks and flows, regardless of who is the owner or by whom and to whom they are paid.

Table 11.1 provides an illustrative set of national accounts in money terms which will be the source of numerical examples in this chapter. The figures have no special significance apart from the fact that they add up (i.e., they satisfy the identities set out in Chapter 1). The bottom part of the table gives the few volume measures which will be needed (final sales, inventories and aggregate output) and the price indices used to convert values into volumes.

The inflation-accounting exercise will start from measurement of real values of assets and debts. We then examine inflation adjustments to accounts for the private sector and the government. The final section shows how real income is defined and demonstrates its relationship to the aggregate volume of output. Note that we are still dealing with a closed economy; the open-economy case is dealt with in the appendix to Chapter 14.

The standard of purchasing power

First let us consider the definition of base-period purchasing power. The approach used here is to measure how much the price of an average assortment of final goods and services purchased in each period differs from the price of the same assortment in the base period. We can find this from Table 11.1 below by comparing the total money value of final purchases by the private sector and government (rows 8 and 11 which in period 2, for example, sum to $384) with the value of the same final purchases at base-period (period 0) prices, which is also the measure chosen in Chapter 1 for the *volume* of final sales (row 17, equal to $333 in period 2). The average price change between 0 and period 2 is measured by the difference between the money value and the base-period value of final sales ($384–$333), divided by the base-period value ($333). In period 2 the result comes to

$$\$51/\$333 = 15\tfrac{1}{2}\%$$

If prices have on average risen by 15½% we may say that the purchasing power of money has fallen by 13½%:

$$1/1.155 = 0.865 = 1-0.135$$

The ratio of the value of expenditure at current prices to the values of the same expenditure at base-period prices is called a price deflator. So the deflator for final purchases (row 20 in Table 11.1) measures what we want (its value in period 2 is 1.155). To convert sums of money to real values we divide them all by this 'deflator' or price index. For example, the real value of aggregate final purchases in period 2, measured as the money value ($384), divided by the price deflator (1.155), is

$$\$384/1.155 = \$333$$

The result in this particular case is, of course, the same as the volume measure from which the price deflator was derived.

Table 11.1 A set of national accounts

	Period:	−1	0	1	2
End-period balance sheets ($ at current prices: assets +, liabilities −)					
1. Private sector: value of inventories		92	100	109	129
2. financial assets		231	250	277	321
3. total assets		323	350	386	450
4. private debt		−136	−150	−163	−191
5. net assets		187	200	223	259
6. Government debt		−95	−100	−114	−130
7. National assets		92	100	109	129
Expenditure on goods and services ($ at current prices)					
8. Private sector: final purchases		185	200	222	256
9. change in value of inventories		...	8	9	20
10. total		...	208	231	276
11. Government final purchases		89	98	110	128
12. National expenditure		...	306	341	404

Disposable income ($ at current prices)

13. Private sector	...	213	245	292
14. Government	...	93	96	112
15. National income	...	306	341	404

Volumes ($ at period 0 prices)

16. End-period inventories	96	100	99	106
17. Aggregate final purchases/sales	293	298	316	333
18. Change in volume of inventories	...	4	-1	7
19. Aggregate output	...	302	315	340

Price deflator (period 0 = 1.000)

20. National final purchases	0.935	1.000	1.050	1.155
21. Inventories	0.958	1.000	1.101	1.217

We can separately deflate final purchases by the private sector and the government (rows 8 and 11) in period 2 to obtain their respective real values:

private sector	$256/1.155 =	$222
government	$128/1.155 =	$111
		——
total	$384/1.155 =	$333

This does not necessarily tell us the *volume* of final purchases actually made by each sector since prices may have risen more for one set of purchases than the other. It tells us what the two sectors could have bought if they had both spent their money on the same things. Note, too, that if there had been no general increase in prices between period 0 and period 2 it is quite likely that the prices of purchases by the two sectors would still have changed relative to one another in much the same way as they actually did. So the real values provide an *estimate* of what the two sets of purchases in period 2 might have cost in the absence of a general rise in prices.

We may now proceed to see how real assets and real income are to be measured.

The real value of assets and debts

Ideally the real value of stocks such as assets and debts which are measured at a *point* in time should be calculated with reference to the level of prices at the same point in time rather than the average level of prices prevailing over a *period* of time. But this complicates the analysis without introducing any important points of principle. So, as in Chapter 9, we shall use the price deflator relevant to flows in each period to convert asset values as well. Our rule is that *end-period* real values of assets and debts are calculated by dividing their money values by the price deflator for the period. For example, the real value of end-period inventories is derived from money values (row 1 of Table 11.1) divided by the price index (row 20) *not* row 21 which would give volumes.

period 0 $100/1.000 = $100
period 1 $109/1.050 = $104
period 2 $129/1.155 = $112

We want to preserve the property that values of assets at the start of each period are the same as their values at the end of the previous period. So *opening* money values of assets must be converted into real terms by dividing by the price deflator for the *previous* period. Price changes may be imagined as taking effect immediately *after* the start of each period. Changes in the real value of assets between two successive periods due to changes in the average price level (which in reality usually occurs fairly continuously) are allocated, somewhat artificially, to the second of the two periods. This is the cost of our simplification.

Inflation adjustments to stock variables

In Chapters 9 and 10 the erosion in real value of a money debt as prices rise was measured as an 'inflation gain' to the debtor and an 'inflation loss' to the creditor. It was shown that such inflation gains and losses can be compensated through higher interest payments. Whether or not the compensation actually occurs, interest payments are included in disposable money incomes as measured in national accounts. But inflation gains and losses are not. To get proper measures of real income it will therefore be necessary to adjust income flows for the effects of inflation on the real value of assets and debts.

To show how the inflation loss on an asset is calculated, let us take the example of private financial assets in period 2. The assets whose real value will be eroded in the period are *start-of-period* assets worth $277 in money terms (the end-period figure for period 1 in row 2 of Table 11.1). The *real* value of these assets at the start of the period is found by dividing the money sum by the price deflator for the previous period:

$277/1.050 = $264

The real value of the same sum of money at the end of the period is

$$\$277/1.155 = 240$$

The inflation loss is the difference –

$$\$264 - \$240 = \$24$$

In the case of a debt the calculation is exactly the same but the fall in real value represents a *gain* to the debtor, not a loss.

Table 11.2 sets out the pattern of inflation adjustments on all assets and debts which enter into national accounting identities. When the price level is rising, values of inventories and financial assets will be adjusted downwards, but there will be inflation 'gains' on debt. Businesses which finance the whole of their inventories by borrowing suffer no *net* inflation loss since they receive an equal inflation gain on their debt. The creditors suffer an inflation loss on the money they have lent but may (or may not) be compensated by higher nominal interest rates. Another aspect of the private sector's exposure to net inflation losses is in respect of financial assets (bonds, notes and deposits) which are the counterpart of government debt. In this case the inflation loss represents a transfer of real purchasing power from the private sector to the government. This, too, may or may not be compensated by interest payments.

When the government's inflation gain is subtracted from the net inflation loss of the private sector, what remains is an inflation loss for the economy as a whole which must be equal to the inflation loss on inventories (gains and losses on financial assets and debts cancel out).*

---

* In a real-life economy with financial assets and liabilities whose money values vary (e.g., equities) and with foreign assets and liabilities, this proposition may not hold. A more comprehensive accounting system is needed to measure the money value of income as well as real income. Inflation adjustments may have to cover tangible fixed assets. Values of financial assets and liabilities may not always net out in the economy as a whole (e.g., equities). Some of the implications are discussed in Chapter 13.

Table 11.2 Inflation adjustments
($, period 0 purchasing power: gains +, losses −)

Period:	0	1	2
Private			
a. inventories	−6	−5	−9
b. financial assets	−16	−12	−24
c. total assets	−22	−17	−33
d. debt	+9	+7	+14
e. net assets	−13	−10	−19
Government			
f. debt	+7	+5	+10
Whole economy			
g. net assets = inventories	−6	−5	−9

Accounts for the private sector

Table 11.3 below gives inflation-adjusted accounts for the private sector. The first row shows the real value of money income (row 13 in Table 11.1 divided by row 20, the general deflator). The second row shows net inflation losses for the private sector calculated in the manner which has just been described (see row e in Table 11.2 above). Deflated money income less net inflation losses defines real income. This definition preserves the budget constraint for the private sector in real terms. In period 2, for example, the real disposable income of the private sector ($234) less real expenditure ($230) yields a financial surplus of $4 which is precisely equal to the increase in real financial assets ($14) less the increase in real debt ($10).

Note that the financial surplus of the private sector is reduced by the net inflation loss in the same way as income. But the 'reduction' is a statistical one, not a proposition about behaviour. It will be argued in the next chapter that inflation normally induces the private sector to increase its money surplus relative to income, leaving the real surplus more or less the same as it would have been in the absence of inflation.

Table 11.3 Inflation-adjusted accounts for the private sector*
($, period 0 purchasing power)

Period:	0		1	2
Flows in period				
a. Deflated money disposable income (13÷20)	213		234	253
less				
b. Inflation loss on net assets (Table 11.2, row e)	−13		−10	−19
c. Real disposable income (a+b)	200		224	234
d. Final purchases (8÷20)	200		211	222
e. Change in real inventories (change in j)	2		4	8
f. Real expenditure (d+e)	202		215	230
g. Real financial surplus (c−f = h+i)	−2		+9	+4
h. Change in real financial assets (change in k)	3		14	14
less				
i. Change in real debt (change in m)	−5		−5	−10
End-period balance sheet (assets +, liabilities −)				
j. Real value of inventories (1÷20)	98	100	104	112
k. Real value of financial assets (2÷20)	247	250	264	278
l. Total real assets (j+k)	345	350	368	390
m. Real debt (4÷20)	−145	−150	−155	−165
n. Net assets (l+m)	200	200	213	225

* Figures in brackets refer to rows in Table 11.1.

The government accounts

Table 11.4 below shows how the inflation gain to the government on its debt reduces the real budget deficit relative to the cash deficit. The bottom part of the table shows the government's income before and after deduction of debt interest. In the case illustrated, real interest is constant, implying that nominal interest rates on government debt have varied in line with changes in the rate of inflation. The resulting variations in deflated interest payments exactly match period-by-period changes in the inflation gain shown in the top part of the table. Changes in the nominal interest rate have compensated holders of government debt for inflation losses.

Table 11.4 Inflation-adjusted government accounts*
($, period 0 purchasing power)

Period:	0	1	2
a. Final purchases (11÷20)	98	105	111
less			
b. Deflated net money income (14÷20)	−93	−91	−97
c. Deflated cash deficit (a+b)	5	14	14
less			
d. Inflation gain on debt (Table 11.2, row f)	−7	−5	−10
e. Real deficit (c+d)	−2	9	4
f. End-period real value of government debt (6÷20)	100	109	113
Deflated money income			
g. Tax revenue less grants, subsidies etc.	102	98	109
less			
h. Interest payments on government debt	−9	−7	−12
i. Net money income (= b)	93	91	97
Net real income			
j. Tax revenue less grants, subsidies etc. (= g)	102	98	109
k. Real interest on government debt (h−d)	−2	−2	−2
l. Net real income (i+k)	100	96	107

* Figures in brackets refer to rows in Table 11.1.

Note that the part of interest on government debt which compensates for inflation losses to holders of the debt does not have to be paid for in any real sense; it is precisely equal to the excess of the deflated cash budget over the real budget deficit. The government could continuously borrow the money needed to pay additional interest* on account of inflation without increasing its debt in real terms.

Real national income and output

Real national income is defined as deflated money national income less the inflation loss on inventories (Table 11.5 below). Now money incomes of the private sector and government add up to money national income, and inflation losses and gains for the two sectors combined are equal to the inflation loss on inventories. This definition of real national income is therefore equal to the sum of real private income and real income of the government. It is also equal to aggregate real expenditure (final purchases plus the change in real inventories). So the money national-accounting identities have been preserved in real terms.

Table 11.5 also illustrates the relationship between real national income and the *volume* of output in a closed economy. The volume of output is defined as the volume of final sales plus the change in the volume of inventories. Our choice of the price index for inflation accounting has meant that the *real value* of final purchases or sales is by identity equal to the *volume* of final sales. So real national income can differ from the volume of output to the extent that changes in the real value of inventories differ from changes in the volume of inventories. Differences between the two latter are caused by 'real' capital gains or losses on inventories which occur when unit costs rise ahead of, or fall behind, selling prices. They are usually small and short-lived.

---

* If capital gains or losses on bonds are taken into account, things are more complicated. For example, the government cannot avoid making an inflation gain on existing bonds when the rate of inflation increases unexpectedly (see Chapter 13).

Table 11.5 Real national income and output*
($, period 0 purchasing power)

Period:	0	1	2
a. Deflated money national income (15÷20)	306	325	350
less			
b. Inflation loss on inventories (Table 11.2, row 1)	−6	−5	−9
c. Real national income (a+b)	300	320	341
d. Final purchases (10+11)	298	316	333
e. Change in real inventories (c−d)	2	4	8
f. Aggregate real expenditure (= c)	300	320	341
g. Change in volume of inventories (= 18)	4	−1	7
h. Aggregate volume of output (d+g)	302	315	340
i. Change in real valuation of inventories (e−g = c−h)	−2	+5	+1

* Figures in brackets refer to rows in Table 11.1.

Conclusion

We have now established a set of accounts for stocks of real assets and debts and for flows of income and expenditure which obey all the same identities as accounts in money terms. The new inflation-adjusted accounts do not describe different things from the money accounts. They measure exactly the same money stocks and flows in a different, for some purposes more revealing, way. Definitions of real income and expenditure have been chosen so that they are in aggregate precisely related to the aggregate volume of output and indeed will usually be very nearly equal to the latter. We are now well on the way to establishing the links between money processes and what happens in the real economy.

12 Real demand

The preceding chapter has shown how a set of accounts describing stocks of financial assets and flows of income and expenditure in money terms can be converted into a second set of accounts describing the same stocks and flows in real terms including the total volume of expenditure and therefore aggregate real output.

The complete model

We now, therefore, have a complete macroeconomic model of a closed economy which in principle could be solved through the following steps:
(1) determine money stocks and flows using the model of Chapters 6 and 7;
(2) determine inflation using the model of Chapters 9 and 10;
(3) use inflation accounting (Chapter 11) to derive real stocks and flows, the total volume of expenditure and aggregate output.

The solution would in practice be complicated because results at steps (2) and (3) feed back into steps (1) and (2). And since, as suggested in Chapter 10, the rate of inflation could be almost anything, it may appear that almost any result could come out from the complete model.

Must we therefore give up all hope of obtaining any analytic understanding of how the whole macroeconomic system works, making us dependent for obtaining knowledge on numerical simulations of computerized models?

A technique for further analysis

We would be able to reach such analytic understanding of the whole system if it were the case that the whole model was 'inflation-neutral'; if, that is to say, it were the case that every proposition about the relationships between stocks and flows measured in money terms also held good for stocks and flows measured in real terms. This gives us the clue to a potentially fruitful line of inquiry. What we shall do is specify the precise conditions under which our model would be inflation neutral in this sense. If we know the conditions under which the solution for real income and output becomes invariant with respect to inflation we may then be able to find out what happens when these special conditions do not hold.

The next section shows how the simple stock-flow model discussed in Chapter 5 can be inflation-neutral. We then explain what inflation neutrality would mean in different parts of a more general model, noting where it is unlikely to be true and what difference that makes.

If stock-flow processes are roughly inflation neutral, it becomes possible to conceive of fiscal policy as an instrument for the control of real income and output, at least in a *closed* economy. This is demonstrated later in the chapter using a hypothetical example of a fiscal planning exercise.

Near the end of the chapter we shall discuss the relationship between real expenditure, the volume of output and the supply side of the economy. Finally some broad conclusions will be drawn about the character of interactions between financial processes, inflation and the 'real economy'.

A simple example of inflation neutrality

Let us start with the simple case of a closed, credit-money economy with no fiscal system where the only debt is borrowing to finance inventories.* The chart below illustrates what would

* This is the model discussed in Chapter 5.

Chart 12.1 A simple example of inflation neutrality

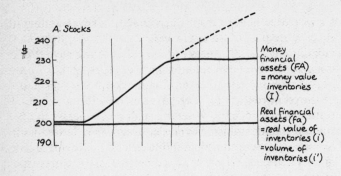

A. Stocks

Money financial assets (FA) = money value inventories (I)

Real financial assets (fa) = real value of inventories (i) = volume of inventories (i')

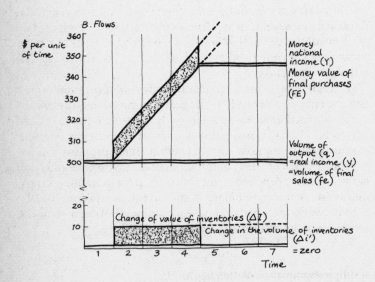

B. Flows

Money national income (Y)

Money value of final purchases (FE)

Volume of output (q) = real income (y) = volume of final sales (fe)

Change of value of inventories (ΔI)

Change in the volume of inventories (Δi') = zero

Time

have to happen for real variables to remain constant while costs, prices and money aggregates increase. There are two *exogenous* variables – the volume of inventories, assumed constant, and the index of unit wage costs, assumed to rise in three consecutive periods by a total of 15%. Everything else is *endogenous*.

The outcome in the chart comes about as follows:

(1) the money value of inventories goes up by the same amount as unit costs (15%), generating an equal increase in money debt and the stock of financial assets;

(2) money income and expenditure rise by 15% which is necessary to induce people to hold the additional financial assets;

(3) the average price of final sales rises in proportion to unit costs (15%);

(4) since money expenditure has risen by 15%, the same as prices, the *volume* of final sales is unchanged;

(5) the volume of output and all *real* (inflation-accounted) variables are then also unchanged.

The result at (5) relies crucially on the money stock/flow process generating a rise in money values which precisely accommodates the increase in unit costs and prices. Notice that in the chart this property holds *period by period* through the transition from one steady state to another. If the property relies on simple and general assumptions we shall have found conditions for inflation-neutrality of real demand. By implication, increases in money costs and prices could continue indefinitely and at varying rates (e.g., along the dotted lines in the chart) without disturbing the 'real economy'.

Conditions for inflation neutrality

Table 12.1 below provides the figures from which the chart was drawn so that the reader can check everything out, period by period. The table explains the steps by which we have calculated the complete solution for money variables, volumes and real

Table 12.1 An inflation-neutral rise in money values
(money values in current \$; real values and volumes in period 1 \$)

	Period:	1	2	3	4	5
Exogenous variables						
1. Volume of inventories, i'		200	200	200	200	200
2. Unit cost index, w'		1.00	1.05	1.10	1.15	1.15
Endogenous variables						
3. Money value of inventories, I = money debt = financial assets, FA = (1)×(2)		200	210	220	230	230
4. Final purchases at current prices, FE = FA/α = (3)÷2/3		300	315	330	345	345
5. Change in money value of inventories, ΔI = change in (3)		0	10	10	10	0
6. Money in national income, Y = (4)+(5)		300	325	340	355	345

	1.00	1.05	1.10	1.15	1.15
7. Price index of final sales, p = (2)	1.00	1.05	1.10	1.15	1.15
8. Volume of final sales, fe = (4)/(7)	300	300	300	300	300
9. Change in volume of inventories, $\Delta i'$ = change in (1)	0	0	0	0	0
10. Volume of output, q = (8)+(9)	300	300	300	300	300
11. Real value of inventories, i = (3)/(7)	200	200	200	200	200
12. Change in real value of inventories, = change in (11)	0	0	0	0	0
13. Real national income, y = (8)+(12)	300	300	300	300	300
14. Real inventory valuation change $\Delta i - \Delta i'$ = (12)−(9)	0	0	0	0	0

variables. Anyone who wants to verify inflation neutrality of this system under different exogenous conditions (e.g., when the volume of inventories changes and when unit costs rise at varying rates) can put new assumptions into rows 1 and 2 of the table and calculate new results, row by row, down to the bottom of the table. It will always be found that the outcome for volumes and real variables depends only on row 1 (the volume of inventories) and is entirely independent of what is assumed in row 2 (unit costs). This is what we mean by inflation neutrality.

There are only three behavioural assumptions in the table; everything else follows from logical identities. The behavioural assumptions are:

(1) The *volume* of inventories (row 1) is independent of inflation (row 2). Otherwise inflation would feed into real stocks and flows from the very beginning.
(2) The adjustment process for holdings of financial assets keeps them in a constant ratio to money expenditure (in row 8 this is used to infer money expenditure). The adjustment process which conforms with this assumption is the one discussed at the end of Chapter 5. It is an *inflation-neutral* asset adjustment process.
(3) The price of final sales (row 7) rises in proportion to unit costs without any lag. (We know from Chapter 9 that this will happen if the real interest rate, the profit mark-up and the rate of sales tax are all constant.)

What happens if any or all of these assumptions does not hold will be explained shortly.

The model in real terms

When real outcomes are invariant with respect to inflation, it must be possible to calculate them directly without having to specify what is happening to costs, prices and money values (i.e., it must be possible to drop rows 2 to 7 from the table above). The appendix to this chapter shows formally in algebraic notation how real outcomes may be determined directly in a general closed-economy model. The analysis starts from debt creation and the fiscal stance (suitably defined in real terms) and then works out implications of the asset adjustment process for real income, expenditure and output. The asset adjustment process itself is expressed in a real (inflation-accounted) form. It is *not* necessary to assume inflation neutrality in order to analyse real stocks and flows in this way. Where inflation neutrality is infringed, an inflation term will appear in the relevant equation of the model.

To illustrate this, let us return once more to the simple example in Table 12.1 above. We now start from the real value of inventories (row 11) as the main exogenous variable of the system. The real value of inventories determines real debt and the real stock of financial assets. The next step is to derive real final expenditure (row 8). Under the same (inflation-neutral) adjustment process for financial assets as before, real final expenditure is given by the real value of financial assets divided by the asset/income norm (fe = fa/α). Finally, real national income (row 13) is given by real final expenditure (row 8) plus the change in real inventories (the change in row 11). Three rows only (8, 11 and 13) suffice for the determination of real outcomes contingent on two behavioural assumptions – inflation neutrality of real debt creation and inflation neutrality of asset adjustment.*

---

* Note that the volume of output (row 10) may in general not be quite the same as real income. Differences between the two arise from real inventory valuation changes (row 14). It was in order to rule out these that we needed to assume above that prices move exactly in line with costs.

In Table 12.1 above the real value of inventories is the same as the volume of inventories because of our assumption that the general price index moves exactly in line with unit costs (see Chapter 11). If unit costs rise faster than the price index there will be a 'real valuation gain' on inventories; the increase in the volume of inventories will be less than the increase in their real value, and the *volume* of output will fall below real income (the reverse is the case when the price index rises faster than unit costs). Since real income and the volume of output depend on changes in inventories, not levels, these effects are transient, nor permanent.

Inflation neutrality with a fiscal system

We now consider in turn the conditions for inflation neutrality of financial asset adjustment, private debt and also the government's fiscal stance. The last is the most important of all because, as shown in earlier chapters, it uniquely determines steady-state income and expenditure flows. If the fiscal stance is fixed in real terms, the outcome for the real economy will be broadly independent of inflation even if private debt and asset adjustment are not inflation-neutral. But if the government fixes the fiscal stance in money terms, irrespective of inflation, the outcome for real income and output will be entirely dependent on what happens to the general price level.

Financial asset adjustment

In the example just discussed we had to assume a specific asset adjustment process in order to ensure that money expenditure went up one for one with the price level in every period. In the appendix it is demonstrated that this particular adjustment process, first discussed at the end of Chapter 5, is the only one which will allow the private sector to preserve an inflation-neutral steady state when the price level rises at varying rates. The process had something going for it, since it is at least plausible that when real income and real debt remain constant people will generally want to arrange their budgets so as to keep their real expenditure and the real value of their financial assets constant as well.

But the plausibility of the process does not mean that it will always be the one which is followed in practice. What happens if asset adjustments are not inflation-neutral?

An important difference would be made if the asset/income norm, α, was affected by changes in the price level. Inflation could then cumulatively and persistently change stock-flow ratios in one direction (e.g., the stock of financial assets might fall relative to money income as the price level went up). Since, for example, inflation at 15% per annum will double the price level every five years, real stocks and flows could then be very strongly affected by inflation. But according to our very general stock-flow axiom this is all rather unlikely to happen.

Even if the asset/income norm is invariant with respect to inflation, the speed of adjustment of holdings of assets may not be what is required for inflation neutrality. If the adjustment is too slow, the ratio of real stocks of assets to real income will be lower when there is inflation. By implication aggregate real expenditure and income will be stimulated by inflation. But the effect will be strictly bounded since, when asset stocks fall behind, the pressure for adjustment rises. It is also possible in principle for asset adjustment to be too fast, in which case inflation would depress real expenditure and income. This latter case requires us to believe that when there is inflation people not merely make good inflation losses but actually hold a higher stock of financial assets relative to income.

Private debt creation

It is plausible to suppose that borrowing to finance inventories will be approximately inflation neutral. The volume of inventories is governed mainly by production and distribution arrangements and by volumes of output and sales. If costs and prices rise, so will the money value of inventories and the money value of debt required to finance them. There are some qualifications. First, real valuation changes (see above, page 231) may temporarily raise or lower real debt on account of inventories when the rate of inflation *changes* (e.g., increase the real debt when inflation is *accelerating*). Second, if interest rates are not adjusted in line with inflation, inventory/sales norms may be affected by variations in real interest rates. Third if banks are not used to inflation, businesses may have some difficulty in expanding their money debt to keep up with the rising cost of inventories.

The point about interest rates also applies to other types of private debt and, indeed, to the government's budget. We may define an inflation-neutral monetary policy as one which adjusts nominal interest rates to preserve real interest rates. Inflation-neutral monetary policy will usually be a necessary condition for neutrality of private debt creation.

Other private debt

In this chapter we still ignore the whole question of equities,* but there is also a wide class of loans financing purchases of durable goods, cars, houses, etc. which will be significantly affected by inflation. For reference later on we shall call such private debt (other than borrowing on inventories) 'personal loans', denoted PL, since the loans are mostly taken out by private individuals and small, personally owned businesses.

A personal loan is usually repaid on a schedule agreed when the loan is first taken out. The aggregate stock of debt outstanding rises or falls depending on the balance between new loans and repayments. For the real value of this debt to be invariant with respect to inflation, real repayments as well as the real value of new loans would have to be inflation-neutral.

How should real repayments be defined? If we want to know what will happen to the real value of loans outstanding, we must take account not only of cash repayments but also of the way in which inflation erodes the real value of money. Unless cash repayment schedules are altered to take account of this, inflation accelerates real repayments and causes the real value of outstanding debt to fall. In other words the real value of the stock of debt is unlikely to be inflation-neutral, even if the real value of the flow of new loans is.

Table 12.2 below illustrates the effect of inflation on a system of personal loans which are paid off in four equal instalments. In periods 1 and 2 there is no inflation and repayments balance

---

* If real profits in a closed economy are not much affected by inflation, then the real valuation of equities should be more-or-less inflation-neutral (see Chapter 13).

Table 12.2 Loans and repayments

Period	(1) Price index	(2) New loans	(3) (current $) Repayments = ¼ of new loans in previous four periods	(4) End-period debt = opening debt + (2) − (3)	(5) Real value of new loans = (2)/(1)	(6) Real repayments = (5) − change in (7)	(7) End-period real debt = (4)/(1)
1	1.00	40	40	100	40	40	100
2	1.00	40	40	100	40	40	100
3	1.10	44	40	104	40	46	94
4	1.21	48	41	111	40	41	91
5	1.33	53	43	121	40	41	91
6	1.46	59	46	134	40	40	91

new loans. From period 3 onwards there is 10% inflation. New loans keep pace with inflation while cash repayments lag behind so the stock of debt rises in money terms. But it does *not* keep up with inflation. The real value of the stock of debt falls cumulatively by 9% up to period 6 when the system reaches a new steady state. If the loans had been paid off over ten years or twenty periods instead of four, the fall in the real value of the stock of debt would have continued for much longer and would eventually have been much greater.

To make loan contracts inflation-neutral, the rule would have to be that cash repayments were varied as necessary so as to pay off real debt at an agreed rate. If the interest rate varies with inflation, total debt service (interest plus cash repayments) would then also be inflation neutral.

The fiscal system

Inflation accounting of the government budget has already been discussed in the preceding chapter. The main adjustment which had to be made to the money accounts was to measure interest on the government's debt in terms of real rather than nominal interest rates. When there is inflation (and assuming that the government is a debtor) the government receives an inflation gain on its debt which makes the inflation-adjusted government deficit smaller than its cash deficit.

The government's real fiscal stance may be defined, by analogy with the money fiscal stance, as the ratio of real government spending, g, to the government's share of *real* national income. This differs from the money fiscal stance not only because spending is measured in real rather than money terms but also because the government's share of real income includes the inflation gain mentioned above which is ignored in money accounts. When there is inflation the money fiscal stance must be higher than the equivalent real fiscal stance. This is one of the mechanisms which in an inflation-neutral system provides the private sector with extra money income (relative to the price level) to finance money asset accumulation

To achieve inflation neutrality the government must give the private sector the money (e.g., by paying more nominal interest or reducing tax rates) to buy extra government debt and must keep its own cash budget in a correspondingly higher deficit.

We may say more generally that fiscal policy is inflation-neutral if the government's real fiscal stance is invariant with respect to inflation. This will be achieved, for example, if government expenditure is decided in real terms, tax rates are fixed in percentage terms, and the real rate of interest on government debt is invariant with respect to inflation. The real fiscal stance may still be inflation-neutral when the real rate of interest does vary with inflation, provided that the government alters tax rates to compensate.

An inflation-neutral fiscal stance implies a cash deficit in the government's budget varying with inflation. This is illustrated by Table 12.3 which shows a set of government accounts given in real terms with their money counterparts at different rates of inflation.

What emerges is that the faster the rate of inflation the larger the government's cash deficit must be in order to keep its real debt constant (or rising at any given rate). Provided the real interest rate is maintained (as in the middle two sections of the table) this happens automatically through the variation in nominal interest payments. But if the real interest rate falls, as illustrated in the bottom part of the table, the real fiscal stance and real government debt can only be maintained by cutting tax rates (or increasing real expenditure) so as to compensate for the fall in real interest paid on government debt.

It may not be easy for a government to maintain an inflation-neutral real fiscal stance, even supposing it wants to. Not only do real interest rates vary with inflation but tax systems are never exactly inflation-neutral. Also, the increased cash deficits required in the presence of inflation are regarded with suspicion by adherents of the 'balanced budget'.

But it is also difficult for a government to maintain a predetermined *money* fiscal stance irrespective of inflation since its expenditure provides real services and infrastructure whose cost goes up with inflation. Government budgeting arrange-

Table 12.3 An inflation-neutral government budget

Period	(1) Government expenditure	(2) Tax revenue	(3) Debt interest	(4) Budget deficit (1)+(3)−(2)	(5) End-period government debt

1. Account in real terms ($, period 0 purchasing power)

Period	(1)	(2)	(3)	(4)	(5)
0	100	105	5	0	100
1	105	107	5	3	103
2	110	111	5	4	107
3	110	115	5	0	107

2. Account in money terms with 5% inflation ($)

Period	(1)	(2)	(3)	(4)	(5)
0	100	105	10	5	100
1	110	112	10	8	108
2	121	122	11	10	118
3	127	133	12	6	124

3. Account in money terms with 10% inflation ($)

Period	(1)	(2)	(3)	(4)	(5)
0	100	105	14	9	100
1	115	118	16	13	113
2	133	135	18	16	129
3	146	153	20	13	142

4. Account in money terms with 10% inflation and zero real interest rate ($)

Period	(1)	(2)	(3)	(4)	(5)
0	100	100	9	9	100
1	115	112	10	13	113
2	133	128	11	16	129
3	146	146	13	13	142

ments often involve a compromise between real and money objectives. The *real* fiscal stance may tighten in response to inflation while the cash deficit expands. If the *real* stance tightens, the net effect will be to deflate real stocks and flows in the economy as a whole. But this does not have to happen; the fiscal stance, real or money, is ultimately a policy choice.

Fiscal planning

To show how fiscal policy could be decided in real terms, Table 12.4 provides figures for a hypothetical planning exercise which assumes that the economy in question does have inflation-neutral stock-flow processes. This example may help the reader to judge how much non-neutrality will matter. The table postulates that the exercise starts in a slump and the government has decided that it wants to expand real demand so that the volume of output can rise as shown in row 1.

The planner's first task is to estimate how the necessary rise in aggregate real demand (row 1) will divide between inventory accumulation and final sales. Row 2 suggests a pattern in which the volume of inventories lags slightly behind in the first period and then catches up through periods 2 and 3. Row 4, representing the target volume of final purchases, is obtained by deducting real inventory accumulation (row 3) from the output target (row 1).

Next the government must decide how it plans to increase its own *real* expenditure within the context of the fiscal plan. This decision determines the division of total final purchases between government (row 5) and the private sector (row 6) which fiscal policy will have to enforce. Given the required level of real private spending we can infer how fast real holdings of financial assets need to rise (assuming an inflation-neutral money adjustment process with $\alpha = 4/5$). The result of this calculation is shown in row 7 of the table.

The real stock of financial assets in row 7 will come in part from borrowing to finance inventories (row 2). Row 9 provides a guess at the real debt that will be generated by private loan-financed

Table 12.4 A fiscal planning exercise
($, period 0 purchasing power)

Accounts in real terms	*Actual*		*Planned*		
Period:	0	1	2	3	4
1. Target volume of output/real income	300	320	341	364	375
2. Assumed end-period inventories	100	104	112	121	125
3. Change in inventories	0	4	8	9	4
4. Required volume of final sales = (1)−(3)	300	316	333	355	371
5. Planned government spending	100	105	111	118	124
6. Required private final purchases = (4)−(5)	200	211	222	237	247
7. Required supply of end period financial assets = 1.25×(6)	250	264	278	296	309
8. Private loan-financed expenditure	10	11	12	12	12
9. End-period debt on account of (8)	50	51	53	55	56
10. Required end-period government debt = (7)−(2)−(9)	100	109	113	120	128
11. Required government deficit	0	9	4	7	8
12. Assumed debt interest charge	3	3	3	3	4
13. Required tax revenue = (5)+(12)−(11)	103	99	110	114	120
14. Tax as percentage of final sales = 100×(13)/(4)	34.3	31.3	33.0	32.1	32.3
15. Government share of aggregate income =[(13−(12)]/(1)	0.333	0.300	0.314	0.305	0.309
16. Fiscal stance = (5)/(15)	300	350	354	387	401

spending (estimated in row 8). The remaining part of the stock of financial assets will have to come from government debt (row 10). This tells us how large the real budget deficit must be in each period (row 11); having estimated real interest charges on government debt (row 12) we can calculate what total tax revenue must be in real terms (row 13) in order to make the whole plan consistent. Finally row 14 shows required tax revenue as a crude tax rate on total final sales (row 4).

Putting the plan into effect

The plan is now almost operational. Government agencies can be told to go ahead with the *real* spending implied by row 5.* If the tax system is inflation-neutral, tax rates can be set immediately for all periods of the plan.† Provided that the assumptions about private debt and asset accumulation are borne out, aggregate real income and output will then grow along the target path as the plan is implemented. It will not matter too much if the assumptions are not quite right since, as shown in Chapter 6, the fiscal system will automatically tend to adjust growth of government debt in a compensating manner. So long as government spending was implemented as planned in real terms (row 5) and the ratio of tax revenue to final sales followed the path shown (row 14) and real interest on government debt was maintained (row 12), it should make little difference to the outcome for real income and output whether prices in general rise, nor how fast they go up. The plan should at least succeed in its objective of bringing the slump to an end.

One possible outcome in money terms is illustrated in Table 12.5. Some readers might find it a useful exercise to construct alternative money outcomes on different assumptions about the price index. The check on this exercise is that all the identities

---

* We have defined real spending to include the effects of *relative* price changes. Budgets of government agencies should therefore be set in *indexed* cash terms; that is to say, they should be denominated as sums of money which automatically get adjusted in line with the *general* rate of inflation.

† Otherwise forecasts in money terms must be made each period to determine appropriate tax rates.

Table 12.5 A possible outcome in money terms
  ($ at current prices)

Accounts in money terms Period:	0	1	2	3	4
Price index	1.00	1.05	1.10	1.20	1.30
1. Aggregate money income	305	341	380	448	499
2. End-period value of inventories	100	109	123	145	162
3. Change in value of inventories	5	9	14	22	17
4. Value of final sales	300	332	366	426	482
5. Cost of government spending	100	110	122	142	161
6. Private final purchases	200	222	244	284	321
7. End-period financial assets	250	277	305	355	401
8. Private loan-financed expenditure	10	12	13	14	16
8a. Cash repayments of debt	8	8	9	6	9
9. End-period debt on account of (8)	50	54	58	66	73
10. End-period government debt	100	114	124	144	166
11. Government deficit	5	14	10	20	22
12. Debt interest	8	8	9	15	17
13. Tax revenue	103	104	121	137	156
14. Tax as percentage of final sales	34.3	31.3	33.0	32.1	32.3
15. Government share of aggregate income $= [(13)-(12)]/(1)$	0.311	0.282	0.295	0.272	0.279
16. Fiscal stance $= (5)/(15)$	321	390	414	522	577

noted in Table 12.4 should hold in money terms, with the same constant ratio of private final purchases to end-period financial assets and with the same ratio of tax revenue to final sales (row 14). The figure for debt interest in money terms (row 12) is calculated by adding the real interest rate (3%) to the percentage increase in the price index in each period to obtain the nominal interest rate, and applying this to the amount of government debt outstanding at the end of the previous period (row 10, lagged).

Table 12.6 Changes in money values of financial aggregates ($ at current prices)

Period	Increase in stock of financial assets	Private borrowing on account of inventories	other	Government borrowing
1	27	9	4	14
2	28	14	4	10
3	50	22	8	20
4	46	17	7	22

Table 12.6 draws together the consequences for financial aggregates. If the central bank refused to accept these consequences, the plan would be in danger. For example, suppose that in period 3 cost and price inflation pushed up the stock of financial assets rather fast. This might lead the central bank to raise nominal (and real) interest rates. This may not make much difference to real demand directly; private borrowing would be discouraged but higher interest on the government debt would push up government borrowing. However, the unpopularity of very high interest rates might persuade the government to raise tax rates or cut spending in order to hold down the budget deficit. The fiscal plan would then have been abandoned. Real income and output would certainly fall short

of the original target. And it is possible that even without the intervention of the central bank the government would react directly to an acceleration of inflation and abandon the original fiscal plan. When there are policy reactions like these, inflation really can become a major obstacle to fiscal expansion.

Real demand and the volume of output

In the example just discussed it was assumed that fiscal expansion can induce a rise in the volume of output, at least when the economy starts from a situation of slump. If all the conditions for inflation neutrality held true, it would have to be the case that real stock-flow processes determine the volume of output irrespective of inflation. There would seem to be no way in which supply conditions could affect aggregate output. This cannot, however, really be correct. What happens to aggregate output cannot in general be determined by real demand alone; it would, for instance, be impossible for total output of an economy to be increased tenfold (or even by one quarter) from one year to the next.

To conclude the main exposition of this book we must now explain how the model of a closed economy which has been deployed will interact with the supply side.

Productive potential and pressure of demand

There is no theory of the 'supply side' of the economy in this book. We are in any case sceptical about the usefulness of theory, logic or accounting to yield useful results about the aggregate productive potential of an economy. We believe that a great deal of specific, empirical knowledge is necessary to explain supply-side characteristics of different sectors (e.g., agriculture, energy, manufacturing, services) and types of enterprise (small-scale, medium or large, local, national or multi-national) in particular regions or countries at various stages of history. But to interpet the significance of propositions about aggregate real income and output we need at the minimum to have a notion of aggregate supply capacity or productive potential.

Different sectors or branches of production and individual units within these branches have varied degrees of flexibility as to the quantity and mix of products they can supply and the conditions under which they will do so. In general as the volume of aggregate spending rises or falls (or grows more or less rapidly) there are many, sometimes contradictory, indications of supply and market constraints such as specific shortages, degrees of capacity-utilization, the state of order books, the degree of difficulty in finding customers, the availability of labour and job opportunities, and so on. Such factors relevant to the volume of output being produced by individual businesses are the subject of surveys in which managers report, for example, whether supply-side or market conditions are currently the main constraint limiting output. Let us define a 'normal pressure of demand' as a situation in which given percentages of respondents to such surveys would identify supply-side costraints on the one hand or product-market constraints on the other as being more important for their business. Now assume that there is a fairly well-defined aggregate volume of output (measured according to our accounting definition as the value of output at base-period prices) that would be produced in an economy in each period at a normal pressure of demand. We regard the (estimated) volume of output that would be produced at a normal pressure of demand as being a measure of the 'productive potential' of the economy. The actual pressure of demand in each period is the ratio of the volume of output actually produced to the estimate for productive potential in the same period. This measure of pressure of demand must take a value of unity if and when it is 'normal' as defined above. As pressure of demand rises above unity, business surveys will increasingly identify supply-side factors as the main bottleneck; as it falls below unity they will increasingly identify product-market problems as the main limit on production.

It is *not* assumed that productive potential rises through time in a predestined manner; in particular the growth of productive potential is not independent of capital investment or of what has been happening or is expected to happen to the pressure of demand. But the fact that the pressure of demand varies considerably in real-life economies (as witnessed by responses to surveys and other types of evidence) implies that productive potential does have exogenous or predetermined elements in the short run.

Profitability and aggregate supply

The contention is sometimes made that there can be a supply-side constraint on the extent to which real output will respond to a rise in real demand when real costs are too high – i.e., additional production is not profitable.

If we consider any individual business, or all businesses in one region or even a whole country within an international trading system, it is indeed possible that when the volume of spending rises, increased production may not be profitable (for example, if costs per unit of additional output exceed prices set by competitors). But this is exceedingly unlikely in a closed economy (unless prices are held down by the government); if demand for additional output is there and prices are too low to justify additional production it must be expected that prices will be increased, one way or another, so as to make it possible for at least some producers to increase the volume of their sales. The outcome *may* be an acceleration of general inflation, and this may in turn have effects on the volume of spending in aggregate. But that is another matter. So although it is true that a rise in the pressure of demand can accelerate inflation, we rule out the possibility that in a closed economy the aggregate volume of production can be prevented from rising (to match a higher volume of real spending) by an excessive level of costs relative to prices.

Effective supply-side limits

We are not, however, asserting that the volume of production can be increased without limit. In the very short run output is relatively inflexible and inventories have to accommodate changes in demand. This itself perturbs the real stock-flow system. At a higher pressure of demand physical shortages become pervasive and/or inflation accelerates. If physical shortages are pervasive frustration of expenditure may force the holding of excess financial assets and depress debt creation. At this point real demand is truly constrained by the supply side.

Money inflation and the real economy

Some economists argue that the volume of output is closely determined by 'supply-side' factors alone. At the same time they are fully aware of the money stock-flow processes which have been our main theme. They resolve these at first sight contra-dictory views by postulating that inflation is determined purely as a by-product of money processes on the one hand and the volume of output on the other. If supply-side conditions happen to make the volume of products for sale go up by 1% while money processes make money expenditure go up by 5%, it is obvious that prices must rise by 5% less 1% – i.e., by 4%.

But this view is not really plausible. For one thing it is not consistent with the observation that, at least in a modern economy, inflation has a dynamic of its own, influenced by social and political factors as well as economic ones. For another thing, product markets are often in prolonged disequilibrium with chronic under-utilization of productive capacity and unemploy-ment. The supply side is not in practice determining the volume of output at all closely.

The analysis of conditions for inflation neutrality suggests a different way of looking at the whole relationship between money, inflation and the real economy. We can think of aggregate real income and output as being determined by real stock-flow processes which are influenced in some degree by the rate of inflation and by supply side conditions. These 'real economy' processes are comparatively stable.

At the same time there may be a comparatively unstable dynamic of inflation, influenced by the pressure of demand and supply side conditions but also by social and political factors.

Money processes, expressed in money terms, are then the joint product of inflation and real stock-flow processes. Money processes are the least stable of all.

Appendix 12.1 *A formal analysis of real demand*

Once income/expenditure accounts and financial balance sheets have been expressed in real terms (Chapter 11) the analysis of real demand is formally much the same as the analysis of money stocks and flows given in Appendix 6.1. We start with exogenous expenditure and private debt creation, then determine changes in the real stock of final assets and the flow of real final purchases by the private sector, and finally solve for real national income and output.

Exogenous expenditure and private debt creation

Government spending, g, will here be treated as if it was exogenously given in real terms. If the cash budgets of government agencies are not fully indexed, it will be necessary to introduce a term for the influence of the price level, p, or the rate of inflation, %p, into the determination of government spending.

We shall distinguish borrowing on inventories from other private debt. Assuming some lag in inventory adjustment, the volume accumulation of inventories, $\Delta i'$, will be given by

$$\Delta i' \equiv i' - i'_{-1} = \gamma' fe_{-1} - i'_{-1} \qquad (A12.1)$$

where γ' is the (volume) inventory/sales norm and i'_{-1} represents the opening volume of inventories carried over from a previous period (cf. A6.4).

Real inventory accumulation, Δi, will be equal to the volume change plus any real valuation change, riv:

$$\begin{aligned} \Delta i &\equiv \Delta i' + riv \\ &= \gamma' fe_{-1} - i'_{-1} + riv \end{aligned} \qquad (A12.2)$$

Note that changes in the rate of cost inflation may induce real valuation changes (riv $\neq 0$).

Changes in the real stock of 'personal loans', pl, will be equal to the real value of new loans (determined by real loan-financed expenditure, lfe) less real loan repayments:

$$\Delta pl = lfe - \varepsilon . pl_{-1} \qquad (A12.3)$$

where ε represents the ratio of real repayments to the opening real stock of loans, pl_{-1}. The rate of inflation may come in as an influence on ε. We shall treat loan-financed expenditure as being exogenous in the current period. It may be affected by monetary policy (the cost of credit), the need for replacement purchases of durables, expectations about future real income and various other specific factors.

Financial aggregates

Changes in the real stock of financial assets, Δfa, will be equal to the sum of changes in real private debt and real government debt:

$$\Delta fa \equiv \Delta i + \Delta pl + \Delta gd \qquad (A12.4)$$

The change in real government debt, Δgd, is given by the government's budget deficit:[*]

$$\Delta gd = g - \theta'.y \qquad (A12.5)$$

where θ' is the government's share of real national income, y. Note that if interest rates and/or the tax system are not inflation-neutral, inflation will affect the government's real income share, θ'.

Real income and expenditure

Assume there is an inflation-neutral adjustment process for real private final purchases, pe, and the real stock of financial assets,[†] which implies

$$pe = fa/\alpha \qquad (A12.6)$$

and recall the national income/expenditure identity

$$y \equiv fe + \Delta i \equiv g + pe + \Delta i \qquad (A12.7)$$

where fe denotes total real final purchases.

The solution for real national income by virtue of A12.4 to A12.7 is similar to the solution (A6.9) for money national income in Appendix 6.1. It is

$$(1 + \frac{\theta'}{\alpha})y = (1 + \frac{1}{\alpha})(g + \Delta i) + \frac{1}{\alpha}(\Delta pl + fa_{-1}) \qquad (A12.8)$$

Real private disposable income, yp, is given by the identity

$$yp \equiv (1 - \theta')y \qquad (A12.9)$$

---

[*] Capital gains or losses on government and private debt are being ignored until Chapter 13.

[†] See Chapter 5 and the discussion further below.

All other real stocks and flows can be derived by putting the solution for real national income back into A12.4 to A12.7 above.

Finally note that the volume of output, q, is equal to real national income less the real inventory valuation change (see Chapter 11):

$$q \equiv y - riv \qquad (A12.10)$$

The asset adjustment process

In this chapter it has been suggested that asset adjustment ought at least to permit the private sector to remain in an inflation-neutral real steady state given a constant flow of real income and a constant real stock of private debt. Netting out debt on account of inventories, the budget constraint for the private sector expressed in real terms is

$$pe + \Delta fa \equiv yp + \Delta pl \qquad (A12.11)$$

A real steady state will have

$$\Delta fa = \Delta pl = 0 \qquad (A12.12)$$
$$\text{and } pe = yp = fa/\alpha.$$

Therefore in the real steady state we must observe money final purchases, PE, satisfying

$$PE = FA/\alpha \qquad (A12.13)$$

where FA is the money stock of financial assets, and this must hold regardless of changes in the price level and the rate of inflation which may arbitrarily perturb money income, YP, and changes in the money stock of personal loans, ΔPL. A12.13 together with the budget constraint for the private sector expressed in money terms –

$$PE + \Delta FA \equiv YP + \Delta PL \qquad (A12.14)$$

uniquely determines the adjustment process in money terms as

$$FA = \frac{\alpha}{1+\alpha} (YP + \Delta PL + FA_{-1}) \qquad (A12.15)$$

PART VI

Developments of the Model

13 Wealth, equity and capital gains

The two final chapters of the book show how the analysis so far can be extended in two quite different directions. One direction, taken up in this chapter, is to generalize the concept of financial assets; this modifies stock-flow dynamics but makes no difference to steady-state flows. The other extension, discussed in Chapter 14, is to introduce 'external' stocks and flows; these change steady states as well as dynamics.

Financial assets and wealth

Our exposition started with money, i.e., notes and bank deposits. There was only one way in which money could be created – by borrowing to finance inventories. Later on, government deficits and personal loans came in as additional processes of debt creation. Money became 'financial assets', which included bonds as well as notes and deposits. Another important type of financial asset has so far been ignored. This is equity – 'stocks' or 'shares' issued by companies. Once equity is brought in, certain other prominent features of capitalist economies come immediately to mind – in particular, stocks of privately owned land, buildings, equipment and other durables which we shall call 'fixed capital', and the private insurance and pension institutions which hold a good part of the equity and fixed capital against future obligations to pay out benefits to clients.

If all these things are brought into our definition of assets we shall have moved from financial assets as such to the more general concept of wealth. Wealth includes such things as pension rights, land, houses and other fixed capital as well as equity, bonds and money.

The generalization also brings into prominence something else which has been left out so far – the effect of capital gains. There may be capital gains or losses* on all components of wealth *except* money. The values of many assets are not well defined, but in principle what we shall need to know is the subjective valuation placed on assets by people or institutions who own them since this, presumably, is what primarily influences their spending decisions.

To which aggregate measure of wealth or assets should our general stock-flow norm apply, how do capital gains affect balance sheets and budget constraints, in what manner will accounts for the economy as a whole add up, and what difference will all this make to flows of expenditure and income?

The purpose of this chapter is to give general answers to these questions, not to elaborate an ever more detailed model. First we discuss which stock variables have to be included in a model if it is to be any use at all, and which may be left out. Then we examine how capital gains come into individual budgets and balance sheets and how adjustment processes are modified. Finally we demonstrate consequences for the dynamic behaviour of aggregate expenditure and income. We shall use equity as the main example of what can happen when the model is extended, so it is useful to start with a brief description of its main features.

Corporate equity

Corporate equity (stocks or shares issued by companies) provides investors with the opportunity to share in the profits of a business and in some of its risks. Unlike loans, equity once issued is never redeemed. Its value to investors depends on future profits which are highly uncertain; market prices of individual equities are volatile and the index for equity in general is prone to large swings as prospects for profits and interest rates improve or deteriorate. In the long run equity tends to rise in value for two reasons. The first is that money profits normally go up with

---

-* In money terms. It is possible to apply inflation accounting to all the concepts and processes in this chapter but we shall not undertake this here.

inflation (see Chapters 9 and 10). The second is that companies usually retain part of their profits to invest in expansion of their business.

Although equity is a saleable asset from the point of view of stockholders, it is only a notional liability for companies. An increase in the market price of equity does not make a company poorer. So we now have an asymmetry. A rise or fall in the value of assets may occur without any change in liabilities. Capital gains or losses on equity are one source of changes in the value of the stock of financial assets as a whole.

The issue of *new* equities is analogous to an increase in private loans. Money raised by new issues comes into the cash budgets of companies in just the same way as the proceeds of loans. In a closed economy the aggregate value of the stock of equity can thus be changed in two ways – by virtue of changes in valuation (i.e., capital gains or losses) and by new issues.

Note on bonds

Note that bonds have some of the same characteristics as equity. The aggregate value of the stock of bonds can alter by virtue of changes in valuation and through new issues and redemptions which are analogous to loan advances and repayments. But there is a major difference between equity and bonds: capital gains on equity can continue indefinitely while gains and losses on bonds are essentially transient – the price of a bond must come back to par when it is due for redemption.* In practice the market value of government debt in aggregate rarely departs far from its par value, but the value of equity in aggregate is constrained by little other than the collective optimism of investors.

The stock of assets

What are the implications of different definitions of the stock of assets in a macroeconomic stock-flow model? In this book we

---

* Assuming the issuing government or corporation has not gone bankrupt.

have started from a minimal definition (money) and have now been working our way towards a maximal definition (wealth). But the maximal definition may not be the most useful for analytic purposes – it may, for example, add greatly to the complexity of the analysis without changing the substance of the main results.

The *minimum* requirement of a definition of the stock of assets in a macroeconomic model is that it should permit us to pin down precisely the flow budgets of the private sector and the government (and, in an open economy, the external world). So we *must* include cumulative budget deficits (or surpluses) of the government in the definition of the private sector's stock of assets. Beyond this the choice of definition is essentially an empirical question, the key issue being which measure of the stock of assets will yield the greatest behavioural regularity of stock-flow ratios.

There is a very strong presumption that certain things must be included if the stock-flow norm, α, is to have behavioural significance. When people hold bank deposits they have no way of telling whether their deposit is financing bank lending to the government or to the private sector. So we must include bank deposits in general, not just the proportion of bank desposits lent to the government. And when people buy government bonds they are concerned with market values (the prices they have paid to buy bonds or the prices they expect to receive for selling them), not with the amount of money the government received when the bonds were issued. So we ought to make allowance for changes in the market prices of government bonds. The general point is that we cannot expect behavioural stability of the stock-flow norm if we leave out assets which are *indistinguishable* from other assets which have been included.

On the other hand it was suggested in Chapter 5 that assets ought definitely to be excluded from the aggregate stock when they are held against debts. We should not include the *whole* of the value of a house as an asset when the house is heavily mortgaged. Similarly we should not include holdings of government bonds or bank deposits financed by bank overdrafts.

It may be a useful simplification in a macroeconomic model to exclude broad classes of assets which do not enter directly into aggregate flow budgets. For example, transactions in equity are almost exclusively between people and institutions within the private sector. They need not appear at all in the flow budget for the private sector as a whole. As we shall see below, capital gains, too, can be excluded from flow accounts. So it is possible to leave out equity altogether. Much the same goes for fixed capital assets. Purchases and sales are implicitly included in the flow accounts as part of final expenditure. Capital gains need not appear at all. So it is possible to leave out equity and fixed capital from the aggregate stock of assets in a macroeconomic stock-flow model.

If a narrow definition of the stock of assets is adopted, adjustments to stocks of assets which have been excluded (e.g., equity and fixed capital) may perturb the stock-flow norm and dynamics of adjustment of assets which have been included (e.g., money and bonds). The extent of these disturbances will depend on the degree to which people regard the assets as substitutes for one another. This is strictly a behavioural issue. The question at stake is, for example, whether a rise in equity and property values will induce people to hold less money and bonds at a given level of income.

If equity and property values do perturb stock-flow relationships for money and bonds, models ought ideally to be expanded to allow for this. There will, however, be a cost as well as a gain. For although it should be possible to give a better representation of asset adjustments, the processes which generate changes in stocks of assets will now include such things as rises and falls in stock markets and property markets which are themselves hard to understand and predict.

Let us now assume that in real life equity values *do* affect other stock-flow processes and see what difference this makes.* We may start with the accounts and balance sheets.

---

* Further extensions to include property values, etc. will be analogous but for clarity of exposition we leave them out.

Accounts for an individual person or institution

The budget constraint for an individual person or institution concerns what we may call cash transactions. The stock of assets, A, at the end of each period now includes money, bonds and equity. We denote cash expenditure in each period on asset purchases less proceeds of sales by TA or 'transactions in assets'.* We must also extend the concept of debt, PD, to include the book value of issues of equity and corporate bonds. The proceeds of new issues and new loans in each period, less loan repayments and bond redemptions, will be denoted by ΔPD. Using 'hats' once again to denote accounts for an individual or group of individuals rather than the private sector as a whole, the budget constraint in any period is

$$\hat{E} + \hat{TA} \equiv \hat{YP} + \Delta\hat{PD} \tag{13.1}$$

This says that expenditure on goods and services, $\hat{E}$, plus asset transactions, $\hat{TA}$, must be equal to disposable income, $\hat{YP}$, plus the change in debt outstanding, $\Delta\hat{PD}$.

The only change we have had to make to the budget constraint is, in effect, to replace the term for changes in the *value* of the stock of assets (formerly $\Delta\hat{FA}$) by *transactions* in assets, $\hat{TA}$. But we still need to know what is happening to the value of the stock of assets. Still considering the accounts of an individual person or institution, the change in each period, $\Delta\hat{A}$, is the sum of transactions, $\hat{TA}$, and capital gains or losses in the period which we write as $R\hat{VA}$ or 'revaluation of assets'. Thus

$$\Delta\hat{A} \equiv \hat{TA} + R\hat{VA} \tag{13.2}$$

There is an element of arbitrariness about when capital gains or losses are brought in. They must be included when an asset is sold but need not be included before. Capital gains on assets which have been sold are called 'realized' capital gains; those on assets which have not yet been sold are 'unrealized' capital gains.

---

* This concept includes 'expenditure' on changes in private bank balances and notes in circulation, i.e., changes in holdings of money.

Chart 13.1 Income and debt financed expenditure with capital gains

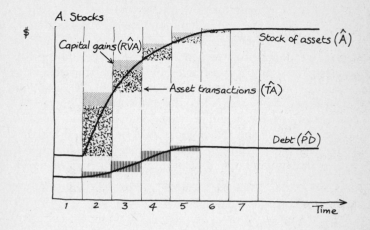

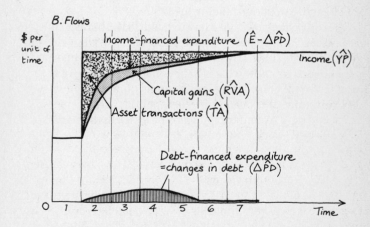

The value and timing of the latter depends on perceptions and anticipations, not on logical requirements of accountancy.

Adjustments of assets and expenditure

Chart 13.1 illustrates adjustments to assets and expenditure when there is a step change in the flow of income, $\hat{Y}P$. The rise in the total value of asset holdings, $\hat{A}$, at the top of the chart is equal to the sum of the two shaded areas in the bottom part of the chart. Since equities have been included the total asset adjustment may be larger than before. But this does not necessarily mean that expenditure will react more slowly to the change in income. Part of the asset adjustment may come from capital gains, not income. The part which has to be financed by a lag of expenditure behind income is net *purchases* of assets, $\hat{TA}$.

What the introduction of capital gains has done is to make the lag in the adjustment of individual expenditure to income less determinate. If the rise in income were accompanied by large capital gains, income-financed expenditure might for a time exceed income (i.e., capital gains would be spent). On the other hand if there were capital losses, expenditure might be held back until these had been made good.

Accounts for the economy as a whole

Now let us consider how equity, capital gains etc. come into aggregated accounts for the private sector and the economy as a whole. Table 13.1 below shows a full set of balance sheets, including fixed capital as well as inventories, equity, bonds and money. Banks have been left out (it is implicit in the table that their assets consist of loans to the government, companies and the personal sector, and that their liabilities consist of deposits). The table illustrates several important points.

First, there is no necessary connection between the stock of physical assets and the value of financial assets and liabilities. Investment in physical assets may have been financed out income (tax revenue, retained profits or personal income). Second, bond liabilities of the government and companies may differ from the value of bonds counted as assets of the personal sector on account of cumulative capital gains or losses (in the table there has been a cumulative *loss* of $10 which appears in the last column). Third, corporate equity is a liability which need never be redeemed; it appears in the balance sheet of companies as a residual item which balances their books, providing a measure of undistributed profits *after* allowing for depreciation and asset revaluations. The value of equity held by the personal sector (which appears in the last column as a net asset of the whole economy) need not bear any close relationship to equity as it appears in corporate balance sheets.

Suppose that we define the stock of private assets for the purposes of our model as money held by the personal sector plus the value of holdings of bonds and equity. In Table 13.1 the value of this stock is

personal money	$200
value of bonds	$80
value of equity	$160
	$440

It has been generated as follows ($):

Government debt at book value		100
= cumulative budget deficits		
Private debt:		
net corporate debt to banks	100	
corporate bond issues	20	
equity issues	40	
personal loans	70	230
Revaluations:		
bonds	−10	
equity	+120	110
Total stock of private assets		440

Table 13.1 Sector balance sheets

($ value)

	Government		Corporate sector		Personal sector		Whole economy
	Assets	*Liabilities*	*Assets*	*Liabilities*	*Assets*	*Liabilities*	*Assets less liabilities*
Money							
	—	Notes and debts to banks 30	—	Net debt to banks 100	Notes and bank deposits 200	Personal loans 70	0
Bonds							
	—	Bonds issued 70	—	Bonds issued 20	Value of bonds 80	—	−10

	Land, buildings infrastructure		Physical assets	Equity	Value of equity		
	150	—	Inventories 100 Fixed capital 100	(Equity issued) 40 (undistributed profits) 40	160	Houses and other fixed capital 100	+160
	—	—	—	—	—	—	450
	150	100	200	120 (200)	540	70	600

There are three flow processes which generate the stock of private assets defined in this way – government deficits, changes in private debt, and capital gains (revaluations). We can write the identity for changes in the stock of assets symbolically as

$$\Delta A \equiv \Delta GD + \Delta PD + RVA \qquad (13.3)$$

where ΔA is the change in the value of the stock of assets in each period, ΔGD is the government's budget deficit (equal to the change in *book value* of government debt), ΔPD is the change in private debt (including corporate bonds and equity at its original issue value), and RVA is capital gains or losses on bonds and equities in the period.

We already know from equation 13.2 that the change in the stock of assets (ΔA) must always be equal to net 'purchases' (TA) plus capital gains (RVA). So net purchases of assets by the private sector in each period, TA, will have to be equal to the first two components of the identity (13.3) above – the government's budget deficit and the change in private debt:

$$TA \equiv \Delta GD + \Delta PD \qquad (13.4)$$

This tells us what the private sector will be able to spend in each period. Private final purchases, PE, are determined as follows:

	disposable income	YP
plus	the change in private debt	$+\Delta PD$
less	asset transactions	$-TA = -\Delta GD - \Delta PD$
less	expenditure on inventories	$-\Delta I$
equals	private final purchases	PE

The result is exactly the same as in the earlier chapters. The difference between private income and private final purchases must be equal to the government's budget deficit plus inventory accumulation:

$$YP - PE \equiv \Delta GD + \Delta I \qquad (13.5)$$

Implications for the stock-flow system

The change as compared with our previous models lies in the fact that the value of the stock of assets can now be altered by capital gains (equation 13.3 above). As always, aggregate flows of private income and expenditure must adjust to levels at which the stock of assets is appropriate relative to income. Capital gains may therefore play the same role as inventory accumulation and personal loans did in the previous models, provoking changes in private income and expenditure. But, as before, if the government's fiscal stance is given, the effects on income and expenditure flows will be moderated and eventually neutralized by induced changes in the budget deficit and the stock of government debt. *Steady-state flows will not be affected.*

Example of a change in the fiscal stance

Chart 13.2 below illustrates the effects of a 50% rise in government spending on the main stock-flow aggregates, depending on whether it provokes large-scale capital gains (dotted lines in the chart) or has no valuation effects (full lines in the chart). In both cases aggregate income/expenditure flows respond with very little lag and settle at the *same* new steady state, determined uniquely by the new fiscal stance.

The capital gains portrayed in the chart are assumed to be huge and come into the stock system quickly. We have assumed the standard asset adjustment process in which people keep their expenditure in a constant ratio to their value of holdings of assets period by period. This has made the capital gains feed *immediately* into the flows of the system. So we have illustrated a very extreme case. What is remarkable is the speed with which the fiscal system intervenes to choke off the rise in aggregate income and bring the economy to its new steady state. The numbers (shown in Table 13.2) from which the chart was drawn

Chart 13.2 A change in fiscal policy with and without capital gains

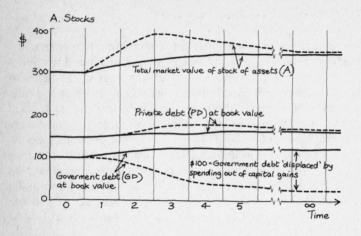

A. Stocks

$

400 ─

300 ─ Total market value of stock of assets (A)

200 ─ Private debt (PD) at book value

100 ─ Goverment debt (GD) at book value · $100 = Government debt 'displaced' by spending out of capital gains

0 ─

0 1 2 3 4 5 ∞ Time

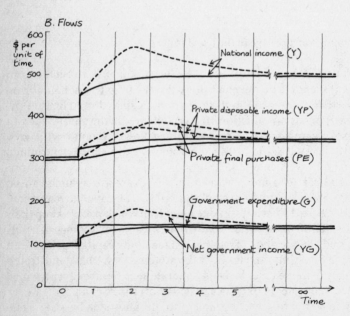

B. Flows

$ per unit of time

600 ─

500 ─ National income (Y)

400 ─ Private disposable income (YP)

300 ─ Private final purchases (PE)

200 ─ Government expenditure (G)

100 ─ Net government income (YG)

0 ─

0 1 2 3 4 5 ∞ Time

assume a *marginal* effective tax rate on national income of 50% which is by no means unrealistic for modern economies. The only other assumptions we had to make concerned inventories (which follow final sales with a slight lag) and other private debt which is held constant in order to focus attention on the effect of capital gains.

It was shown in Chapter 6 that the mean lag in the response of the aggregate income flow to an expansion of the fiscal stance is determined by the increase in the steady-state level of government debt. In the chart above the steady-state book value of government debt has to *fall* to accommodate the private sector's large-scale capital gains. Thus in the revaluation case (dotted lines) the mean lag is negative – i.e., the income/expenditure flow for a time substantially overshoots its new steady-state level. (In the absence of revaluations there is a small positive mean lag.)

The figures underlying Chart 13.2 and the whole series of steps required to obtain them are displayed in Table 13.2 which follows. Readers who wish to understand better why the results come out as they do may enter alternative assumptions and derive alternative solutions. The solutions have been obtained using the same adjustment parameters as in Appendix 6.1.

The process illustrated in Chart 13.2 and Table 13.2 is not essentially different from that described in Chapters 5 and 6. The reader may be tempted to ask where the money 'comes from' when, as postulated here, the private sector as a whole spends more because capital gains have occurred. The answer is that the collective decision to spend more because people feel richer creates income (just as more borrowing creates income) on whatever scale is necessary to finance that expenditure without any net sales of financial assets by the sector taken as a whole actually taking place. But the additional income so created feeds into the fiscal system and starts to reduce the amount of government debt outstanding, thereby bringing the whole system quite quickly to a steady state.

Table 13.2 Effects of a change in the fiscal stance

($ value)

Period:	0	1	2	3	4	5	∞
1. Government spending, G	100	150	150	150	150	150	150
2. End-period value of inventories, I	100	105 (105)	120 (110)	130 (120)	130 (125)	125 (125)	125
3. Change in other private debt, ΔPD−ΔI	0	0	0	0	0	0	0
4. Capital gains, RVA	0	50 (0)	50 (0)	0 (0)	0 (0)	0 (0)	0
5. Opening value stock of assets, A_{-1}	300	300 (300)	352 (318)	390 (330)	380 (340)	370 (345)	350
6. National income $Y = 2/3(100+2(G+\Delta I)+ \Delta PD+RVA+A_{-1})$	400	507 (473)	555 (485)	540 (500)	520 (500)	507 (497)	500
7. Net government income $YG = 1/2Y-100$	100	153 (137)	177 (143)	170 (150)	160 (150)	153 (148)	150
8. Government budget deficit, $\Delta GD = G-YG$	0	-3 (13)	-27 (7)	-20 (0)	-10 (2)	-3	0
9. Increase in value of stocks and assets, $\Delta A = \Delta GD + \Delta PD + RVA$	0	52 (18)	38 (12)	-10 (10)	-10 (5)	-8 (2)	0

10. End-period value of stocks of assets, $A = A_{-1} + \Delta A$ Private final purchases, $PE = A$	300	352 (318)	390 (330)	380 (340)	370 (345)	362 (347)	... 350
11. Private disposable income, $YP = Y - YG$	300	354 (336)	378 (342)	370 (350)	360 (350)	354 (349)	... 350
12. Total final sales, $FE = PE + G$	400	502 (468)	540 (480)	530 (490)	520 (495)	512 (497)	... 500
13. End-period book value of government debt, $GD = GD_{-1} + \Delta GD$	100	97 (113)	70 (120)	50 (120)	40 (120)	37 (122)	... 25 (125)
14. End-period book value of private debt, $PD = PD_{-1} + \Delta PD$	150	155 (155)	170 (160)	180 (170)	180 (175)	175 (175)	... 175
15. Cumulative revaluations (cumulative RVA)	50	100 (50)	150 (50)	150 (50)	150 (50)	150 (50)	... 150 (50)

Note: figures in brackets assume no capital gains in the current episode.
See Appendix 6.1 for general method of calculation. Note that here $\alpha = 1$ and the *marginal* tax rate is $\theta = 1/2$; the constant term in the solution for national income, Y, accommodates the difference between the marginal and the average tax rate (25% when Y = $400, 30% when Y = $500).

Conclusions

If there were no fiscal system, the introduction of equity, capital
gains etc. would make what is already an unstable model (see
Chapter 5) even less determinate and more unstable. Stock
market booms or slumps would feed into expenditure flows,
causing profits and inventories to fluctuate. The whole stock-
flow system could conceivably be regulated by an active
monetary policy but the task of stabilization would be
complicated and difficult.

Once there is a fiscal system, stock-flow processes are
inevitably dictated closely by the fiscal stance, and with a short
mean lag. Private debt creation and capital gains can produce
only short-lived disturbances. This is true, at least, for a closed
economy. We must now, finally, see what happens when the
stock-flow system is opened to external transactions.

14 The open economy

This chapter extends our macroeconomic model to the case of an open economy which forms part of a wider international system. We shall not seek to analyse properties of the international system as such – a task beyond the scope of this book.* The main question examined here is how stocks and flows in a single national economy are affected by external transactions with the rest of the world. We shall also briefly examine problems connected with the existence of different national currencies. The most important result in this chapter is the demonstration of how, in an open economy, foreign trade performance constrains aggregate flows of income and output and the government's fiscal stance.

The national economy

Let us first define the boundaries of the national economy we are dealing with. It will comprise a group of 'national' institutions – households, businesses, banks and government – operating mainly but not exclusively in their own country. The national economy as such will not include 'foreign' institutions. operating in the country or elsewhere.† But we shall have to take account

---

* Although the world as a whole is a closed economy, the models of earlier chapters are not applicable, if only because the world economy has many governments and many currencies. The outcome for the world as a whole is strongly affected by interactions between policies of different governments, which are themselves influenced by problems of currency stabilization.

† Note, however, that subsidiaries of foreign enterprises operating in the country may be regarded as national institutions although *owned* by foreigners. Subsidiaries of national enterprises operating in other countries may similarly be regarded as 'foreign' institutions.

of transactions of foreign institutions which affect the national economy.

Income/expenditure flows and stocks of assets and debts relevant to our national economy may variously be denominated in the national currency or in foreign currencies. But we shall *measure* all stocks and flows in terms of a single currency – the national currency – in order to obtain a unified system of accounts.* Throughout a large part of the chapter we shall be discussing properties of the stock-flow system which are logically independent of currency problems per se. These are properties of an open economy which must hold irrespective of which currencies are actually used to pay for external trade or to denominate external assets and debts. Problems of currency markets and exchange rates will come in towards the end of the chapter; they may impose additional constraints on stock-flow outcomes.

The plan of the chapter is as follows. First we shall see how the income and expenditure flows of a national economy fit into the wider pattern of flows in the world as a whole. The main problem at this stage is to determine what part of the world income flow accrues specifically to our national economy. It will be shown that the national income must always be equal to national expenditure plus the country's 'external balance' (the excess of exports over imports).†

The next part of the chapter examines constraints on the private sector's accumulation of financial assets. For this purpose we have to extend the analysis of debt creation and capital gains given in previous chapters to incorporate financial transactions with the rest of the world.

In the open economy exports and imports play a similar role to government spending and taxation, stabilizing private sector stocks and flows and defining steady states for the private sector. The third part of the chapter shows that the combined influence

---

* The implicit assumption is that in each accounting period there are unique, well-defined exchange rates for the various currencies which preserve flow identities. Note that changes in exchange rates may imply revaluations of stocks of assets and debts which are discussed further below.

† See below, page 00, for a precise definition.

of the fiscal system and external trade on private stocks and flows is very powerful indeed. But despite this, aggregate stock-flow processes are no longer sufficient to bring the open economy as a whole to a full steady state. Instead there will be *quasi* steady states in which income/expenditure flows are constant but the government's budget remains unbalanced and external transactions are in continuous surplus or deficit.

This brings us to the last part of the chapter which discusses currency problems. These will usually constrain stock-flow processes and thereby prevent unbalanced, *quasi* steady states from continuing indefinitely. If the open economy does come to a *full* steady state, the flow of aggregate income will necessarily be equal to a measure analogous to the fiscal stance, which we call the 'trade performance ratio'. Either the fiscal stance must adjust to conform with foreign trade performance, or the other way round. What is impossible, in a full steady state, is that the two should be independent of one another. In practice governments try to procure adjustments of the foreign trade performance of their national economy but at the same time often find themselves compelled by currency problems to adjust their fiscal stance. In the long run fiscal policy can only be used to sustain growth of real income and output in an open economy provided that foreign trade performance so permits. This is the most important practical conclusion of our book.

Let us start by considering some flow identities.

Income/expenditure flows and the external balance

Table 14.1 below portrays a national economy as one part of a world system. *National* income or expenditure is defined as the sum of the income or expenditure of the private sector and government. There is nothing more to the *definition* than that. The two sectors may be earning their income and spending their money in their own country or anywhere else in the world.* The constraint that all income ultimately derives from expenditure is

---

* Note that national inventory accumulation may include goods on land, sea or air in the course of shipment; so there need be no problems about balances of trade failing to add up for the world as a whole.

true for the world as a whole but *not* for any one country. What the constraint implies, however, is that if one country does not spend all its income, thereby earning a financial surplus ($40 in the table), the rest of the world as a whole must be spending in excess of its income, incurring an equal and opposite collective deficit. To remind ourselves of this we shall call the difference between national income and national expenditure the country's *external* balance. The external balance is the sum of the financial balances of the private sector and government.

Table 14.1 Income and expenditure flows
($ per period)

	(1) Disposable income	(2) Final purchases and inventory accumulation	(3) Surplus (+) or deficit (−) = (1)−(2)
Private	450	400	+50
Government	150	160	−10
National economy	600	560	+40
Rest of world	6900	6940	−40
World	7500	7500	0

Next let us investigate what governs the national economy's share of the world income flow. Table 14.2 illustrates how income from production depends on the allocation of expenditure between purchases of national products and foreign products. In the table the private sector and government are spending $380 on products of their own country and the rest of the world is spending a further $200 on the country's products, so its total income from production is

$$\$380 + \$200 = \$580$$

The money spent by our country's private sector and government on goods and services produced by the rest of the world ($180) contributes to the income of the latter.

Table 14.2 The distribution of income and expenditure ($ per period)

	Expenditure on goods and services produced by the national economy	Expenditure on goods and services produced by the rest of the world	Total
Expenditure by:			
Private sector	260	140	400
Government	120	40	160
National economy	380	180	560
Rest of world	200	6740	6940
World	580	6920	7500

	Income of national economy	Income of rest of world	World income
Income from production	580	6920	7500
Net transfers	+20	−20	0
Disposable income	600	6900	7500

In the table above national disposable income differs from income from production on account of *transfers* paid between national sectors and the rest of the world (shown as a net flow of $20 in favour of the national economy). Transfer *receipts* may include wages and salaries earned by nationals working for foreign businesses, interest and dividends paid to nationals by foreign debtors and companies, taxes paid by foreign institutions to the national government etc. Transfer *payments* comprise similar flows in the reverse direction.

The next table below brings together expenditure flows and transfers which contribute to the country's external balance and thereby determine national income, conditional on national expenditure. To keep our model simple we use the term 'exports' to cover all flows from the rest of the world which contribute to national income. Exports therefore include purchases of national products by the rest of the world ($200) and transfer receipts ($50). Similarly we use the term 'imports' to cover all flows from the national economy which contribute to the income of the rest of the world, including purchases of foreign products ($180) and transfer payments ($30).

Table 14.3 The external balance of the national economy and national income
($ per period)

Exports:

Expenditure by rest of world on goods and services produced by national economy	200
Income transfers received by the private sector and government from the rest of the world	50
Total	250

Imports:

Expenditure by national economy on goods and services produced by the rest of the world	180
Income transfers paid by the private sector and government to the rest of the world	30
Total	210

External balance = exports − imports	40
National expenditure (final purchases and inventory accumulation)	560
National income	600

The external balance, defined originally as the difference between national income and national expenditure ($40), is equal to exports ($250) less imports ($210). This is an important result. It tells us that, given any level of national expenditure, national income will be higher (lower) than national expenditure by the amount by which exports exceed (fall short of) imports.

Foreign trade performance

Unless allocations of expenditure between national and foreign products are strictly controlled by governments, exports and imports are influenced by supply-side conditions (the capacity and competitiveness of producers) as well as by aggregate expenditure flows. Many factors enter into the determination of exports and imports, including levels of costs and prices in different markets. Recall also that we have defined the terms 'exports' and 'imports' to include transfers as well as flows of trade in goods and services. At some risk of over-simplification we shall now regard exports, X, as *exogenous* (being determined by external market conditions and the competitiveness of national producers) and imports, M, as *endogenous*, being determined by the flow of national income, Y, and an 'import propensity', μ. We write the determination of imports as

$$M = \mu Y \qquad (14.1)$$

which says that imports are equal to national income multiplied by the import propensity.* For example, in Table 14.3 above imports (including transfer payments) were $210 compared with national income of $600. The implied import propensity was

$$\$210/\$600 = 35\%$$

---

* Note than this is equivalent to regarding imports as a given fraction of the *sum* of national expenditure, E, and exports, X. It was shown above that national income equals expenditure plus exports less imports ($Y = E+X-M$). So

$$M = \mu Y = \mu(E+X-M) = \frac{\mu}{1+\mu} (E+X)$$

In a simple model we assume that this ratio is invariant with respect to income.

Exports and the import propensity, although exogenous, will both change through time. In general, if world markets expand exports will rise. If technology and spending patterns become more international, the import propensity will rise. If national producers become more competitive, exports will rise faster and the import propensity *may* fall. These variables may also be influenced by trade policy (export subsidies, say, or import restrictions).

Foreign trade and national income

At this stage we cannot make a full evaluation of the effects on national income of changes in exports or the import propensity because we have not yet examined how private expenditure and government expenditure will react to changes in national income. But we can see the direction of the likely effects. A rise in exports adds to national income, inducing higher national expenditure *and* a rise in imports. On the other hand an increase in the import propensity means a diversion of national expenditure away from national products to foreign ones. It therefore reduces national income, inducing a fall in national expenditure.

What cannot yet be determined at all is the outcome for the external balance. It might seem obvious that a rise in exports will 'improve' the external balance (move it towards surplus). But this may not be the case. It is possible that national income and expenditure will rise enough to induce an increase in imports equal to, or greater than, the initial rise in exports. For similar reasons it is *possible* that a rise in the import propensity will not in the end increase the flow of imports.

To sort out all this we must now examine how external transactions affect asset and expenditure adjustments.

Changes in assets and debts

In the world as a whole net purchases of assets (including increases in money balances) must be equal to net increases in debt. Net purchases of assets by each sector in each country depend on the sector's financial surplus or deficit (the excess or shortfall of its income compared with expenditure) and on changes in its debt. Table 14.4 below portrays a pattern of asset and debt transactions in the world economy. The financial surpluses and deficits shown are the same as in Table 14.1, being generated by income/expenditure flows. From this table we can see where assets purchased by the private sector in our national economy must come from.

Table 14.4 Asset and debt transactions
($ per period)

	(1) Financial surplus (+) or deficit (−)	(2) Debt transactions (3)−(1)	(3) Asset transactions (1)+(2)
Private sector	+50	+10	+60
Government	−10	+10	0
National economy	+40	+20	+60
Rest of world	−40	+230	+190
World	0	+250	+250

The net purchase of assets by the private sector in the top row of the table is $60. From the private sector's own point of view this represents the cash flow provided by a $50 excess of income over expenditure (column (1)) plus $10 from an increase in debt (column (2)). But the purchase of assets by the private sector as a whole is also constrained by what is happening in the rest of the table. In fact, assuming that the government does not hold financial assets, net private purchases of assets must be equal to the increase in private and government debt combined ($210) plus the external balance ($40) generated by exports less imports. This is another important result. Net private purchases of assets (which we called 'asset transactions', TA, in Chapter 13) must be equal to changes in private and government debt (which we shall now call 'debt transactions', TPD and TGD) plus the external balance, B:

$$TA \equiv TPD + TGD + B \qquad (14.2)$$

In other words the external balance adds to (or if in deficit, subtracts from) debt creation by national sectors in determining the net amount of money and other financial assets which the private sector as a whole can acquire.

Revaluations

As seen in Chapter 13, net private purchases of assets, TA, may be supplemented by capital gains or 'asset revaluations', RVA. In fact the change in the stock of assets is the sum of transactions and revaluations:

$$\Delta A \equiv TA + RVA \qquad (14.3)$$

In the open economy revaluations occur not only because of rises or falls in equity and bond prices but also on account of changes in currency exchange rates. For example, if the private sector holds foreign currency assets (e.g., $F100 where $F denotes foreign currency) and there is a fall in the exchange rate for the national currency (e.g., 10%), there will be a capital gain on the foreign currency assets measured in terms of national currency (e.g., their value rises from, say, $N180 to $N200 where $N represents national currency). Debts also may be subject to revaluation.*

The overall change in the value of assets held by the private sector may be expressed as in the following example:

	(national currency)
Transactions	
external balance = exports−imports, B	40
government budget deficit, TGD	10
private debt transactions, TPD	10
	—
	60
Revaluations	
private asset, RVA (say)	25
	—
Change in private stock of assets, ΔA	85
	—

Completing the model

Throughout this book we have pointed out that income/expenditure flows must adjust in such a way that the private sector is content with its stock of assets. In this sense it is changes in the stock of assets which 'drive' the flow system, determining private

---

* Changes in exchange rates affect the value of debts denominated in foreign currency. This is why we have used the term 'debt transactions', TPD and TGD, rather than changes in stocks of debt, ΔPD and ΔGD, in the table and identity 14.2 above. Changes in stocks of debt, like changes in the stock of assets, are the sum of transactions and revaluations. Debt revaluations do not directly affect cash flows. Their influence on flows is felt when they feed back into debt *transactions*. Consider the example of a company which has to redeem foreign currency bonds which have reached maturity. Suppose that $F100 of bonds yielded $N180 when first issued. If the exchange rate for the national currency has fallen 50% by the time the bonds mature, the company will have to find $N360 to redeem them. Note that revaluations may also affect the national banking system, implying that it must undertake financial transactions to keep total assets equal to total liabilities. The transactions may be treated as part of TA (commercial banks) or TGD (central bank).

expenditure and income. But the process is a two-way one. Income/expenditure flows themselves change the private sector's stock of assets, e.g., in the present case through the government's budget and the external balance. The stock-flow system as a whole therefore has to be solved as a sequential, interactive process.

The logic of the solution for an open economy is as follows. Government expenditure and exports are the main *exogenous* variables (together with the government's income share, θ, and the import propensity, μ). Given these, the income/expenditure flow in each period has to be such as to reconcile the change in the private stock of assets with the sum of the various sources of assets listed above (the external balance, the government budget deficit, increases in private debt and asset revaluations).

The algebra of the solution is given in Appendix 14.1. Here we use a numerical example, illustrated in Chart 14.1 below, to show how the national economy responds to a simultaneous step change in exports and government expenditure. In period 0 *all* stocks are stationary. Government revenue equals government expenditure, imports are equal to exports, private expenditure is equal to private income. This is a full steady state. We have shocked the system in period 1 by increasing exports from $200 to a new, constant level of $220 and simultaneously raising government expenditure from $150 to a new, constant level of $180. We have also assumed that this stimulus is reinforced by major capital gains as equity prices rise and by substantial increases in private debt. Yet all the flows in the lower part of the chart quickly reach new, steady levels. Imports and taxation act together as stabilizers. When private expenditure rises, half or more than half of the extra income flow is taken by other countries (imports) and the government (taxation), leaving half or less than half as an addition to private income in the country.

Imports and taxation also work together in adjusting the stock of assets available to the private sector. But they do not necessarily work in the same direction. In Chart 14.1 imports exceed exports so external transactions are continuously depriving the economy of assets. On the other hand the government budget remains in deficit, continuously feeding in

Chart 14.1 Income determination of an open economy with a fiscal system

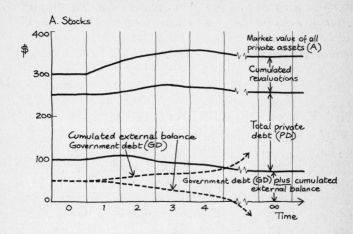

A. Stocks

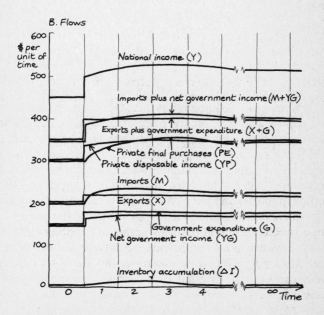

B. Flows

additional government debt. Because these two processes can work in opposite directions, the economy settles into a situation in which private sector stocks and flows are constant but the government's debt is continuously rising and external transactions are continuously in deficit. The counterpart is a chronic external deficit. We call this a *quasi* steady state because it cannot persist indefinitely.

Quasi steady states

What determines the level of income and the degree of imbalance in the government's budget in a quasi steady state?

The quasi steady state is a situation in which stocks of private assets and debts are constant. There may be continuing changes in government debt but these must be accommodated by the rest of the world. Suppose for example that the government's budget is in deficit. If aggregate private assets and debts are not to be disturbed, the rest of the world will have to be buying government debt or other assets from the national economy as payment for an external flow deficit (i.e., an excess of imports over exports). Similarly if the government has a budget surplus and is reducing its debt, the country's private sector can only be in a steady state if foreigners are selling back government debt or other assets to the national economy to cover a deficit in their accounts (i.e., an external *surplus* for 'our' country).

In quasi steady states the government's budget surplus or deficit must therefore be equal to the external surplus or deficit. This implies that government income less spending is equal to exports less imports,

$$YG - G = X - M$$

In other words the sum of the two *exogenous* variables, government expenditure and exports, must be equal to the sum of the two stabilizing *endogenous* variables, government income and imports:

$$G + X = YG + M$$

External transactions and the government's budget are *together* operating like the fiscal system in a closed economy. The quasi steady state is the same as steady states in earlier chapters except that the transitions which lead to it and the levels at which income/expenditure flows settle down are now determined by the joint action of external transactions and the national fiscal system.

The analogue of the fiscal stance in the open economy is the ratio of government spending *plus* exports $(G+X)$ to the government's income share *plus* the import propensity $(\theta+\mu)$. The quasi-steady-state level of income will not only be determined by this ratio, but will be equal to it – i.e.,

$$Y = \frac{G+X}{\theta+\mu} \qquad (14.4)$$

In the chart above the initial steady state and the final quasi steady state are given as follows:

	initial steady state	final quasi steady state
(i) government spending plus exports, $G+X$	$350	$400
(ii) government share plus the propensity to import, $\theta+\mu$	0.778	
(iii) national income, Y = (i)/(ii)	$450	$514

The final outcome for national income would have been the same if government spending had risen less and exports had risen more (or the other way round) so long as the sum of the two had gone up by the same amount (i.e., from $350 to $400).

The fiscal stance and trade performance ratio

By analogy with the fiscal stance, G/θ, it is useful to give a name to the ratio of exports to the import propensity

$$X/\mu$$

We have called this ratio the 'trade performance ratio'. The level of income in quasi steady states (equation 14.4 above) can be regarded as a weighted average of the foreign trade performance ratio and the fiscal stance – i.e.,

$$Y = w_1 \frac{X}{\mu} + w_2 \frac{G}{\theta} \tag{14.5}$$

where the weights w_1 and w_2 are proportionate to imports and government income (μ compared with θ).

A full steady state in which the stock of government debt is constant and the external balance is zero will only be achieved if the fiscal stance and the foreign trade performance ratio happen to be equal to one another. The first column of Table 14.5 below illustrates such a situation. Government spending ($150) divided by the government's income share (33.3%) happens to be exactly equal to exports ($200) divided by the import propensity (44.4%). Both ratios come to $450 and this will be the steady-state level of national income. Government income then balances government spending and imports are equal to exports.

The other two columns of the table show steady states in which the fiscal stance and the foreign trade performance ratio differ. When the fiscal stance is higher there will be ongoing government deficits and external deficits. When the foreign trade performance ratio is higher both the government's budget and the external balance will be in surplus. There is nothing in the money adjustment processes assumed so far in this book which might tend to bring such a situation to an end. The deficits in the middle column might continue indefinitely, implying a never-

Table 14.5 Alternative steady states

	($)		
	Full steady state	20% higher fiscal stance	20% higher foreign trade performance
1. Government spending	150	180	150
2. Government income share	0.333	0.333	0.333
3. Fiscal stance = (1)/(2)	450	540	450
4. Exports	200	200	240
5. Import propensity	0.444	0.444	0.444
6. Foreign trade performance = (4)/(5)	450	450	540
Steady-state flows			
7. National income = weighted average of (3) & (6)	450	489	501
8. Government income	150	163	167
9. Imports	200	217	223
10. Government deficit	0	17	−17
11. External balance	0	−17	+17
12. Private income = private expenditure	300	326	334

ending rise in government debt relative to the constant, steady-state level of national income.

As a long-term proposition the hypothesis of ever-increasing government debt relative to income accompanied by continuous external deficits is implausible. A full steady state could be restored by a reduction in the fiscal stance *or* by a rise in the trade performance ratio. There are two, related sets of pressures which might cause such adjustments to occur. One is the potential difficulty of financing the government budget when increases in government debt must directly or indirectly be taken up by foreigners. The other is the probability that continuous external deficits will make the national currency less and less acceptable in currency markets, provoking rapid falls in the exchange rate for the currency.

Appendix 14.1 *A formal stock-flow analysis for an open economy*

This appendix sets out an algebraic model of money stocks and flows, analogous to the one in Chapter 6. We also comment briefly on how the model can be expressed in real terms and note the relationship between real income and the volume of output.

A model in money terms

Budgets for the government and the private sector in an open economy are not in principle different from those in a closed economy, except that there may now be debt revaluations. The government's budget may be written as

$$TGD \equiv G - YG \qquad (A14.1)$$

where TGD represents debt transactions which finance the excess of government spending, G, over government income, YG. The private sector's budget is

$$TA \equiv YP + TPD - PE - \Delta I \qquad (A14.2)$$

where TA denotes the net asset transactions in each period implied by private income, YP, and debt transactions, TPD, less final purchases, PE, and inventory accumulation, ΔI.

As shown in the preceding chapter, the flow of national income, Y, is given by national expenditure plus the external balance, B:

$$YP + YG \equiv Y \equiv PE + G + \Delta I + B \qquad (A14.3)$$

The external balance is the difference between exports and transfer receipts, X, and imports and transfer payments, M:

$$B \equiv X - M \tag{A14.4}$$

From A14.1 to A14.3 we obtain the constraint on asset and debt transactions:

$$TA \equiv TPD + TGD + B \tag{A14.5}$$

The end-period value of private assets, A, will be the opening value, A_{-1}, plus transactions, TA, and revaluations, RVA, during the period:

$$A \equiv A_{-1} + TA + RVA \tag{A14.6}$$

Now assume (see Appendix 6.1) that the private sector's asset adjustment process maintains

$$A = \alpha PE \tag{A14.7}$$

Net government income, YG, is given by

$$YG \equiv \theta Y \tag{A14.8}$$

and imports by

$$M = \mu Y \tag{A14.9}$$

where θ is the government's share of national income and μ is the import propensity.

We can solve A14.3 to A14.9 to obtain period-by-period solutions for national income as

$$(1 + \mu + \frac{\mu + \theta}{\alpha})Y = \Delta I + (1 + \frac{1}{\alpha})(G + X) + \frac{1}{\alpha}(TPD + RVA + A_{-1}) \tag{A14.10}$$

Table A14.1 Numerical example of the response to a rise in exports and government expenditure

Period:	0	1	2	3	4	…	∞
1. Government expenditure, G	150	180	180	180	180	…	180
2. Exports, X	200	220	220	220	220	…	220
3. Change in inventories, ΔI	0	5	10	5	0	…	0
4. Private debt transactions, TPD	0	10	13	7	0	…	0
5. Private asset revaluations, RVA	0	20	10	10	0	…	0
6. Opening value of private assets, A_{-1}	300	300	333	348	355	…	343
7. National income $Y = 9/20 \times (2G + 2X + \Delta I + TPD + RVA + A_{-1})$	450	511	525	526	520	…	514
8. Net government income $YG = 1/3 \times Y$	150	170	175	176	173	…	171
9. Government budget deficit, $TGD = G - YG$	0	10	5	4	7	…	9

10. Imports, M = 4/9×Y	200	227	233	234	231	…	229
11. External balance, B = X−M	0	−7	−13	−14	−11	…	−9
12. Private asset transactions, TA =TPD+TGD+B	0	13	5	−3	−4	…	0
13. Private final purchases = end-period value of private assets, PE = A = A_{-1}+TA+RVA	300	333	348	355	351	…	343
14. Private disposable income, YP = Y−YG	300	341	350	350	347	…	343
End-period stocks							
15. Government debt	50	60	65	69	76	…	⎫
16. Cumulated external balance	50	43	30	16	5	…	⎬ 73
17. Borrowing to finance inventories	100	105	115	120	120	…	120
18. Other private debt	50	55	58	60	60	…	60
19. Cumulated private asset revaluations	50	70	80	90	90	…	90
20. Value of private stock of assets	300	333	348	355	351	…	343

Values for other endogenous variables are then found by substituting back into A14.3 to A14.9.

Quasi steady states

Assume that $\Delta I = TPD = RVA = 0$

and that

$$A_{-1} = A = \alpha YP$$

Substituting into the solution for national income we obtain

$$Y = \frac{G+X}{\mu+\theta} \qquad (A14.11)$$

This is the quasi steady state discussed in Chapter 14. Its properties can be inferred from A14.3 to A14.9 above.

Numerical example

Table A14.1 sets out the steps by which the simulation in Chart 14.1 was calculated. The simulation assumes

$$\alpha = 1, \mu = 4/9, \theta = 1/3$$

Substituting these values in A14.10 above yields the period-by-period solution for national income

$$Y = \frac{9}{20} \times (2G+2X+\Delta I+TPD+RVA+A_{-1}) \quad (A14.12)$$

The series for G, X, ΔI, TPD and RVA at the top of the table have been written down. All other variables are formally endogenous.

The model in real terms

To express the model in inflation-accounted terms it is necessary to make adjustments for inflation gains and losses – or real interest effects. Note that external transfer receipts and payments are affected; the 'real external balance', b, is not quite the same as the deflated money balance B/p. Also the 'real import propensity'

$$\mu' \equiv m/y$$

is not quite the same as the money import propensity, μ. With appropriate choice of definitions all the usual identities can be maintained, yielding a model expressed in terms of real variables which is formally identical to the one specified by A14.1 to A14.10 above.

Real national income is given by

$$y \equiv fe + \Delta i + x - m \tag{A14.13}$$

while the volume of national output is measured by

$$q \equiv fe + \Delta i' + x' - m' \tag{A14.14}$$

where x' and m' denote volumes of exports and imports *excluding* transfer receipts and payments. The difference between real national income and the volume of national output resolves into three components:

(i)   changes in real inventory valuations, $\Delta i - \Delta i'$
(ii) net real transfer receipts, tr
(iii) real terms of trade effects, tt, given by

$$tt \equiv (b - tr)\left(1 - \frac{p}{pm}\right) + x'\left(\frac{px}{pm} - 1\right)$$

where px and pm denote the price deflators for exports and

imports of goods and services (i.e., excluding transfers). This can be proved as follows. Note that

$$b = tr + x'.\frac{px}{p} - m'\,\frac{pm}{p}$$

so

$$y - q - (\Delta i - \Delta i') = b - x' + m'$$

$$= tr + b - tr - (\frac{x'.px}{p} - \frac{m'.pm}{p}).\frac{p}{pm} + x'\frac{px}{pm} - x'$$

$$= tr + tt$$

where tt is defined as above.

Epilogue

Our claim is to have provided a framework for an orderly analysis of whole economic systems evolving through time. This logical framework is neither 'monetarist' nor 'Keynesian'; it is non-denominational both in theoretical and in political terms. As we have relied only on certain general behavioural assumptions, and as no data relating to real economies have been supplied, our book cannot by itself enable detailed conclusions to be drawn about economic policy or performance.

We end, all the same, by expressing some opinions about the broad conclusions which it is possible to draw.

The most important result is, we believe, to reestablish the quintessentially Keynesian principle of effective demand as the determinant of real output and employment. In a closed economy real demand itself is determined, with quite a short time lag, by fiscal policy; the effects of monetary (as distinct from fiscal) policy are transitory. The rate of inflation is largely indeterminate in terms of economic forces and, although it has a dynamic of its own, is likely to be rather unstable. But the instability of inflation does not significantly alter the fact that real output can be regulated by fiscal policy subject to capacity constraints.

In sum, we have reestablished something very like the Keynesian position as perceived by policy-makers through the 1950s and 1960s, when economic performance throughout the developed world was more consistently successful than in any other period of history. In the absence of external constraints government, by its fiscal decisions, would inevitably be choosing the degree of capacity utilization and the level of employment. Inflation cannot be controlled directly by monetary policy. If it accelerates whenever there is a high pressure of demand, there will be a conflict between full employment and price stability which could only be resolved by political and institutional means.

The important qualifications to all this is that in real-life open economies, fiscal policy alone may not be enough. It is also necessary for a country's international trade performance – the growth of its exports (in real terms) less import penetration – to expand as much as the desired level of output. Unless this condition is met, fiscal policy will have to give, and full employment cannot be achieved.

So we end on a note of heavily qualified optimism. We believe that it is possible for the world to achieve, once again, sustained real growth with high employment. Inflation might then be more rapid although this is not inevitable. Yet we cannot hope even to see the beginnings of such a recovery until the peoples and governments of the world are convinced that the achievement is indeed within their power, and work together towards coordinated growth based on expansionary fiscal and trade policies that are mutually compatible.

List of charts
and their numerical simulations*

* Numerical simulations for the charts can be found, where relevant, in the tables referred to in brackets.

Index

Index

Fontana Paperbacks: Non-fiction

Fontana is a leading paperback publisher of non-fiction, both popular and academic. Below are some recent titles.

- [ ] THE POLITICS OF INDUSTRIAL RELATIONS (second edition) Colin Crouch £2·95
- [ ] NATTER NATTER Richard Briers £1·50
- [ ] KITCHEN HINTS Hilary Davies £1·25
- [ ] MRS WEBER'S DIARY Posy Simmonds £2·50
- [ ] A TREASURY OF CHRISTMAS Frank & Jamie Muir £2·95
- [ ] THE VIDEO HANDBOOK John Baxter & Brian Norris £1·95
- [ ] A BOOK OF SEA JOURNEYS Ludovic Kennedy (ed.) £3·50
- [ ] BEDSIDE GOLF Peter Alliss £1·95
- [ ] DAY CARE Alison Clarke-Stewart £1·95
- [ ] THE WOMAN QUESTION: READINGS ON THE SUBORDINATION OF WOMEN Mary Evans (ed.) £3·95
- [ ] WAR FACTS NOW Christy Campbell £2·50
- [ ] CHRONICLE OF YOUTH Vera Brittain £2·75
- [ ] FRIGHTENED FOR MY LIFE Geoff Coggan & Martin Walker £1·95
- [ ] HIGH PRESSURE: WORKING LIVES OF WOMEN MANAGERS Cary Cooper & Marilyn Davidson £1·95
- [ ] TRADE UNIONS: THE LOGIC OF COLLECTIVE ACTION Colin Crouch £2·50
- [ ] THE KINGDOM Robert Lacey £2·95
- [ ] A FOREIGN FLAVOUR Rose Elliot £2·95
- [ ] SEVEN DAYS TO DISASTER Des Hickey & Gus Smith £2·50
- [ ] P.S. I LOVE YOU Michael Sellers £1·75

You can buy Fontana paperbacks at your local bookshop or newsagent. Or you can order them from Fontana Paperbacks, Cash Sales Department, Box 29, Douglas, Isle of Man. Please send a cheque, postal or money order (not currency) worth the purchase price plus 10p per book (or plus 12p per book if outside the UK).

NAME (Block letters) _____

ADDRESS _____

_____

_____

Errata

Page 91, line 9: *for* $50 \times 4/7$ *read* $50 + 4/7$

Page 91, line 10: *for as read* from

Page 92, line 9: *for* income *read* income spent

Page 96 (A5.22): *for* $-\dfrac{(1-\alpha\phi)}{\alpha\phi}$ *read* $=\dfrac{(1-\alpha\phi)}{\alpha\phi}$

Page 119, line 16: *for* B2 *read* B3

Page 159, line 26: *for* $2/3 \times \$1667$ *read* $3/5 \times \$1667$

Page 175, line 7 up: *for* 000 *read* 72

Page 177, line 2 up: *for* r *read* R

Table 10.2, row 1, col. 7: *for* 1.00 *read* 100